ULTIMATE 9x13 COOKBOOK

Taste of Home BOOKS

RDA ENTHUSIAST BRANDS, LLC
MILWAUKEE, WI

Taste of Home. Reader's digest

A TASTE OF HOME/READER'S DIGEST BOOK
© 2015 RDA Enthusiast Brands, LLC 1610 N. 2nd St., Suite 102, Milwaukee WI 53212. All rights reserved.
Taste of Home and Reader's Digest are registered trademarks of The Reader's Digest Association, Inc.

EDITORIAL

Editor-in-Chief: Catherine Cassidy
Creative Director: Howard Greenberg
Editorial Operations Director: Kerri Balliet

Managing Editor, Print & Digital Books: Mark Hagen
Associate Creative Director: Edwin Robles Jr.

Editor: Christine Rukavena
Art Director: Jessie Sharon
Layout Designer: Catherine Fletcher
Editorial Production Manager: Dena Ahlers
Copy Chief: Deb Warlaumont Mulvey
Copy Editors: Mary-Liz Shaw, Dulcie Shoener, Joanne Weintraub
Contributing Copy Editor: Steph Kilen
Editorial Intern: Michael Welch
Content Operations Assistant: Shannon Stroud
Editorial Services Administrator: Marie Brannon

Food Editors: James Schend; Peggy Woodward, RD
Recipe Editors: Mary King; Jenni Sharp, RD; Irene Yeh

Test Kitchen & Food Styling Manager: Sarah Thompson
Test Cooks: Nicholas Iverson (lead), Matthew Hass, Lauren Knoelke
Food Stylists: Kathryn Conrad (lead), Leah Rekau, Shannon Roum
Prep Cooks: Bethany Van Jacobson (lead), Megumi Garcia, Melissa Hansen, Sara Wirtz

Photography Director: Stephanie Marchese
Photographers: Dan Roberts, Jim Wieland
Photographer/Set Stylist: Grace Natoli Sheldon
Set Stylists: Melissa Franco, Stacey Genaw, Dee Dee Jacq
Photo Studio Assistant: Ester Robards

Editorial Business Manager: Kristy Martin
Editorial Business Associate: Samantha Lea Stoeger

BUSINESS

Vice President, Group Publisher: Kirsten Marchioli
Publisher: Donna Lindskog
General Manager, Taste of Home Cooking School: Erin Puariea
Executive Producer, Taste of Home Online Cooking School: Karen Berner

THE READER'S DIGEST ASSOCIATION, INC.

President and Chief Executive Officer: Bonnie Kintzer
Chief Financial Officer: Tom Callahan
Vice President, Chief Operating Officer, North America: Howard Halligan
Chief Revenue Officer: Richard Sutton
Chief Marketing Officer: Leslie Dukker Doty
Vice President, Content Marketing & Operations: Diane Dragan
Senior Vice President, Global HR & Communications: Phyllis E. Gebhardt, SPHR
Vice President, Brand Marketing: Beth Gorry
Vice President, Chief Technology Officer: Aneel Tejwaney
Vice President, Consumer Marketing Planning: Jim Woods

For other Taste of Home books and products, visit us at **tasteofhome.com.**

For more Reader's Digest products and information, visit **rd.com** (in the United States) or **rd.ca** (in Canada).

International Standard Book Number: 978-1-61765-420-6
Library of Congress Control Number: 2015937042

Cover Photography:
Taste of Home Photo Studio

Pictured on front cover:
Hawaiian Joy Bars, page 181; Creamy Cavatappi & Cheese, page 97; Patriotic Dessert, page 234; Make Once, Eat Twice Lasagna, page 58.

Pictured on back cover:
Italian Apricot-Pancetta Strata, page 9; Mrs. Thompson's Carrot Cake, page 203; Pesto Chicken Strata, page 15.

Printed in China.
1 3 5 7 9 10 8 6 4 2

GRAHAM STREUSEL
COFFEE CAKE, 152

PEPPERONI
MACARONI, 53

DILLY VEGGIE PIZZA, 30

Contents

HOLIDAY BRUNCH CASSEROLE, 17

ARGENTINE LASAGNA, 69

Grab Your **9x13** Pan & Let's Get **Cooking!**

SMOKY CHICKEN NACHOS, 27

It's no secret...we home cooks *love* our 9x13 baking pans! When it comes to baking, storing, freezing and serving, nothing beats **the versatility of a 9x13**. It's one of the **first pans we purchase** and the pan we turn to for **weeknight dinners** and **special celebrations** alike.

In fact, this classic pan is ready to meet every need—from appetizers and entrees to side dishes and desserts. Let these **315 home-cooked specialties** show you how. After all, each is made with the **most popular pan in the house!**

At-a-glance icons highlight these convenient recipes:

⑤ INGREDIENTS
Dish uses 5 or fewer ingredients (may call for salt, pepper, water or cooking oil).

FREEZE IT
Keep these favorites on ice for a busy day.

IT'S THE PAN THAT CAN!

The versatile 9x13 comes in many materials. The recipes in this book call for baking pans (made of metal) or baking dishes (from glass or other materials). Here are some considerations as you choose the 9x13 for the job.

METAL BAKING PANS

These great conductors of heat create nice browning on rolls, coffee cakes and other baked goods. Metal is a safe, smart choice for under the broiler. It may react with acidic foods such as tomato sauce or cranberries and create a metallic taste or discoloration.

GLASS BAKING DISHES

Glass provides slower, more even baking for egg dishes, custards and casseroles. It takes longer to heat than metal but, once heated, the dish holds the heat longer. This is undesirable for many desserts, because a sugary batter may overbrown in glass. If you wish to bake in glass dish even though the recipe calls for a metal pan, decrease the oven temperature by 25°.

OTHER BAKING DISHES

Ceramic or stoneware baking dishes generally perform like glass, but are more attractive. They may also be safe for higher temperatures than glass; refer to the manufacturer's instructions.

SAUSAGE & PEPPER PIZZA, 92

GET MORE FROM YOUR 9x13!

▶ **Double any recipe** that calls for an 8-in.-square (or 1½-qt.) baking dish. Bake at the same temperature, for longer, in a glass or ceramic 9x13 dish.

▶ **Bake three loaves** of your favorite yeast bread side by side in a metal 9x13 pan.

▶ **Give a freezer-friendly gift** of Make Once, Eat Twice Lasagna (page 58) in a new ceramic 9x13. Include the thawing and baking directions from the recipe. Or, attach these directions to the lasagna of your choice.

▶ **Share the love** with casseroles baked in disposable aluminum 9x13 pans. For best results, check the food 10-15 minutes early, as it may cook faster. Bake with pan on a cookie sheet for added support.

**NAYLET LAROCHELLE'S ITALIAN
APRICOT-PANCETTA STRATA**
PAGE 9

Brunch

MELISSA MILLWOOD'S HAM, EGG & CHEESE CASSEROLE *PAGE 13*

LIN KOPPEN'S HOT SPICED FRUIT *PAGE 18*

RENA CHARBONEAU'S POTATO EGG BAKE *PAGE 22*

Dutch Baby Tropicale

A Dutch baby is a cross between a pancake and a popover. It puffs up golden brown, then collapses when taken out of the oven and filled.

—**CINDY RAPPUHN** STARTUP, WA

PREP: 15 MIN. • **BAKE:** 20 MIN.
MAKES: 8 SERVINGS

- 5 eggs
- 1 cup 2% milk
- 1 cup all-purpose flour
- ⅓ cup butter, cubed

FILLING

- 3 tablespoons butter
- 2 large bananas, sliced
- 1 medium papaya, peeled and sliced
  Lime wedges, optional

1. In a blender, combine eggs, milk and flour; cover and process just until smooth. Place cubed butter in an ungreased 9x13-in. baking dish. Place in a 425° oven for 5 minutes or until melted.
2. Pour batter into hot dish. Bake, uncovered, 20 minutes or until puffy and golden brown.
3. For filling, melt butter in a large skillet. Add bananas and papaya. Cook over medium heat until tender, stirring frequently. Spoon into Dutch baby. Serve immediately with lime wedges.

TOP TIP

For a classic spin on the dish that's also quite easy, squeeze some fresh lemon juice over the plain Dutch baby and dust it generously with confectioners' sugar.

Italian Apricot-Pancetta Strata

For me, the combination of sweet and savory makes this Italian-inspired strata a winning dish. It can be served for breakfast, brunch or as a late afternoon meal.

—NAYLET LAROCHELLE MIAMI, FL

PREP: 35 MIN. + CHILLING
BAKE: 35 MIN. • **MAKES:** 12 SERVINGS

- ⅓ pound pancetta, finely chopped
- 2 tablespoons butter, divided
- 1⅓ cups finely chopped sweet onion
- 2 cups sliced fresh mushrooms
- 3 cups fresh baby spinach, coarsely chopped
- 5 cups cubed multigrain bread
- ½ cup sliced almonds, optional
- 6 eggs
- 1 cup heavy whipping cream
- ¼ teaspoon salt
- ¼ teaspoon pepper
- 1 carton (8 ounces) mascarpone cheese
- 1 cup (4 ounces) shredded part-skim mozzarella cheese
- ½ cup shredded Asiago cheese
- 1 cup apricot preserves
- 3 tablespoons minced fresh basil

1. In large skillet, cook pancetta until crisp, stirring occasionally. Remove with a slotted spoon; drain on paper towels. Discard the drippings, reserving 1 tablespoon in pan.
2. Add 1 tablespoon butter to drippings; heat over medium-high heat. Add onion; cook and stir 4-6 minutes or until tender. Transfer onion to a large bowl.

3. Heat remaining butter in pan. Add mushrooms; cook and stir 2-3 minutes or until tender. Stir in spinach; cook until wilted.
4. Add bread cubes, mushroom mixture, pancetta and, if desired, almonds to the onion; toss to combine. Transfer to a greased 9x13-in. baking dish.
5. In a large bowl, beat eggs, cream, salt and pepper until blended. Beat in mascarpone cheese just until blended; pour over bread. Sprinkle with mozzarella cheese and Asiago cheese; spoon preserves over top. Refrigerate, covered, several hours or overnight.
6. Preheat oven to 350°. Remove strata from refrigerator while oven heats. Bake strata, uncovered, 35-45 minutes or until golden brown and a knife inserted near the center comes out clean. Sprinkle with basil. Let stand 5-10 minutes before cutting.

⑤INGREDIENTS
Corned Beef Brunch

One of my daughters shared this recipe with me. She made it for her first overnight guests after she was married.

—KATHLEEN LUTZ STEWARD, IL

PREP: 10 MIN. • **BAKE:** 35 MIN.
MAKES: 8-10 SERVINGS

- 3 cans (14 ounces each) corned beef hash
- 12 slices (1 ounce each) American cheese
- 12 eggs
- ½ teaspoon pepper
    Chopped chives, optional

1. Spread hash in the bottom of a greased 9x13-in. baking dish. Layer cheese slices over hash. Beat eggs and pepper; pour over top.
2. Bake at 350° for 35-40 minutes or until a knife inserted near the center comes out clean. Garnish with chives if desired.

Crustless Quiche Bake

Chock-full of veggies, cheese, bacon and eggs, this delicious recipe would be great served with fresh muffins or toasted bread and assorted fruits.

—**JUNE MARIE RACUS**

SUN CITY WEST, AZ

PREP: 30 MIN.
BAKE: 40 MIN. + STANDING
MAKES: 12 SERVINGS

- 14 **bacon strips, chopped**
- 1 **pound sliced fresh mushrooms**
- ½ **cup chopped green pepper**
- 8 **green onions, thinly sliced**
- 1 **jar (2 ounces) diced pimientos, drained**
- 2 **tablespoons sherry, optional**
- 12 **eggs**
- 1½ **cups 2% milk**
- ¾ **teaspoon dried thyme**
- ¾ **teaspoon seasoned salt**
- ½ **teaspoon ground mustard Dash dill weed**
- 4 **cups (16 ounces) shredded Gruyere or Swiss cheese, divided**

1. In a large skillet, cook bacon over medium heat until crisp. Remove to paper towels with a slotted spoon; drain, reserving 2 tablespoons drippings.

2. In the drippings, saute the mushrooms, green pepper and onions until tender. Add the pimientos and, if desired, sherry; cook until liquid is evaporated.

3. In a large bowl, whisk the eggs, milk, thyme, seasoned salt, mustard and dill. Add the bacon, mushroom mixture and 3 cups cheese. Transfer to a greased 9x13-in. baking dish.

4. Bake, uncovered, at 350° for 35 minutes. Sprinkle with remaining cheese. Bake for 5-10 minutes longer or until a knife inserted near the center comes out clean and cheese is melted. Let stand for 10 minutes before cutting.

FREEZE OPTION *Freeze unbaked quiche and remaining cheese separately in freezer containers. To use, remove from freezer 30 minutes before baking (do not thaw). Preheat oven to 350°. Bake quiche as directed, increasing time as necessary for a knife inserted near the center to come out clean.*

Green Chili Egg Puff

PREP: 15 MIN. • **BAKE:** 35 MIN.
MAKES: 12 SERVINGS

- 10 **eggs**
- ½ **cup all-purpose flour**
- 1 **teaspoon baking powder**
- ½ **teaspoon salt**
- 4 **cups (16 ounces) shredded Monterey Jack cheese**
- 2 **cups (16 ounces) 4% cottage cheese**
- 1 **can (4 ounces) chopped green chilies**

1. In a large bowl, beat eggs on medium-high for 3 minutes or until light and lemon-colored. Combine the flour, baking powder and salt; gradually add to eggs and mix well. Stir in the cheeses and green chilies.

2. Pour into a greased 9x13-in. baking dish. Bake, uncovered, at 350° for 35-40 minutes or until a knife inserted near the center comes out clean. Let stand for 5 minutes before serving.

Green chilies add a touch of Southwest flavor to this fluffy egg dish. The cottage cheese offers nice texture, and people always adore the gooey Monterey Jack cheese melted throughout.
—**LAUREL LESLIE** SONORA, CA

the eggs, sausage and bacon, sauteed vegetables, tomatoes and mozzarella.

5. Bake at 375° for 15-18 minutes or until cheese is melted. Serve with picante sauce and additional sour cream if desired.

Chocolate-Peanut Granola Bars

Everyone always thinks they're eating something naughty when I serve these, but they're full of oats and healthy fats.

—BRENDA L. CAUGHELL DURHAM, NC

START TO FINISH: 30 MIN.
MAKES: 2 DOZEN

- 2½ cups old-fashioned oats
- ¾ cup lightly salted dry roasted peanuts, coarsely chopped
- ¾ cup wheat germ
- ¾ cup sunflower kernels
- ½ cup honey
- ¼ cup packed brown sugar
- 3 tablespoons butter
- ⅓ cup creamy peanut butter
- ⅓ cup Nutella

1. In an ungreased 15x10x1-in. baking pan, combine the oats, peanuts, wheat germ and sunflower kernels. Bake at 400° for 8-12 minutes or until toasted, stirring occasionally. Cool.
2. In a small saucepan, combine honey, brown sugar and butter. Cook and stir over medium heat until mixture comes to a boil; cook 2 minutes longer. Remove from heat; stir in peanut butter and Nutella until blended.
3. Transfer oat mixture to a large bowl; add honey mixture and toss to coat. Press into a greased 9x13-in. pan. Cool.

Contest-Winning Brunch Pizza

This is one of my family's favorite breakfast dishes. Hearty and satisfying with all the veggies, this pizza always garners raves when I serve it to guests.

—MARTY SCHWARTZ SARASOTA, FL

PREP: 35 MIN. • **BAKE:** 15 MIN.
MAKES: 12 PIECES

- 1 tube (8 ounces) refrigerated crescent rolls
- ½ pound bacon strips, chopped
- ½ pound bulk pork sausage
- ½ pound sliced fresh mushrooms
- 1 small onion, finely chopped
- 1 small green pepper, finely chopped
- 1 tablespoon butter
- 8 eggs, lightly beaten
- 1 package (3 ounces) cream cheese, softened
- ⅓ cup sour cream
- 1 garlic clove, minced
- ¼ teaspoon Italian seasoning
- 2 plum tomatoes, chopped

- 1½ cups (6 ounces) shredded part-skim mozzarella cheese
  Picante sauce and additional sour cream, optional

1. Unroll crescent dough into a greased 9x13-in. baking dish; seal seams and perforations. Bake at 375° for 6-8 minutes or until golden brown.
2. Meanwhile, in a small skillet, cook bacon and sausage over medium heat until bacon is crisp and sausage is no longer pink. Using a slotted spoon, remove meat to paper towels; drain, reserving 2 tablespoons of the drippings. In the drippings, saute the mushrooms, onion and green pepper. Remove and set aside.
3. Heat butter in a large skillet over medium heat. Add eggs; cook and stir until almost set.
4. In a small bowl, beat the cream cheese, sour cream, garlic and Italian seasoning; spread over crust. Layer with

Ham, Egg & Cheese Casserole

I put a twist on a classic French cafe sandwich, croque madame, and turned it into a saucy, impossible-to-resist casserole.
—**MELISSA MILLWOOD** LYMAN, SC

PREP: 35 MIN.
BAKE: 40 MIN. + STANDING
MAKES: 12 SERVINGS

- 1 loaf (1 pound) frozen bread dough, thawed
- ¾ cup butter, cubed
- ⅓ cup all-purpose flour
- 2½ cups 2% milk
- 3 tablespoons Dijon mustard
- ¾ teaspoon pepper
- ½ teaspoon salt
- ½ teaspoon ground nutmeg
- ½ cup grated Parmesan cheese
- 1 pound sliced smoked deli ham
- 2 cups (8 ounces) shredded Swiss cheese
- 6 eggs
- ¼ cup minced fresh parsley

1. Preheat oven to 350°. On a lightly floured surface, roll the dough into a 10x14-in. rectangle. Transfer to a greased 9x13-in. baking dish; build up edges slightly.

2. In a large saucepan, melt butter over medium heat. Stir in flour until smooth; gradually whisk in milk. Bring to a boil, stirring constantly; cook and stir 3-4 minutes or until thickened. Stir in mustard, pepper, salt and nutmeg. Remove from heat; stir in Parmesan cheese.

3. Place a third of the ham over the dough; top with 1 cup sauce and ⅔ cup Swiss cheese. Repeat layers twice. Bake, uncovered, 30 minutes or until bubbly and crust is golden brown.

4. Using the back of a spoon, make six indentations in top of the casserole to within 2 in. of edges. Carefully break an egg into each indentation.

5. Bake 10-15 minutes longer or until egg whites are completely set and yolks begin to thicken but are not hard. (If desired, bake an additional 5 minutes for firmer eggs.) Sprinkle with parsley. Let stand 10 minutes before cutting.

Beef, Potato & Egg Bake

To keep my family going all morning, I start with lean ground beef and spices, then sneak some spinach into this protein-packed dish.
—**JENNIFER FISHER** AUSTIN, TX

PREP: 25 MIN. • **BAKE:** 45 MIN.
MAKES: 12 SERVINGS

- 1 **pound lean ground beef (90% lean)**
- 2 **teaspoons onion powder**
- 1½ **teaspoons salt, divided**
- 1 **teaspoon garlic powder**
- ½ **teaspoon rubbed sage**
- ½ **teaspoon crushed red pepper flakes**
- 1 **package (10 ounces) frozen chopped spinach, thawed and squeezed dry**
- 4 **cups frozen shredded hash brown potatoes**
- 14 **large eggs**
- 1 **cup fat-free ricotta cheese**
- ⅓ **cup fat-free milk**
- ¾ **to 1 teaspoon pepper**
- ¾ **cup shredded Colby-Monterey Jack cheese**
- 1⅓ **cups grape tomatoes, halved**

1. Preheat oven to 350°. In a large skillet, cook beef with onion powder, ½ teaspoon salt, garlic powder, sage and pepper flakes over medium heat for 6-8 minutes or until no longer pink, breaking up the beef into crumbles; drain. Stir in spinach. Remove from heat.

2. Spread potatoes in a greased 9x13-in. baking dish; top with beef mixture. In a large bowl, whisk eggs, ricotta cheese, milk, pepper and remaining salt; pour over top. Sprinkle with cheese. Top with tomatoes.

3. Bake casserole, uncovered, 45-50 minutes or until a knife inserted in center comes out clean. Let stand 5-10 minutes before serving.

Pesto Chicken Strata

I like this rustic strata because it's nice to have something savory to go with sweet brunch dishes. It has the fresh flavors of homemade pesto.

—**MICHAEL COHEN** LOS ANGELES, CA

PREP: 25 MIN. + CHILLING
BAKE: 40 MIN.
MAKES: 12 SERVINGS

- 1 **pound boneless skinless chicken thighs, cut into 1-inch pieces**
- ¾ **teaspoon salt, divided**
- ¾ **teaspoon coarsely ground pepper, divided**
- 1 **tablespoon plus ½ cup olive oil, divided**
- 1 **cup chopped fresh basil**
- 1½ **cups grated Parmesan cheese, divided**
- 1 **cup (4 ounces) shredded part-skim mozzarella cheese**
- ⅔ **cup pine nuts, toasted**
- 5 **garlic cloves, minced**
- 10 **eggs**
- 3 **cups 2% milk**
- 8 **cups cubed Italian bread**

1. Sprinkle the chicken with ¼ teaspoon salt and ¼ teaspoon pepper. In a large skillet, heat 1 tablespoon oil over medium heat. Add chicken; cook and stir 6-8 minutes or until no longer pink. Drain.
2. In a large bowl, mix basil, 1 cup Parmesan cheese, mozzarella cheese, pine nuts and garlic. In another bowl, whisk eggs, milk, remaining oil, salt and pepper.
3. In a greased 9x13-in. baking dish, layer half of the bread cubes, a third of the cheese mixture and half of the chicken. Repeat layers. Top with the remaining cheese mixture. Pour egg mixture over top; sprinkle with remaining Parmesan cheese. Refrigerate, covered, several hours or overnight.
4. Preheat oven to 350°. Remove strata from refrigerator while oven heats. Bake, uncovered, 40-50 minutes or until golden brown and a knife inserted near the center comes out clean. Let casserole stand 5-10 minutes before serving.

Broccoli-Mushroom Bubble Bake

I got bored with the same old breakfast casseroles served at our monthly moms' meeting, so I created something new. Judging by the reactions of the other moms, this one's a keeper.

—**SHANNON KOENE** BLACKSBURG, VA

PREP: 20 MIN. • **BAKE:** 25 MIN.
MAKES: 12 SERVINGS

- 1 **teaspoon canola oil**
- ½ **pound fresh mushrooms, finely chopped**
- 1 **medium onion, finely chopped**
- 1 **tube (16.3 ounces) large refrigerated flaky biscuits**
- 1 **package (10 ounces) frozen broccoli with cheese sauce**
- 3 **eggs**
- 1 **can (5 ounces) evaporated milk**
- 1 **teaspoon Italian seasoning**
- ½ **teaspoon garlic powder**
- ½ **teaspoon salt**
- ¼ **teaspoon pepper**
- 1½ **cups (6 ounces) shredded Colby-Monterey Jack cheese**

1. Preheat oven to 350°. In a large skillet, heat oil over medium-high heat. Add the mushrooms and onion; cook and stir 4-6 minutes or until tender.
2. Cut each biscuit into eight pieces; place in a greased 9x13-in. baking dish. Top with the mushroom mixture.
3. Cook broccoli with cheese sauce according to package directions. Spoon over the mushroom mixture.
4. In a large bowl, whisk eggs, milk and seasonings; pour over top. Sprinkle with cheese. Bake for 25-30 minutes or until golden brown.

HOW TO

CLEAN MUSHROOMS

Gently remove dirt by rubbing with a mushroom brush or a damp paper towel. Or quickly rinse mushrooms under cold water, then drain and pat dry with paper towels. Trim any tough stems.

for 50-55 minutes or until a knife inserted near center comes out clean. Let stand 10 minutes before cutting.

5. In a microwave, heat the reserved sauce. Drizzle warm sauce over strata.

Spicy Egg Bake

This family favorite makes a yummy morning meal. It's also a great way to use up extra taco meat. Adjust the heat by choosing a hotter or milder salsa. It's delicious with muffins and fresh fruit.

—**MICHELLE JIBBEN** SPRINGFIELD, MN

START TO FINISH: 30 MIN.
MAKES: 8 SERVINGS

- 1 tube (8 ounces) refrigerated crescent rolls
- 10 eggs
- ⅓ cup water
- 3 tablespoons butter
- 1½ cups prepared taco meat
- 1 cup (4 ounces) shredded cheddar cheese
- 1 cup (4 ounces) shredded Monterey Jack cheese
- 1 cup salsa

1. Unroll crescent roll dough into a greased 9x13-in. baking dish. Seal the seams and perforations; set aside.

2. In a small bowl, whisk eggs and water. In a large skillet, heat butter until hot. Add egg mixture; cook and stir over medium heat until eggs are almost set. Remove from the heat.

3. Sprinkle taco meat over dough. Layer with eggs, cheeses and salsa. Bake, uncovered, at 375° for 14-16 minutes or until bubbly and cheese is melted.

Caramel Apple Strata

If you're planning to host a breakfast or brunch, you'll appreciate this overnight strata. It works great as your something sweet, tastes like a sticky bun and won't dry out like coffee cakes sometimes do.

—**KELLY BOE** WHITELAND, IN

PREP: 20 MIN. + CHILLING
BAKE: 50 MIN. + STANDING
MAKES: 12 SERVINGS

- 2 cups packed brown sugar
- ½ cup butter, cubed
- ¼ cup corn syrup
- 3 large apples, peeled and chopped
- 2 tablespoons lemon juice
- 1 tablespoon sugar
- 1 teaspoon apple pie spice
- 1 loaf (1 pound) day-old cinnamon bread
- ½ cup chopped pecans

- 10 eggs
- 1 cup 2% milk
- 1 teaspoon salt
- 1 teaspoon vanilla extract

1. In a small saucepan, combine the brown sugar, butter and corn syrup. Bring to a boil over medium heat, stirring constantly. Cook and stir 2 minutes or until thickened. Set aside.

2. In a small bowl, combine apples, lemon juice, sugar and pie spice. Arrange half of the bread slices in a greased 9x13-in. baking dish. Spoon apples over bread; drizzle with half of the caramel sauce. Sprinkle with pecans; top with remaining bread.

3. In a large bowl, combine eggs, milk, salt and vanilla. Pour over top. Cover and refrigerate strata overnight. Cover and refrigerate remaining caramel sauce.

4. Remove the strata from refrigerator 30 minutes before baking. Bake, uncovered, at 350°

Holiday Brunch Casserole

Consider this hearty casserole the next time you're hosting overnight company. Guests will be impressed with both the bountiful filling and scrumptious flavor.

—NELDA CRONBAUGH

BELLE PLAINE, IA

PREP: 20 MIN. + CHILLING
BAKE: 30 MIN. + STANDING
MAKES: 12 SERVINGS

- 4 **cups frozen shredded hash brown potatoes, thawed**
- 1 **pound bulk pork sausage, cooked and drained**
- ½ **pound bacon strips, cooked and crumbled**
- 1 **medium green pepper, chopped**
- 1 **green onion, chopped**
- 2 **cups (8 ounces) shredded cheddar cheese, divided**
- 4 **eggs**
- 3 **cups 2% milk**
- 1 **cup reduced-fat biscuit/ baking mix**
- ½ **teaspoon salt**

1. In a large bowl, combine the first five ingredients; stir in 1 cup cheese. Transfer to a greased 9x13-in. baking dish.
2. In another bowl, whisk eggs, milk, baking mix and salt until blended; pour over top. Sprinkle with the remaining cheese. Refrigerate, covered, overnight.
3. Preheat oven to 375°. Remove casserole from refrigerator while oven heats. Bake, uncovered, 30-35 minutes or until a knife inserted near the center comes out clean. Let stand 10 minutes before cutting.

Cheese Strata with Ham & Sun-Dried Tomatoes

Brimming with ham, cheese and sun-dried tomatoes, this pretty breakfast casserole feeds a crowd while adding visual appeal to your brunch's spread. It's elegant comfort food at its best.

—KIM DEANE FENTON, MO

PREP: 30 MIN. + CHILLING
BAKE: 45 MIN. • **MAKES:** 12 SERVINGS

- 1 **cup cubed fully cooked ham**
- 1 **cup sun-dried tomatoes (not packed in oil), chopped**
- 1 **tablespoon minced fresh parsley**
- 1½ **teaspoons minced chives**
- 1 **loaf sourdough bread (1 pound), crust removed and cut into 1-inch cubes**
- 2 **cups (8 ounces) shredded cheddar cheese**
- 12 **eggs**
- 1½ **cups 2% milk**
- ½ **cup heavy whipping cream**
- 1 **teaspoon salt**
- ¼ **teaspoon coarsely ground pepper**
- ⅛ **teaspoon ground nutmeg**
- ⅛ **teaspoon cayenne pepper**
- 1 **tablespoon butter, melted**

1. In a small bowl, mix ham, tomatoes, parsley and chives. In a greased 9x13-in. baking dish, layer half of each of the following: bread cubes, ham mixture and cheese. Repeat layers.
2. In a large bowl, whisk eggs, milk, cream and seasonings; pour over layers. Drizzle with melted butter. Refrigerate, covered, overnight.
3. Preheat oven to 350°. Remove strata from refrigerator while oven heats. Bake, uncovered, 45-50 minutes or until a knife inserted near the center comes out clean. (Cover loosely with foil if top browns too quickly.) Let stand 5-10 minutes before cutting.

Hot Spiced Fruit

My baked pears, apples and cranberries have a touch of sweetness and spice—like a pie without the crust. Spiced fruit warms up any occasion.

—LIN KOPPEN ORCHARD PARK, NY

PREP: 25 MIN.
BAKE: 30 MIN. + COOLING
MAKES: 12 SERVINGS

- ¼ **cup packed brown sugar**
- 2 **tablespoons cornstarch**
- ¼ **teaspoon ground cinnamon**
- ¼ **teaspoon ground ginger**
- ⅛ **teaspoon ground cloves**
- 1 **cup cranberry or white grape juice**
- 3 **medium pears, peeled and sliced**
- 3 **medium apples, peeled and sliced**
- 1 **cup fresh or frozen cranberries, thawed and chopped**
- 1 **can (11 ounces) mandarin oranges, drained**

1. Preheat oven to 375°. In a small bowl, mix the first five ingredients; gradually whisk in cranberry juice.
2. In a greased 9x13-in. baking dish, combine remaining ingredients. Pour cranberry juice mixture over top.
3. Bake fruit, uncovered, for 30-35 minutes or until pears and apples are tender, stirring once. Let stand 10 minutes before serving. Serve warm or cold.

Spinach & Sausage Egg Bake

I've occasionally brought this recipe to work, and it's always gone in no time. Leftovers are good, too. Pop a serving in the microwave, and it's just as good as fresh.

—**PAULA CROCKETT**
WEST COLUMBIA, SC

PREP: 20 MIN. • **BAKE:** 30 MIN.
MAKES: 12 SERVINGS

- 1 **pound bulk pork sausage**
- 1 **package (10 ounces) frozen chopped spinach, thawed and squeezed dry**
- 6 **bacon strips, cooked and crumbled**
- ¼ **cup finely chopped onion**
- ¼ **cup finely chopped sweet red pepper**
- 1 **cup (4 ounces) shredded Monterey Jack cheese**
- 1 **cup (4 ounces) shredded cheddar cheese**
- 10 **eggs**
- ¾ **cup 2% milk**
- 2 **teaspoons snipped fresh dill or ½ teaspoon dill weed**
- 1½ **teaspoons chili powder**
- 1 **teaspoon garlic powder**
- 1 **teaspoon pepper**
- ¼ **teaspoon salt**

1. Preheat oven to 375°. In a large skillet, cook sausage over medium heat until no longer pink; drain. Spoon into a greased 9x13-in. baking dish. Layer with the spinach, bacon, onion, red pepper and cheeses.
2. In a large bowl, whisk eggs, milk and seasonings; pour over top. Bake for 30-35 minutes or until a knife inserted near center comes out clean. Let stand 5 minutes before cutting.

Ham, Cheese & Chilies Casserole

Don't you just love it when you find a holiday recipe that can be folded into the everyday repertoire? This strata, layered with sourdough, cheddar and savory ham, is egg-cellent for Easter but just as wonderful for any other brunch.

—**THERESA KREYCHE** TUSTIN, CA

PREP: 20 MIN. + CHILLING
BAKE: 40 MIN. • **MAKES:** 8 SERVINGS

- 6 **slices sourdough bread (1 inch thick)**
- ¼ **cup butter, softened**
- 2½ **cups (10 ounces) shredded cheddar cheese, divided**
- 1 **cup cubed fully cooked ham**
- 1 **can (4 ounces) chopped green chilies**
- ¼ **cup finely chopped onion**
- 2 **tablespoons minced fresh cilantro**
- 5 **eggs**
- 1½ **cups 2% milk**
- ¼ **teaspoon salt**
- ¼ **teaspoon ground cumin**
- ¼ **teaspoon ground mustard**

1. Remove and discard crust from bread if desired. Butter bread; cube and place in a greased 9x13-in. baking dish. Sprinkle with 1¾ cups cheese, ham, chilies, onion and cilantro.
2. Whisk the eggs, milk, salt, cumin and mustard in a large bowl. Pour over bread mixture; cover and refrigerate overnight.
3. Remove from the refrigerator 30 minutes before baking. Bake, covered, at 350° for 30 minutes.
4. Uncover; sprinkle with the remaining cheese. Bake for 10-15 minutes or until a knife inserted near the center comes out clean. Let stand 5 minutes before cutting.

Baked Banana French Toast

This easy overnight recipe makes a delightful breakfast or brunch entree. The decadent flavor is reminiscent of banana pudding.

—**NANCY ZIMMERMAN**
CAPE MAY COURT HOUSE, NJ

PREP: 20 MIN. + CHILLING
BAKE: 55 MIN. + STANDING
MAKES: 12 SERVINGS

- 2 **cups sliced ripe bananas**
- 2 **tablespoons lemon juice**
- 9 **cups cubed French bread**
- 1 **package (8 ounces) cream cheese, cubed**
- 9 **eggs**
- 4 **cups 2% milk**
- ½ **cup sugar**
- ¼ **cup butter, melted**
- ¼ **cup maple syrup**
- ½ **teaspoon ground cinnamon**

1. In a small bowl, toss bananas with lemon juice. Place half of bread in a greased 9x13-in. baking dish; layer with cream cheese, bananas and remaining bread.

2. In a large bowl, whisk the eggs, milk, sugar, butter, syrup and cinnamon; pour over the bread. Cover and refrigerate for 8 hours or overnight.

3. Remove from the refrigerator 30 minutes before baking. Bake, uncovered, at 350° for 55-65 minutes or until a knife inserted near the center comes out clean. Let stand for 10 minutes before serving.

Bacon & Cheddar Strata

We love to have this sunrise specialty on Christmas and other holiday mornings. The no-fuss breakfast casserole is ready to pop into the oven when you wake up.

—**DEB HEALEY** COLD LAKE, AB

PREP: 20 MIN. + CHILLING
BAKE: 45 MIN. • **MAKES:** 10 SERVINGS

- 1 **pound bacon strips**
- 1 **medium sweet red pepper, finely chopped**
- 8 **green onions, thinly sliced**
- ½ **cup chopped oil-packed sun-dried tomatoes**
- 8 **slices white bread, cubed**
- 2 **cups (8 ounces) shredded cheddar cheese**
- 6 **eggs, lightly beaten**
- 1½ **cups 2% milk**
- ¼ **cup mayonnaise**
- ½ **teaspoon salt**
- ¼ **teaspoon ground mustard**
- ⅛ **teaspoon pepper**

1. In a large skillet, cook bacon in batches until crisp; drain on paper towels. Crumble into a small bowl. Add red pepper, onions and tomatoes. In a greased 9x13-in. baking dish, layer half of the bread, bacon mixture and cheese. Top with the remaining bread and bacon mixture.

2. In another bowl, combine the eggs, milk, mayonnaise and seasonings. Pour over top. Sprinkle with remaining cheese. Cover and refrigerate overnight.

3. Remove from refrigerator 30 minutes before baking. Preheat oven to 350°. Bake, covered, 40 minutes. Uncover and bake 5-10 minutes or until a knife inserted near center comes out clean. Let stand 5 minutes before cutting.

Spinach and Artichoke Bread Pudding

Bread pudding is usually considered a dessert, but this savory version packed with spinach, artichokes and cheese is a perfect side for dinner or brunch.

—KATHLEEN FRAHER
FLORISSANT, MO

PREP: 20 MIN. + CHILLING
BAKE: 35 MIN. + STANDING
MAKES: 15 SERVINGS

- 2 packages (9 ounces each) fresh spinach
- 2 cans (14 ounces each) water-packed artichoke hearts, rinsed, drained and quartered
- 9 eggs
- 2¾ cups heavy whipping cream
- 1 cup (4 ounces) shredded Monterey Jack cheese
- 1 cup (4 ounces) shredded cheddar cheese
- ½ cup shredded Parmesan cheese
- ½ cup shredded Romano cheese
  Dash salt
- 8 cups day-old cubed French bread

1. In a large saucepan, bring ½ in. of water to a boil. Add spinach; cover and boil for 3-5 minutes or until wilted. Drain.
2. In a large bowl, combine the artichokes, eggs, cream, cheeses and salt. Gently stir in bread cubes and spinach. Transfer to a greased 9x13-in. baking dish. Cover and refrigerate overnight.
3. Remove from the refrigerator 30 minutes before baking. Bake, uncovered, at 350° for 35-40 minutes or until a knife inserted near the center comes out clean. Let stand for 10 minutes before cutting.

Spring Morning Casserole

My mom gave me this recipe, and it has quickly become my favorite breakfast casserole. I love that it can be made the night before and popped in the oven for a special breakfast.

—MELODY HOLLAND LEBANON, PA

PREP: 25 MIN. + CHILLING
BAKE: 40 MIN. + STANDING
MAKES: 12 SERVINGS

- 2 cups cut fresh asparagus (1-inch pieces)
- 1 small sweet red pepper, chopped
- 1 small onion, chopped
- 3 tablespoons butter
- 8 cups cubed day old French bread
- 1 cup cubed fully cooked ham
- 2 cups (8 ounces) shredded cheddar cheese
- 8 eggs, beaten
- 2 cups 2% milk
- ⅓ cup honey
- ½ teaspoon salt
- ½ teaspoon pepper

1. In a large skillet, saute the asparagus, red pepper and onion in butter until tender; set aside.
2. Place bread in a greased 9x13-in. baking dish. Layer with ham, 1 cup cheese and vegetable mixture. Sprinkle with remaining cheese. In a large bowl, combine the eggs, milk, honey, salt and pepper. Pour over the top. Cover and refrigerate overnight.
3. Remove from the refrigerator 30 minutes before baking. Bake casserole, uncovered, at 350° for 40-45 minutes or until a knife inserted near the center comes out clean. Let stand 10 minutes before cutting.

Croissant Breakfast Casserole

Here's a wonderful breakfast treat for overnight guests. The first time I tried the recipe, my family instantly declared it a winner.

—JOAN HALLFORD
NORTH RICHLAND HILLS, TX

PREP: 15 MIN. + CHILLING
BAKE: 25 MIN. • **MAKES:** 12 SERVINGS

- 1 jar (18 ounces) orange marmalade
- ½ cup apricot preserves
- ⅓ cup orange juice
- 3 teaspoons grated orange peel
- 6 croissants, split
- 5 eggs
- 1 cup half-and-half cream
- 1 teaspoon almond or vanilla extract
  Fresh strawberries

1. In a small bowl, mix the marmalade, preserves, orange juice and peel. Arrange croissant bottoms in a greased 9x13-in. baking dish. Spread with 1½ cups marmalade mixture. Cover with croissant tops.
2. In another bowl, whisk eggs, cream and extract; pour over croissants. Spoon remaining marmalade mixture over tops. Refrigerate, covered, overnight.
3. Preheat oven to 350°. Remove casserole from refrigerator while oven heats. Bake, uncovered, 25-30 minutes or until a knife inserted near the center comes out clean. Let stand 5 minutes before serving. Serve with strawberries.

Potato Egg Bake

No one will ever guess how nutritious this mouthwatering breakfast bake is. Potatoes give it a hearty base while cheese and veggies pile on the flavor.

—RENA CHARBONEAU
GANSEVOORT, NY

PREP: 20 MIN. • **BAKE:** 35 MIN.
MAKES: 8 SERVINGS

- 2 pounds Yukon Gold potatoes (about 6 medium), peeled and diced
- ½ cup water
- 1 cup frozen chopped broccoli, thawed
- 6 green onions, thinly sliced
- 1 small sweet red pepper, chopped
- 6 eggs
- 8 egg whites
- 1 cup (8 ounces) 1% cottage cheese
- 1 cup (4 ounces) shredded reduced-fat cheddar cheese
- ½ cup grated Parmesan cheese
- ½ cup fat-free milk
- 2 tablespoons dried parsley flakes
- ½ teaspoon salt
- ¼ teaspoon pepper

1. Place potatoes and water in a microwave-safe dish. Cover and microwave on high for 7 minutes or until tender; drain.
2. Spread potatoes in a 9x13-in. baking dish coated with cooking spray. Top with the broccoli, onions and red pepper.
3. In a large bowl, whisk the remaining ingredients. Pour over vegetables. Bake, uncovered, at 350° for 35-40 minutes or until center is set.

Maple-Bacon French Toast

This is my favorite Sunday breakfast. It's easy to put together Saturday night and pop in the fridge until morning. It gives me more time for enjoying family on Sundays. Plus, we all get to enjoy a wonderful breakfast together!

—**ERIN WRIGHT** WALLACE, KS

PREP: 20 MIN. + CHILLING
BAKE: 30 MIN. • **MAKES:** 8 SERVINGS

- 6 **eggs**
- 2 **cups half-and-half cream**
- 1 **cup 2% milk**
- ¼ **cup maple syrup**
- 2 **tablespoons sugar**
- ¼ **teaspoon ground cinnamon**
  Dash salt
- 16 **slices French bread (1 inch thick)**
- 10 **bacon strips, cooked and crumbled**
  Additional maple syrup

1. In a shallow bowl, whisk eggs, cream, milk, syrup, sugar, cinnamon and salt. Dip both sides of bread in egg mixture. Arrange bread slices into two shingled rows in a greased 9x13-in. baking dish. Pour the remaining egg mixture over top. Refrigerate, covered, overnight.

2. Preheat oven to 350°. Remove French toast from refrigerator while oven heats. Bake, covered, 25 minutes. Sprinkle with bacon. Bake, uncovered, 5-10 minutes longer or until a knife inserted in French toast comes out clean. Let stand for 5 minutes before serving. Serve French toast with additional syrup.

WHITNEY SMITH'S
SMOKY CHICKEN NACHOS
PAGE 27

Appetizers
& Snacks

HEATHER AHRENS' DILLY
VEGGIE PIZZA *PAGE 30*

CAROL WERKMAN'S
CHEDDAR-BACON DIP *PAGE 41*

MARY PONINSKI'S
MEATBALLS IN PLUM SAUCE
PAGE 43

Spicy Shrimp

Not too hot but full of flavor, these shrimp are one of a kind. They're ideal for parties because they're so easy to prepare.

—**BOB GEBHARDT** WAUSAU, WI

START TO FINISH: 30 MIN.
MAKES: 10 SERVINGS

- 6 bacon strips, diced
- 1 cup butter, cubed
- 2 tablespoons seafood seasoning
- 2 tablespoons Dijon mustard
- 1½ teaspoons chili powder
- 1 teaspoon pepper
- ½ to 1 teaspoon Louisiana-style hot sauce
- ¼ teaspoon each dried basil, oregano and thyme
- 2 garlic cloves, minced
- 1½ pounds uncooked shell-on medium shrimp

1. In a large skillet, cook bacon over medium heat until partially cooked but not crisp; drain. Stir in the butter, seafood seasoning, mustard, chili powder, pepper, hot sauce, basil, oregano and thyme. Cook over low heat for 5 minutes. Add garlic; cook 1 minute longer.

2. Place the shrimp in an ungreased 9x13-in. baking dish. Add butter mixture and stir to coat. Bake, uncovered, at 375° for 20-25 minutes or until shrimp turn pink, stirring twice.

Smoky Chicken Nachos

What's a game-day celebration without can't-stop-munching nachos? Loaded with layers of crunchy tortilla chips, black beans and a creamy, smoky chicken mixture, this snack will disappear well before halftime.

—WHITNEY SMITH WINTER HAVEN, FL

PREP: 20 MIN. • **BAKE:** 15 MIN.
MAKES: 12 SERVINGS

- 1 **pound ground chicken**
- ⅔ **cup water**
- 1 **envelope taco seasoning**
- ¼ **cup cream cheese, softened**
- 3 **tablespoons minced fresh chives**
- 2 **tablespoons plus 1½ teaspoons 2% milk**
- 2 **tablespoons dry bread crumbs**
- 1 **teaspoon prepared mustard**
- ½ **teaspoon paprika**
- ¾ **teaspoon liquid smoke, optional**
- 6 **cups tortilla chips**
- 1 **can (15 ounces) black beans, rinsed and drained**
- 1 **cup (4 ounces) shredded cheddar-Monterey Jack cheese**
   Optional toppings: chopped tomatoes and sliced ripe olives

1. In a large skillet over medium heat, cook chicken until no longer pink; drain. Add water and taco seasoning; bring to a boil. Reduce heat and simmer for 5 minutes.
2. Combine the cream cheese, chives, milk, bread crumbs, mustard, paprika and, if desired, liquid smoke; stir into chicken mixture until blended.
3. In an ungreased 9x13-in. baking dish, layer half of the chips, chicken mixture, beans and cheese. Repeat layers.
4. Bake at 350° for 15-20 minutes or until cheese is melted. Serve with tomatoes and olives if desired.

Hoisin Cocktail Meatballs

These saucy meatballs make a fun and flavorful appetizer for all kinds of get-togethers. Sometimes I prep them a day ahead so I can just pop them into the oven.

—DEIRDRE COX KANSAS CITY, MO

PREP: 20 MIN. • **BAKE:** 20 MIN.
MAKES: ABOUT 2½ DOZEN

- 2 **tablespoons hoisin sauce**
- 1 **tablespoon reduced-sodium soy sauce**
- 1 **teaspoon sesame oil**
- ¼ **cup dry bread crumbs**
- 3 **tablespoons chopped green onions**
- 3 **tablespoons minced fresh parsley**
- 2 **garlic cloves, minced**
- 1 **teaspoon minced fresh gingerroot**
- 1½ **pounds lean ground beef**
  SAUCE
- ¼ **cup rice vinegar**
- ¼ **cup hoisin sauce**
- 2 **tablespoons water**
- 2 **tablespoons sesame oil**
- 2 **tablespoons reduced-sodium soy sauce**
- 1 **tablespoon honey**
- 2 **garlic cloves, minced**
- 1 **teaspoon minced fresh gingerroot**

1. In a large bowl, combine the first eight ingredients. Crumble beef over mixture and mix well.
2. Shape into scant 1-in. meatballs. Place in a 9x13-in. baking dish coated with cooking spray. Bake, uncovered, at 350° for 20-25 minutes or until meat is no longer pink.
3. Meanwhile, in a small saucepan, combine the sauce ingredients; heat through. Serve with meatballs.

Hearty Ham Balls

When I worked at a nursing home, a very special resident asked me to make ham balls and shared her recipe with me. Everybody enjoyed them there—and my family loves them, too.

—**EULALA SCHWABAC**
STANBERRY, MO

PREP: 25 MIN. • **BAKE:** 45 MIN.
MAKES: 4 DOZEN

- 2 **cups graham cracker crumbs**
- 2 **eggs, lightly beaten**
- ⅔ **cup milk**
- 2 **pounds ground fully cooked ham**
- 1 **pound ground beef**
- 1 **pound ground pork**
- 1 **can (10¾ ounces) condensed tomato soup, undiluted**
- ½ **cup packed brown sugar**
- 2 **to 4 tablespoons honey**
- 2 **tablespoons white vinegar**
- 1 **to 2 tablespoons ground mustard**

1. In a large bowl, combine the cracker crumbs, eggs and milk; crumble the ham, beef and pork over the mixture and mix well. Shape into 1¼-in. balls. Place the meatballs in two greased 9x13-in. baking dishes.
2. Combine the remaining ingredients; pour over ham balls.
3. Bake, uncovered, at 350° for 45-50 minutes or until the meatballs are browned and fully cooked, basting occasionally with cooking liquid.

Sun-Dried Tomato Spread

This creamy, bubbly spread is truly outstanding. Baked to a golden brown, it gets its richness from cream cheese and mayonnaise.

—**VALERIE ELKINTON** GARDNER, KS

PREP: 15 MIN. • **BAKE:** 20 MIN.
MAKES: 7 CUPS

- 2 **packages (8 ounces each) cream cheese, softened**
- 2 **cups mayonnaise**
- ¼ **cup finely chopped onion**
- 4 **garlic cloves, minced**
- 1 **jar (7 ounces) oil-packed sun-dried tomatoes, drained and chopped**
- ⅔ **cup chopped roasted sweet red peppers**
- 2 **cups (8 ounces) shredded part-skim mozzarella cheese**
- 2 **cups (8 ounces) shredded Italian cheese blend**
- 1 **cup shredded Parmesan cheese, divided**
  Assorted crackers

1. In a large bowl, combine the first four ingredients. Stir in tomatoes and red peppers. Add the mozzarella, cheese blend and ¾ cup Parmesan cheese.
2. Transfer to a greased 9x13-in. baking dish. Sprinkle with the remaining Parmesan cheese. Bake, uncovered, at 350° for 18-22 minutes or until the edges are bubbly and lightly browned. Serve with crackers.

Artichoke Crescent Appetizers

These irresistible appetizers are guaranteed to please. My family loves them both warm and cold.

—**MARY ANN DELL** PHOENIXVILLE, PA

PREP: 20 MIN. • **BAKE:** 15 MIN.
MAKES: ABOUT 2 DOZEN

- 1 **tube (8 ounces) refrigerated crescent rolls**
- 2 **tablespoons grated Parmesan cheese**
- 2 **packages (3 ounces each) cream cheese, softened**
- ½ **cup sour cream**
- 1 **egg**
- ½ **teaspoon dill weed**
- ¼ **teaspoon seasoned salt**
- 1 **can (14 ounces) water-packed artichoke hearts, rinsed, drained and chopped**
- ⅓ **cup thinly chopped green onions**
- 1 **jar (2 ounces) diced pimientos, drained**

1. Unroll crescent dough and press onto the bottom and ½ in. up the sides of an ungreased 9x13-in. baking dish; seal seams and perforations. Sprinkle with the Parmesan cheese. Bake at 375° for 8-10 minutes or until lightly browned.

2. Meanwhile, in a small bowl, beat the cream cheese, sour cream and egg until smooth. Stir in the dill and seasoned salt. Spread over the crust. Sprinkle with artichokes, green onions and pimientos.

3. Bake for 15-20 minutes or until edges are golden brown. Cut into squares.

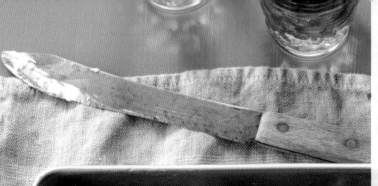

Dilly Veggie Pizza

This is one of my favorite ways to use up leftover chopped veggies. It's a cinch to prepare, and you can change the mixture to match your kids' taste buds. Always popular at special events, it tastes just as good the next day.

—HEATHER AHRENS COLUMBUS, OH

PREP: 20 MIN.
BAKE: 10 MIN. + COOLING
MAKES: 15 SERVINGS

- 1 tube (8 ounces) refrigerated crescent rolls
- 1½ cups vegetable dill dip
- 2 medium carrots, chopped
- 1 cup finely chopped fresh broccoli
- 1 cup chopped seeded tomatoes
- 4 green onions, sliced
- 1 can (2¼ ounces) sliced ripe olives, drained

1. Unroll crescent dough into one long rectangle. Press onto the bottom of a greased 9x13-in. baking pan; seal seams. Bake at 375° for 10-12 minutes or until golden brown. Cool completely on a wire rack.
2. Spread the vegetable dip over the crust; sprinkle with the carrots, broccoli, tomatoes, onions and olives. Cut into squares. Refrigerate leftovers.

Layered Mediterranean Dip

Family and friends will dive into this delightful dip. I created the blend when I wanted to make something like layered taco dip but with Greek and Italian flavors.

—**MARY FRUCELLI** WAKE FOREST, NC

PREP: 20 MIN. + CHILLING
MAKES: 10 CUPS

- 2 **cans (15 ounces each) pinto beans, rinsed and drained**
- ⅓ **cup prepared pesto**
- 2 **cups (16 ounces) reduced-fat sour cream**
- 1 **package (8 ounces) reduced-fat cream cheese**
- 1½ **teaspoons Italian seasoning**
- ½ **teaspoon pepper**
- 4 **plum tomatoes, seeded and finely chopped**
- 1 **medium green pepper, finely chopped**
- 3 **green onions, finely chopped**
- 2 **cups (8 ounces) shredded Italian cheese blend**
- 1 **cup crumbled feta cheese**
- 2 **cans (2¼ ounces each) sliced ripe olives, drained**
  Baked pita chips

1. Place beans in a large bowl; stir in pesto until blended. Spread into a 9x13-in. dish.
2. In another bowl, beat the sour cream, cream cheese, Italian seasoning and pepper until smooth; layer over bean mixture. Sprinkle with vegetables, cheeses and olives. Refrigerate for at least 30 minutes. Serve with chips.

Hot Antipasto

My husband's family requests this meaty appetizer for our annual Christmas Eve potluck. Everyone loves that there are so many delicious ingredients to nibble on. It's a real crowd-pleaser.

—**SUSAN LEIGHTON** PORTLAND, CT

PREP: 25 MIN. • **BAKE:** 25 MIN.
MAKES: 28 SERVINGS (½ CUP EACH)

- 1 **pound sweet Italian sausage links, cut into ½-inch slices**
- 1 **pound hot Italian sausage links, cut into ½-inch slices**
- 1 **jar (16 ounces) pepperoncini, drained**
- 1 **jar (16 ounces) pickled hot cherry peppers, drained**
- 1 **can (16 ounces) kidney beans, rinsed and drained**
- 1 **can (15 ounces) garbanzo beans or chickpeas, rinsed and drained**
- 1 **jar (8 ounces) marinated whole mushrooms, drained**
- 1 **jar (7½ ounces) marinated quartered artichoke hearts, drained**
- 1 **jar (7 ounces) pimiento-stuffed olives, drained**
- 1 **can (6 ounces) pitted ripe olives, drained**
- 1 **package (3½ ounces) sliced pepperoni**
- 2 **cups (8 ounces) shredded Italian cheese blend**

1. In a large skillet, cook the sausages over medium heat until no longer pink; drain and place in a large bowl.
2. Stir in the pepperoncini, hot cherry peppers, beans, mushrooms, artichokes, olives and pepperoni. Transfer to an ungreased 9x13-in. baking dish (dish will be full).
3. Bake, uncovered, at 350° for 20 minutes. Sprinkle with cheese. Bake 4-5 minutes longer or until cheese is melted.
NOTE *Look for pepperoncini (pickled peppers) in the pickle and olive section of your grocery store.*

Praline Pecans & Cranberries

This pretty mix is so easy to prepare and fun to snack on. I made a few batches for Christmas parties and everyone wanted the recipe.

—**NANCY ROMAN** HACKENSACK, NJ

PREP: 15 MIN.
BAKE: 1 HOUR + COOLING
MAKES: 5½ CUPS

- 3½ cups pecan halves
- ¼ cup packed brown sugar
- ¼ cup light corn syrup
- 2 tablespoons butter
- 1 teaspoon vanilla extract
- ¼ teaspoon baking soda
- 1½ cups dried cranberries

1. Place pecans in a greased 9x13-in. baking pan; set aside. In a small saucepan, combine the brown sugar, corn syrup and butter. Bring to a boil over medium heat, stirring constantly. Remove from the heat. Stir in vanilla and baking soda. Drizzle over pecans; stir until coated.
2. Bake at 250° for 1 hour, stirring every 20 minutes. Add cranberries; toss to combine. Immediately transfer to a waxed paper-lined baking sheet; cool completely. Break into pieces. Store in an airtight container.

DID YOU KNOW?

Pecans have a higher fat content than other nuts, so they're more prone to going rancid. They will stay fresh for twice as long in the freezer as they would at room temperature.

Pimiento Cheese-Stuffed Artichoke Bottoms

When your friends take a look at this vibrant appetizer, they'll know they're at a party. There's nothing better than noshing on one of these bites while mingling or watching football. They are cheesy, bacony and superb.

—**ELIZABETH BENNETT** MILL CREEK, WA

PREP: 30 MIN. • **BAKE:** 20 MIN.
MAKES: ABOUT 2 DOZEN

- 3 cans (14 ounces each) artichoke bottoms, drained
- ¾ cup shredded sharp cheddar cheese
- ½ cup shredded Monterey Jack cheese
- 1 jar (4 ounces) diced pimientos, drained
- ¼ cup mayonnaise
- 3 cooked bacon strips, chopped, divided
- 1 garlic clove, minced
- 1 teaspoon Worcestershire sauce
- ⅛ teaspoon salt
- ⅛ teaspoon pepper
- ⅛ teaspoon cayenne pepper
- 2 green onions, chopped

1. Cut a thin layer from bottoms of artichokes to level if necessary. Place in a greased 9x13-in. baking dish. In a small bowl, combine the cheeses, diced pimientos, mayonnaise, half of the bacon, garlic, Worcestershire sauce, salt, pepper and cayenne.
2. Place 1 tablespoon mixture in each artichoke; top with the remaining bacon. Bake at 350° for 15-18 minutes or until golden brown. Sprinkle with onions.

Chorizo Bean Dip

With zesty flavors and tempting toppings, this Mexican dip is always a hit. I serve it with extra-thick tortilla chips for some serious scooping!

—ELAINE SWEET DALLAS, TX

PREP: 25 MIN. • **BAKE:** 20 MIN.
MAKES: 20 SERVINGS

- 1 pound ground sirloin
- ⅓ pound uncooked chorizo or bulk spicy pork sausage
- 1 medium onion, chopped
- 1 envelope taco seasoning
- 2 cans (16 ounces each) refried black beans
- 1 cup (4 ounces) shredded Monterey Jack cheese
- 1⅓ cups salsa
- 2 cans (2¼ ounces each) sliced ripe olives, drained
- 2 cups guacamole
- 6 green onions, thinly sliced
- 1 cup (8 ounces) sour cream
- ½ cup minced fresh cilantro
- ¾ cup jalapeno-stuffed olives, sliced
  Tortilla chips

1. Crumble beef and chorizo into a large skillet; add onion and taco seasoning. Cook over medium heat until meat is no longer pink; drain.

2. Spread the beans into a greased 9x13-in. baking dish. Layer with the meat mixture, cheese, salsa and ripe olives.

3. Cover and bake at 350° for 20-25 minutes or until mixture is heated through.

4. Spread guacamole over the top. Combine the green onions, sour cream and cilantro; spread over guacamole. Sprinkle with stuffed olives. Serve immediately with tortilla chips.

⑤ INGREDIENTS

Smoky Jalapenos

When I make these spicy snacks, I never have leftovers. It's easy to dial down the heat with mild banana peppers instead of jalapenos.

—**MELINDA STRABLE** ANKENY, IA

PREP: 25 MIN. • **BAKE:** 20 MIN.
MAKES: 14 APPETIZERS

- 14 jalapeno peppers
- 4 ounces cream cheese, softened
- 14 miniature smoked sausages
- 7 bacon strips

1. Cut a lengthwise slit in each pepper; remove the seeds and the membranes. Spread a teaspoonful of cream cheese into each pepper; stuff each with a sausage.
2. Cut bacon strips in half widthwise; cook in a microwave or skillet until partially cooked. Wrap a bacon piece around each pepper; secure with a toothpick.
3. Place in an ungreased 9x13-in. baking dish. Bake, uncovered, at 350° for 20 minutes for spicy flavor, 30 minutes for medium and 40 minutes for mild.

NOTE *Wear disposable gloves when cutting hot peppers; the oils can burn skin. Avoid touching your face.*

⑤ INGREDIENTS

Barbecued Peanuts

These zippy seasoned peanuts are perfect for football parties, movie nights or after-school munching. I like to prepare them at the holidays to give as presents.

—**ABBEY BOYLE** TAMPA, FL

PREP: 10 MIN.
BAKE: 20 MIN. + COOLING
MAKES: 3 CUPS

- ⅓ cup barbecue sauce
- 2 tablespoons butter, melted
- 1 teaspoon garlic powder
- ¼ to ½ teaspoon cayenne pepper
- 1 jar (16 ounces) dry roasted peanuts

1. In a large bowl, combine the barbecue sauce, butter, garlic powder and cayenne. Add the peanuts; stir until evenly coated. Transfer to a greased 9x13-in. baking pan.
2. Bake, uncovered, at 325° for 20-25 minutes, stirring every 10 minutes. Spread on waxed paper; cool completely. Store in an airtight container.

Sweet & Sour Meatballs

When we entertain friends for Sunday dinner, I frequently serve these tangy meatballs. Everyone loves the distinctive sauce, and people are often surprised to learn that it's made with gingersnaps.

—MELODY MELLINGER
MYERSTOWN, PA

PREP: 30 MIN. • **BAKE:** 40 MIN.
MAKES: 10 SERVINGS

- 3 **eggs**
- 1 **medium onion, chopped**
- 1½ **cups dry bread crumbs**
- 1 **teaspoon salt**
- 2 **pounds ground beef**
- 2 **tablespoons canola oil**

SAUCE
- 3½ **cups tomato juice**
- 1 **cup packed brown sugar**
- 10 **gingersnaps, finely crushed**
- ¼ **cup white vinegar**
- 1 **teaspoon onion salt**

1. In a large bowl, combine the eggs, onion, bread crumbs and salt. Crumble the beef over the mixture and mix well. Shape into 1½-in. balls.

2. In a large skillet, brown meatballs in batches in oil. Transfer to a greased 9x13-in. baking dish.

3. In a large saucepan, combine the sauce ingredients. Bring to a boil over medium heat, stirring until the cookie crumbs are dissolved. Pour over meatballs.

4. Bake, uncovered, at 350° for 40-45 minutes or until meat is no longer pink.

⑤ INGREDIENTS

Apple Sausage Appetizers

Bake sausage slices in this sweet glaze for a tasty no-fuss appetizer. The recipe yields a big batch, so it's perfect for holiday parties and other large gatherings.

—DOLORES BARNAS BLASDELL, NY

PREP: 10 MIN. • **BAKE:** 40 MIN.
MAKES: 20 SERVINGS

- 2 **jars (23 ounces each) unsweetened chunky applesauce**
- ½ **cup packed brown sugar**
- 2 **pounds fully cooked kielbasa or Polish sausage, cut into ½-inch slices**
- 1 **medium onion, chopped**

In a bowl, combine applesauce and brown sugar. Stir in sausage and onion. Transfer to a greased 9x13-in. baking dish. Bake the mixture, uncovered, at 350° for 40-50 minutes or until bubbly.

Oven-Fried Sesame Chicken Wings

Made with a zesty sesame-bread crumb coating, these buttery wings "fry" easily in the oven. I made a large batch to serve at my sister's wedding. They're delicious served hot or cold.

—**PATRICE EHRLICH** MERCED, CA

PREP: 15 MIN. • **BAKE:** 40 MIN.
MAKES: 2½ DOZEN

- 15 **whole chicken wings**
- ¾ **cup dry bread crumbs**
- 2 **tablespoons sesame seeds, toasted**
- 1 **teaspoon paprika**
- ½ **teaspoon salt**
- ⅓ **cup heavy whipping cream**
- ¼ **cup butter, melted**

1. Cut the chicken wings into three sections; discard wing tip sections. In a large resealable plastic bag, combine the bread crumbs, sesame seeds, paprika and salt. Place cream in a shallow bowl. Dip chicken wings in the cream, then place in the bag and shake to coat evenly.

2. Pour butter into a 9x13-in. baking dish; add chicken, turning to coat. Bake, uncovered, at 375° for 40-45 minutes or until juices run clear, turning every 10 minutes.

NOTE *Uncooked chicken wing sections (wingettes) may be substituted for the whole chicken wings.*

Shrimp Lover Squares

PREP: 20 MIN. + CHILLING
MAKES: 2 DOZEN

- 1 **tube (8 ounces) refrigerated crescent rolls**
- 1 **package (8 ounces) cream cheese, softened**
- ¼ **cup sour cream**
- ½ **teaspoon dill weed**
- ⅛ **teaspoon salt**
- ½ **cup seafood cocktail sauce**
- 24 **cooked medium shrimp, peeled and deveined**
- ½ **cup chopped green pepper**
- ⅓ **cup chopped onion**
- 1 **cup (4 ounces) shredded Monterey Jack cheese**

1. In a greased 9x13-in. baking dish, unroll crescent dough into one long rectangle; seal seams and perforations. Bake at 375° for 10-12 minutes or until golden brown. Cool completely on a wire rack.

2. In a small bowl, beat the cream cheese, sour cream, dill and salt until smooth. Spread over the crust. Top with the cocktail sauce, shrimp, green pepper, onion and cheese. Cover and refrigerate for 1 hour. Cut into squares.

During the holiday season, my family enjoys having a variety of appetizers as a meal while playing a board game or watching a movie. These delicious shrimp squares are part of the buffet I prepare every year. —**ARDYCE PIEHL** POYNETTE, WI

Crab-Stuffed Baby Portobellos

Our Christmas is always capped off with these irresistible mushrooms.

—**DEBBIE JOHNSTON** OWATONNA, MN

PREP: 45 MIN. • **BAKE:** 25 MIN.
MAKES: 3 DOZEN

- 1 **pound baby portobello mushrooms**
- ¾ **cup butter, divided**
- 2 **garlic cloves, minced**
- 2 **cans (6 ounces each) crabmeat, drained, flaked and cartilage removed**
- ¼ **cup grated Romano cheese**
- 1 **tablespoon minced fresh parsley**
- 3 **teaspoons garlic powder**
- 1½ **teaspoons onion powder**
- ¼ **cup grated Parmesan cheese**
- 1 **teaspoon garlic salt**
- ½ **cup shredded part-skim mozzarella cheese**

1. Remove stems from the mushrooms; set caps aside. Finely chop stems.
2. In a large skillet, saute the chopped mushrooms in ¼ cup butter for 5 minutes or just until tender. Add garlic; saute 1-2 minutes longer or until garlic is golden. Remove from the heat; stir in the crab, Romano, parsley, garlic powder and onion powder.
3. Melt remaining butter; pour into a 9x13-in. baking dish. Fill mushroom caps with crab mixture; place in dish. Sprinkle with Parmesan and garlic salt.
4. Bake, uncovered, at 350° for 20-25 minutes or until the mushrooms are tender. Sprinkle with mozzarella cheese. Bake 2-4 minutes longer or until cheese is melted. Serve warm.

⑤ INGREDIENTS

Bacon Water Chestnut Wraps

In our house, family gatherings just wouldn't be the same without these classic wraps. It's impossible to eat just one!

—**LAURA MAHAFFEY** ANNAPOLIS, MD

PREP: 20 MIN. • **BAKE:** 30 MIN.
MAKES: ABOUT 2½ DOZEN

- 1 **pound bacon strips**
- 2 **cans (8 ounces each) whole water chestnuts, drained**
- ½ **cup packed brown sugar**
- ½ **cup mayonnaise**
- ¼ **cup chili sauce**

1. Cut bacon strips in half. In a large skillet over medium heat, cook bacon until almost crisp; drain. Wrap each bacon piece around a water chestnut and secure with a toothpick. Place in an ungreased 9x13-in. baking dish.
2. In a small bowl, combine the brown sugar, mayonnaise and chili sauce; pour over water chestnuts. Bake, uncovered, at 350° for 30 minutes or until hot and bubbly.

Spinach Squares

Go for the green! Even people who don't usually care for spinach can't pass up these colorful and satisfying appetizer squares.

—**PATRICIA KILE** ELIZABETHTOWN, PA

PREP: 10 MIN. • **BAKE:** 30 MIN.
MAKES: 4 DOZEN

- 2 **tablespoons butter, melted, divided**
- 1 **cup all-purpose flour**
- 1 **teaspoon baking powder**
- ¾ **teaspoon salt**
- ½ **teaspoon dried oregano**
- ¼ **teaspoon dried basil**
- ¼ **teaspoon dried thyme**
- ¼ **teaspoon pepper**
- 3 **eggs**
- 1 **cup milk**
- 2 **packages (10 ounces each) frozen chopped spinach, thawed and squeezed dry**
- 2 **cups (8 ounces) shredded cheddar cheese**
- 2 **cups (8 ounces) shredded Monterey Jack cheese**
- 1 **cup chopped onion**
  Sliced pimientos

1. Brush the bottom and sides of a 9x13-in. baking dish with 1 tablespoon butter; set aside. In a large bowl, combine the flour, baking powder, seasonings, eggs, milk and remaining butter. Stir in the spinach, cheeses and onion. Spread in prepared pan.
2. Bake, uncovered, at 350° for 30-35 minutes or until a toothpick inserted in the center comes out clean. Cut into squares. Garnish each with a slice of pimiento.

Double-Nut Stuffed Figs

We have a diabetic in the family, and we love this recipe because it's sweet and delicious without compromising on good nutrition.

—**BOB BAILEY** COLUMBUS, OH

PREP: 20 MIN. • **BAKE:** 30 MIN.
MAKES: 3 DOZEN

- 36 **dried Calimyrna figs**
- ⅔ **cup finely chopped pecans**
- ⅔ **cup finely chopped walnuts**
- 7 **tablespoons agave nectar, divided**
- 3 **tablespoons baking cocoa**
- ¼ **teaspoon ground cinnamon**
- ⅛ **teaspoon ground cloves**
- ½ **cup pomegranate juice**
- 4½ **teaspoons lemon juice**

1. Preheat oven to 350°. Remove stems from figs. Cut an "X" in the top of each fig, about two-thirds of the way down.

2. In a small bowl, combine pecans, walnuts, 3 tablespoons agave nectar, cocoa, cinnamon and cloves; spoon into the figs. Arrange in a 9x13-in. baking dish coated with cooking spray.

3. In a small bowl, mix the pomegranate juice, lemon juice and remaining agave nectar; drizzle over figs. Bake, covered, 20 minutes. Bake, uncovered, 8-10 minutes longer or until heated through, basting figs occasionally with cooking liquid.

Queso Baked Nachos

I modified a nachos recipe I found, and my family loves it! It is now a regular at our dinner table.

—**DENISE WHEELER** NEWAYGO, MI

START TO FINISH: 25 MIN.
MAKES: 12 SERVINGS

- 1 **pound ground beef**
- 1 **enevelope taco seasoning**
- ¾ **cup water**
- 1 **package (13 ounces) tortilla chips**
- 1 **cup refried beans**
- 1 **jar (15½ ounces) salsa con queso dip**
- 2 **plum tomatoes, chopped**
- ½ **cup sour cream**
- ¼ **cup minced fresh chives, optional**

1. In a large skillet, cook beef over medium heat 6-8 minutes or until no longer pink, breaking into crumbles; drain. Stir in taco seasoning and water. Bring to a boil. Reduce heat; simmer, uncovered, 3-5 minutes or until thickened, stirring occasionally.

2. In an ungreased 9x13-in. baking dish, layer a third of each of the following: tortilla chips, beans, meat mixture and queso dip. Repeat layers twice.

3. Bake, uncovered, for 10-15 minutes or until heated through. Top with tomatoes, sour cream and, if desired, minced chives. Serve immediately.

Cheddar-Bacon Dip

Both children and adults enjoy this savory dip. I like to make it for special occasions, such as birthdays and holiday parties, because it's so quick and easy to prepare.

—CAROL WERKMAN NEERLANDIA, AB

PREP: 15 MIN. + CHILLING
MAKES: 10-12 SERVINGS

- 1 package (8 ounces) cream cheese, softened
- 1 cup (8 ounces) sour cream
- 5 green onions, thinly sliced
- 4 medium tomatoes, chopped
- 1 large green pepper, chopped
- 1 jar (16 ounces) taco sauce
- 2 cups (8 ounces) shredded cheddar cheese
- 1 pound sliced bacon, cooked and crumbled
  Tortilla or nacho tortilla chips

1. In a bowl, beat cream cheese and sour cream until smooth. Spread in an ungreased 9x13-in. dish or on a 12-in. plate. Combine the onions, tomatoes and green pepper; sprinkle over the cream cheese layer.

2. Pour the taco sauce over the vegetables. Sprinkle with the cheddar cheese. Refrigerate. Just before serving, sprinkle with bacon. Serve with chips.

I love a Reuben sandwich, and this recipe combines all of its flavors into a great party dip.

—**SYLVIA METZLER** CHILLICOTHE, OH

Baked Reuben Dip

PREP: 10 MIN. • **BAKE:** 25 MIN.
MAKES: 8 CUPS

- 1 jar (32 ounces) sauerkraut, rinsed and well drained
- 10 ounces sliced deli corned beef, chopped
- 2 cups (8 ounces) shredded sharp cheddar cheese
- 2 cups (8 ounces) shredded Swiss cheese
- 1 cup mayonnaise
- ¼ cup Russian salad dressing
- 1 teaspoon caraway seeds, optional
  Rye crackers

In a large bowl, mix the first six ingredients; stir in caraway seeds if desired. Transfer to a greased 9x13-in. baking dish. Bake at 350° for 25-30 minutes or until bubbly. Serve with rye crackers.

Meatballs in Plum Sauce

A topping made of plum jam and chili sauce beautifully coats tender meatballs. You'll want to have these delightful appetizers on your party menu.
—**MARY PONINSKI** WHITTINGTON, IL

PREP: 50 MIN. + STANDING
BAKE: 30 MIN.
MAKES: 10-12 SERVINGS

- ½ cup milk
- 1 cup soft bread crumbs
- 1 egg, lightly beaten
- 1 tablespoon Worcestershire sauce
- 1 medium onion, finely chopped
- ¼ teaspoon salt
- ¼ teaspoon pepper
- ⅛ teaspoon ground cloves
- ½ pound lean ground beef
- ½ pound ground pork
- ½ pound ground veal
- 2 tablespoons canola oil
- ½ teaspoon beef bouillon granules
- ½ cup boiling water
- 3 tablespoons all-purpose flour
- 1 cup plum jam
- ½ cup chili sauce

1. In a large bowl, pour milk over the bread crumbs; let stand for 10 minutes. Add the egg, Worcestershire sauce, onion, salt, pepper and cloves. Crumble beef, pork and veal over mixture and mix well (mixture will be soft). Shape into 1-in. balls.

2. In a large skillet, brown the meatballs in oil in batches. Drain on paper towels. Place in a greased 9x13-in. baking dish.

3. In a small bowl, dissolve the bouillon in water. Stir flour into pan drippings until blended; add the bouillon mixture, jam and chili sauce. Bring to a boil; cook and stir for 1-2 minutes or until thickened. Pour over meatballs.

4. Cover and bake at 350° for 30-45 minutes or until meat is no longer pink and sauce is bubbly.

Praline Cereal Crunch

A sweet and salty snack like this is hard to resist. The recipe makes 10 cups, so you'll have plenty to serve when hosting a party.

—GELENE BOLIN PARADISE, CA

PREP: 10 MIN.
BAKE: 1 HOUR + COOLING
MAKES: 10 CUPS

- 8 **cups Crispix cereal**
- 2 **cups pecan halves**
- ½ **cup packed brown sugar**
- ½ **cup light corn syrup**
- ½ **cup butter, cubed**
- 1 **teaspoon vanilla extract**
- ½ **teaspoon baking soda**

1. In a 9x13-in. baking pan, combine cereal and pecans; set aside. In a microwave-safe bowl, combine the brown sugar, corn syrup and butter. Microwave, uncovered, on high for 2 -2½ minutes or until mixture comes to a boil, stirring occasionally. Stir in vanilla and baking soda.
2. Pour over cereal mixture; stir to coat evenly. Bake at 250° for 1 hour, stirring every 20 minutes. Turn onto waxed paper to cool. Break into bite-size pieces.

Glazed Orange Chicken Wings

Orange juice concentrate is the tasty, sweet-and-tangy base for these moist and tender chicken wings. Well-glazed but not too sticky, they're easy to eat while you're mingling with friends and family.

—MARIE BROWN CARTHAGE, MS

PREP: 10 MIN. • **BAKE:** 30 MIN.
MAKES: 1½ DOZEN

- 2 **pounds chicken wingettes and drumettes**
- 1 **can (6 ounces) frozen orange juice concentrate, thawed**
- 2 **tablespoons reduced-sodium soy sauce**
- ½ **teaspoon salt**
- ½ **teaspoon celery seed**
- ½ **teaspoon hot pepper sauce**
- ¼ **teaspoon ground ginger**

1. Place chicken in a greased 9x13-in. baking dish.
2. Combine the remaining ingredients; pour over chicken. Bake, uncovered, at 375° for 30-40 minutes or until chicken juices run clear, basting occasionally with glaze.

DID YOU KNOW?

Most vanilla comes from Madagascar and Reunion Island—formerly known as the Bourbon Islands—off the southeast coast of Africa. Bourbon vanilla is celebrated for its strong, clear vanilla flavor and creamy finish.

Stuffed Butterflied Shrimp

One of my fondest memories is preparing this dish for my father on Christmas Eve. The flavorful shrimp can be an appetizer or entree. I've handed out this recipe to many friends and family over the years.

—**JOAN ELLIOTT** DEEP RIVER, CT

PREP: 20 MIN. + STANDING
BAKE: 20 MIN. • **MAKES:** 2 DOZEN

- **24 uncooked unpeeled large shrimp**
- **1 cup Italian salad dressing**
- **1½ cups seasoned bread crumbs**
- **1 can (6½ ounces) chopped clams, drained and minced**
- **6 tablespoons butter, melted**
- **1½ teaspoons minced fresh parsley**

1. Peel shrimp, leaving tail section on. Make a deep cut along the top of each shrimp (do not cut all the way through); remove the vein. Place the shrimp in a shallow dish; add the salad dressing. Set aside for 20 minutes.

2. Meanwhile, in a large bowl, combine the bread crumbs, clams, butter and parsley. Drain shrimp and discard the salad dressing. Arrange shrimp in a greased 9x13-in. baking dish. Open shrimp and press flat; fill each with 1 tablespoon of crumb mixture. Bake, uncovered, at 350° for 20-25 minutes or until shrimp turn pink.

**DOLORES BETCHNER'S
EASY STUFFED SHELLS**
PAGE 50

Beef & Pork

BETTY WINSCHER'S
CHEESEBURGER PEPPER
CUPS *PAGE 54*

BERNICE KNUTSON'S PIZZA
NOODLE BAKE *PAGE 59*

LINDA KOBELUCK'S
MAPLE-GLAZED RIBS *PAGE 62*

Sausage Ravioli Lasagna

You can easily alter this lasagna to please any palate—substitute ground beef or turkey for the sausage or use beef ravioli instead of cheese ravioli.

—NICOLE GAZZO BONDURANT, IA

PREP: 20 MIN.
BAKE: 35 MIN. + STANDING
MAKES: 8 SERVINGS

- 1 package (25 ounces) frozen cheese ravioli
- 1½ pounds bulk Italian sausage
- 1 container (15 ounces) ricotta cheese
- 1 egg, lightly beaten
- 1 teaspoon dried basil
- ½ teaspoon Italian seasoning
- 2 jars (one 26 ounces, one 14 ounces) spaghetti sauce
- 2 cups (8 ounces) shredded Italian cheese blend

1. Cook ravioli according to package directions. Meanwhile, in a large skillet, cook sausage over medium heat until no longer pink; drain. Combine ricotta cheese, egg, basil and Italian seasoning; set aside. Drain ravioli.

2. Spoon 1⅓ cups spaghetti sauce into a greased 9x13-in. baking dish. Layer with half of the ravioli and sausage. Spoon ricotta mixture over sausage; top with 1⅓ cups sauce. Layer with remaining ravioli and sausage. Spread remaining sauce over top; sprinkle with shredded cheese.

3. Cover and bake at 350° for 30 minutes. Uncover; bake for 5-10 minutes or until cheese is melted. Let stand 10 minutes before cutting.

Stuffed Zucchini

An abundance of squash from my garden inspired me to make up this recipe, which is now a favorite.

—MARJORIE ROBERTS

WEST CHAZY, NY

PREP: 25 MIN. • **BAKE:** 45 MIN.
MAKES: 8-10 SERVINGS

- 1½ **pounds lean ground beef (90% lean)**
- 1 **large onion, chopped**
- 1 **large green pepper, chopped**
- 1 **jalapeno pepper, minced**
- 1¼ **cups soft bread crumbs**
- 1 **egg, beaten**
- 1 **tablespoon dried parsley flakes**
- 1 **teaspoon dried basil**
- 1 **teaspoon Italian seasoning**
- 1 **teaspoon salt**
- ⅛ **teaspoon pepper**
- 2 **cans (8 ounces each) tomato sauce, divided**
- 2 **medium tomatoes, coarsely chopped**
- 4 **to 5 medium zucchini**
- 2 **cups (8 ounces) shredded mozzarella cheese**

1. In a large bowl, combine first 11 ingredients and one can of the tomato sauce; mix well. Stir in tomatoes. Halve the zucchini lengthwise; scoop out seeds. Fill with meat mixture; place in two 9x13-in. baking dishes. Top with remaining tomato sauce.

2. Bake, uncovered, at 375° for 45 minutes or until the zucchini is tender. Sprinkle the zucchini with cheese during the last few minutes of baking.

NOTE *Wear disposable gloves when cutting hot peppers; the oils can burn skin. Avoid touching your face.*

Andouille-Stuffed Peppers

I was inspired by the important role of green peppers in Cajun dishes when I created my spiced-up recipe. For a healthy choice, substitute chicken sausage or cubed cooked chicken breast for the andouille.

—SARAH LARSON CARLSBAD, CA

PREP: 40 MIN. • **BAKE:** 40 MIN.
MAKES: 4 SERVINGS

- 1 **package (8 ounces) jambalaya mix**
- 4 **small green peppers**
- ¾ **pound fully cooked andouille sausage links, chopped**
- 1 **jalapeno pepper, seeded and minced**
- 1 **can (16 ounces) tomato juice Louisiana-style hot sauce, optional**

1. Prepare the jambalaya mix according to package directions. Meanwhile, cut peppers in half lengthwise; remove seeds.

2. In a large skillet, cook and stir sausage over medium-high heat until browned. Add jalapeno; cook 1 minute longer.

3. Stir sausage mixture into prepared jambalaya. Spoon into pepper halves. Place in a greased 9x13-in. baking dish; pour the tomato juice over and around the peppers.

4. Bake, uncovered, at 350° for 40-45 minutes or until peppers are tender. Serve with hot sauce if desired.

NOTE *This recipe was prepared with Zatarain's New Orleans-style Jambalaya mix. Wear disposable gloves when cutting hot peppers; the oils can burn skin. Avoid touching your face.*

loaf. Bake, uncovered, at 350° for 55-60 minutes or until no pink remains and a thermometer reads 160°. Drain; let stand for 10 minutes before slicing.

4. Serve immediately or cover unbaked meat loaf and freeze for up to 3 months.

TO USE FROZEN MEAT LOAF *Thaw in the refrigerator overnight. Bake as directed.*

⑤INGREDIENTS

Easy Stuffed Shells

I created a super-easy way to fill pasta shells—just use meatballs. Put the kids on stuffing duty. They'll be proud to help, and they'll have another reason to love the dish come dinnertime.

—**DOLORES BETCHNER** CUDAHY, WI

PREP: 20 MIN. • **BAKE:** 40 MIN.
MAKES: 12 SERVINGS

- 36 **uncooked jumbo pasta shells**
- 1 **jar (24 ounces) spaghetti sauce**
- 36 **frozen fully cooked Italian meatballs (½ ounce each), thawed**
- 2 **cups (8 ounces) shredded part-skim mozzarella cheese**

1. Preheat oven to 350°. Cook pasta shells according to package directions; drain and rinse in cold water.
2. Spread ½ cup sauce into a greased 9x13-in. baking dish. Fill each shell with a meatball; place over sauce. Top with remaining sauce and cheese.
3. Bake, covered, 35 minutes. Uncover; bake 3-5 minutes longer or until bubbly and cheese is melted.

FREEZE IT

Sun-Dried Tomato Meat Loaf

Meat loaf gets Italian flair with herbs and sun-dried tomatoes. The recipe yields a large loaf, and extra slices make tasty sandwiches.

—*TASTE OF HOME* TEST KITCHEN

PREP: 25 MIN.
BAKE: 55 MIN. + STANDING
MAKES: 10 SERVINGS

- 1¼ **cups sun-dried tomatoes (not packed in oil)**
- 3 **cups boiling water**
- ½ **cup chopped onion**
- ½ **cup chopped green pepper**
- 2 **teaspoons canola oil**
- 1 **egg, lightly beaten**
- ½ **cup milk**
- 1 **cup soft bread crumbs**
- 2 **teaspoons dried basil**
- 1 **teaspoon dried oregano**
- 1 **teaspoon salt**
- 1 **teaspoon pepper**
- ½ **teaspoon dried thyme**
- 1½ **pounds ground beef**
- ¼ **cup ketchup**

1. In a large bowl, combine tomatoes and water; let stand for 15 minutes or until softened. Meanwhile, in a small skillet, saute onion and green pepper in oil until tender. In a large bowl, combine egg, milk and bread crumbs.
2. Drain and chop the tomatoes; set aside ¼ cup for topping meat loaf. Add onion mixture, basil, oregano, salt, pepper, thyme and remaining chopped tomatoes to the egg mixture. Crumble beef over the mixture and mix well. Shape into a loaf in an ungreased 9x13-in. baking dish.
3. Combine the ketchup and reserved tomatoes; spread over

Oven Stew and Biscuits

Here's a hearty stick-to-the-ribs stew that's sure to warm up any day. The recipe came from my brother, who was a wonderful cook.

—BERTHA BROOKMEIER
EL CAJON, CA

PREP: 20 MIN. • **BAKE:** 45 MIN.
MAKES: 6-8 SERVINGS

- ⅓ cup all-purpose flour
- 1 teaspoon salt
- ½ teaspoon pepper
- 2 pounds beef top sirloin, cut into 1-inch cubes
- ¼ cup canola oil
- 1 can (14½ ounces) stewed tomatoes
- 1 jar (4½ ounces) sliced mushrooms, drained
- 1 large onion, thinly sliced
- 3 tablespoons soy sauce
- 3 tablespoons molasses
- 1 medium green pepper, cut into 1-inch pieces
- 1 tube (12 ounces) refrigerated buttermilk biscuits
- 1 teaspoon butter, melted
  Sesame seeds

1. In a large resealable plastic bag, combine flour, salt and pepper. Add beef in batches; shake to coat. In a large skillet, brown beef in batches in oil . Return all to the pan; stir in tomatoes, mushrooms, onion, soy sauce and molasses.
2. Transfer to a greased 9x13-in. baking dish. Cover and bake at 375° for 20 minutes. Stir in the green pepper. Cover and bake 10 minutes longer.
3. Uncover; top with biscuits. Brush biscuits with butter; sprinkle with sesame seeds. Bake 15-18 minutes more or until the biscuits are golden brown.

Parm-Breaded Pork Chops

The king of Italian cheeses brings a sweet, nutty taste to the buttery cracker coating in these tasty chops. I love how easy the dish is to make on a school night, but it tastes like you spent a long time.

—MELANIE HOGAN BIRMINGHAM, AL

PREP: 10 MIN. • **BAKE:** 35 MIN.
MAKES: 6 SERVINGS

- ¼ cup all-purpose flour
- 1 egg
- 2 tablespoons 2% milk
- 1 cup crushed Ritz crackers
- 3 tablespoons grated Parmesan cheese
- ½ teaspoon salt
- ⅛ teaspoon pepper
- 6 boneless pork loin chops (4 ounces each)
- ¼ cup butter, melted

1. Place flour in a shallow bowl. In a separate shallow bowl, whisk egg and milk. In a third bowl, combine the crackers, cheese, salt and pepper. Dip pork chops in the flour, egg mixture, then cracker mixture.
2. Place butter in a 9x13-in. baking dish; add pork chops. Bake, uncovered, at 350° for 25-30 minutes or until a thermometer reads 145°.
3. Let pork chops stand for 5 minutes before serving.

Ham and Broccoli Bake

This satisfying casserole is a snap to bake up for a casual lunch or brunch because you can prep it the night before. Just add fruit juice and a green salad.

—HARMONY TARDUGNO
VERNON CENTER, NY

PREP: 15 MIN. + CHILLING
BAKE: 35 MIN.
MAKES: 8 SERVINGS

- 1 loaf (8 ounces) day-old French bread, cubed
- ½ cup butter, melted
- 2 cups (8 ounces) shredded cheddar cheese
- 2 cups frozen chopped broccoli, thawed
- 2 cups cubed fully cooked ham
- 4 eggs
- 2 cups 2% milk
- ¼ teaspoon pepper

1. Toss bread cubes with butter. Place half in a greased 9x13-in. baking dish. Layer with half of the cheese and broccoli; sprinkle with ham. Layer with remaining broccoli, cheese and bread cubes.
2. In a large bowl, whisk the eggs, milk and pepper. Pour over casserole. Cover the dish and refrigerate overnight.
3. Remove from the refrigerator 30 minutes before baking. Bake, uncovered, at 350° for 35-40 minutes or until a knife inserted near the center comes out clean. Let casserole stand for 5 minutes before cutting.

⑤ INGREDIENTS

Sausage Spaghetti Spirals

My family loves this casserole with hearty chunks of sausage and green pepper. The recipe makes a big pan, so it's nice for gatherings.

—CAROL CAROLTON WHEATON, IL

PREP: 15 MIN. • **BAKE:** 30 MIN.
MAKES: 6 SERVINGS

- 1 pound bulk Italian sausage
- 1 medium green pepper, chopped
- 5 cups spiral pasta, cooked and drained
- 1 jar (24 ounces) spaghetti sauce
- 1½ cups (6 ounces) shredded part-skim mozzarella cheese

1. In a large skillet, cook sausage and green pepper over medium heat until meat is no longer pink; drain. Stir in cooked pasta and the spaghetti sauce.
2. Transfer to a greased 9x13-in. baking dish. Cover and bake at 350° for 25 minutes. Uncover; sprinkle with cheese. Bake pasta 5-10 minutes longer or until cheese is melted.

Pepperoni Macaroni

Because this jazzed-up macaroni can be assembled in advance and baked right before serving, it's my handy go-to when I need something on the fly.

—**MARLENE MOHR** CINCINNATI, OH

PREP: 15 MIN. • **BAKE:** 40 MIN.
MAKES: 8 SERVINGS

2½ cups uncooked elbow
    macaroni
1 **pound bulk Italian sausage**
1 **large onion, chopped**
1 **can (15 ounces) pizza sauce**

1 **can (8 ounces) tomato sauce**
⅓ **cup milk**
1 **package (3½ ounces) sliced
    pepperoni, halved**
1 **jar (4½ ounces) sliced
    mushrooms, drained**
1 **can (2¼ ounces) sliced ripe
    olives, drained**
1 **cup (4 ounces) shredded
    part-skim mozzarella cheese**

1. Cook macaroni according to package directions. Meanwhile, in a large skillet, cook sausage and onion over medium heat until meat is no longer pink; drain. Drain macaroni.

2. In a large bowl, combine the pizza sauce, tomato sauce and milk. Stir in the sausage mixture, macaroni, pepperoni, mushrooms and olives.

3. Transfer to a greased 9x13-in. baking dish. Cover and bake at 350° for 30 minutes. Uncover; sprinkle with cheese. Bake for 10-15 minutes more or until heated through and the cheese is melted.

Cheeseburger Pepper Cups

I like to serve my grandkids special meals, and this dish is one of their favorites. They prefer red or yellow peppers because they're sweeter than green.

—BETTY WINSCHER ROYALTON, MN

PREP: 15 MIN. • **BAKE:** 35 MIN.
MAKES: 4 SERVINGS

- 4 medium sweet red, yellow or green peppers
- ½ pound ground beef
- ¼ cup finely chopped onion
- 2 cups cooked brown rice
- 1 can (6 ounces) tomato paste
- 2 tablespoons ketchup
- 1 tablespoon Worcestershire sauce
- 1 tablespoon spicy brown mustard
- ½ teaspoon garlic salt
- ¼ teaspoon pepper
- 1 cup vegetable broth
- 1 cup (4 ounces) shredded cheddar cheese

1. Cut peppers in half lengthwise and remove seeds; set aside. In a large skillet, cook beef and onion over medium heat until meat is no longer pink; drain. Stir in the rice, tomato paste, ketchup, Worcestershire sauce, mustard, garlic salt and pepper. Spoon into the peppers.

2. Place in a greased 9x13-in. baking dish; pour broth around the peppers. Cover and bake at 350° for 30 minutes. Sprinkle with cheese. Bake, uncovered, 5 minutes longer or until cheese is melted.

Reuben Crescent Bake

It may not be a true Reuben, but my recipe tastes just like one! Plus, it's easy to whip up eight servings of the classic with this casserole. I like to serve it with homemade soup.

—**KATHY KITTELL** LENEXA, KS

PREP: 20 MIN. • **BAKE:** 15 MIN.
MAKES: 8 SERVINGS

- 2 **tubes (8 ounces each) refrigerated crescent rolls**
- 1 **pound sliced Swiss cheese, divided**
- 1¼ **pounds sliced deli corned beef**
- 1 **can (14 ounces) sauerkraut, rinsed and well drained**
- ⅔ **cup Thousand Island salad dressing**
- 1 **egg white, lightly beaten**
- 3 **teaspoons caraway seeds**

1. Preheat oven to 375°. Unroll one tube of crescent dough into one long rectangle; seal seams and perforations. Press onto the bottom of a greased 9x13-in. baking dish. Bake 8-10 minutes or until golden brown.
2. Layer with half of the cheese and all the corned beef. Combine sauerkraut and salad dressing; spread over beef. Top with the remaining cheese.
3. On a lightly floured surface, press or roll second tube of crescent dough into a 9x13-in. rectangle, sealing seams and perforations. Place over cheese. Brush with egg white; sprinkle with caraway seeds.
4. Bake for 12-16 minutes or until heated through and crust is golden brown. Let stand for 5 minutes before cutting.

Stuffed Burger Bundles

I changed up my mom's recipe to make it my own. Add some mashed potatoes and pour the sauce over both the potatoes and the bundles. This is real comfort food!

—**DEBBIE CARTER** KINGSBURG, CA

PREP: 30 MIN. • **BAKE:** 35 MIN.
MAKES: 4 SERVINGS

- 1 **cup stuffing mix**
- ⅓ **cup evaporated milk**
- ½ **teaspoon salt**
- ½ **teaspoon dried thyme**
- 1 **pound ground beef**

MUSHROOM SAUCE
- 1 **cup sliced fresh mushrooms**
- 1 **tablespoon butter**
- 1 **can (10¾ ounces) condensed cream of mushroom soup, undiluted**
- 1 **tablespoon ketchup**
- 2 **teaspoons Worcestershire sauce**
- ¼ **teaspoon dried thyme**

1. Prepare stuffing according to package directions. Meanwhile, in a large bowl, combine the milk, salt and thyme. Crumble beef over milk mixture and mix well. Shape mixture into eight thin patties. Divide stuffing among four patties; top with remaining patties and press edges firmly to seal.
2. Place in an ungreased 9x13-in. baking dish. Bake, burgers, uncovered, at 350° for 35-40 minutes or until a thermometer reads 160° and juices run clear.
3. For sauce, in a large skillet, saute mushrooms in butter until tender. Stir in the remaining ingredients; heat through. Serve with burgers.

Chicago Deep-Dish Pizza

Because I live near Chicago, I've managed to sample more than my share of deep-dish pizzas. This recipe lets you re-create the best of my hometown—right in yours!

—LYNN HAMILTON NAPERVILLE, IL

PREP: 40 MIN. + RISING
BAKE: 40 MIN.
MAKES: 12 SERVINGS

- 2 to 2½ cups all-purpose flour
- ¼ cup cornmeal
- 1 package (¼ ounce) quick-rise yeast
- 1½ teaspoons sugar
- ½ teaspoon salt
- 1 cup water
- ⅓ cup olive oil

TOPPINGS

- ½ pound sliced fresh mushrooms
- 4 teaspoons olive oil, divided
- 1 can (28 ounces) diced tomatoes, well drained
- 1 can (8 ounces) tomato sauce
- 1 can (6 ounces) tomato paste
- 2 to 3 garlic cloves, minced
- ½ teaspoon salt
- ¼ teaspoon dried basil
- ¼ teaspoon dried oregano
- ¼ teaspoon pepper
- 3 cups (12 ounces) shredded part-skim mozzarella cheese, divided
- 1 pound bulk Italian sausage, cooked and crumbled
- 24 slices pepperoni, optional
- ½ cup grated Parmesan cheese
  Thinly sliced fresh basil

1. In a large bowl, combine 1½ cups flour, cornmeal, yeast, sugar and salt. In a small saucepan, heat water and oil to 120°-130°. Add to the dry ingredients; beat just until moistened. Stir in enough of the remaining flour to form a soft dough.

2. Turn onto a floured surface; knead until smooth and elastic, about 6-8 minutes. Place in a greased bowl, turning once to grease the top. Cover and let rise in warm place until doubled, about 30 minutes.

3. In a large skillet, saute the mushrooms in 2 teaspoons of the oil until tender. In a large bowl, mix the tomatoes, tomato sauce, tomato paste, garlic and seasonings.

4. Generously grease a 9x13-in. baking pan or dish with the remaining 2 teaspoons of oil. Punch dough down. Roll into an 11x15-in. rectangle. Transfer to prepared pan, pressing onto the bottom and halfway up the sides of pan. Sprinkle with 2 cups of the mozzarella cheese.

5. Spoon half of the sauce over the cheese (save remaining sauce for another use or for dipping). Layer with the sausage, sauteed mushrooms and, if desired, pepperoni; top with remaining mozzarella cheese and the Parmesan cheese.

6. Cover and bake at 450° for 35 minutes. Uncover; bake about 5 minutes longer or until lightly browned. Sprinkle with sliced basil if desired.

Pork Chops with Scalloped Potatoes

Mom always managed to put a delicious, hearty meal on the table for our family and the farmhands. This dish reminds me of home.

—**BERNICE MORRIS** MARSHFIELD, MO

PREP: 25 MIN. • **BAKE:** 1½ HOURS
MAKES: 6 SERVINGS

- 3 tablespoons butter
- 3 tablespoons all-purpose flour
- 1½ teaspoons salt
- ¼ teaspoon pepper
- 1 can (14½ ounces) chicken broth
- 6 pork rib or loin chops (¾ inch thick)
- 2 tablespoons canola oil
  Additional salt and pepper, optional
- 6 cups thinly sliced peeled potatoes
- 1 medium onion, sliced
  Paprika and minced fresh parsley, optional

1. In a small saucepan, melt butter; stir in the flour, salt and pepper until smooth. Add broth. Bring to a boil; cook and stir for 1 minute or until thickened. Remove from heat; set aside.
2. In a large skillet, brown the pork chops on both sides in oil; sprinkle with additional salt and pepper if desired.
3. In a greased 9x13-in. baking dish, layer potatoes and onion. Pour broth mixture over layers. Place pork chops on top.
4. Cover dish and bake at 350° for 1 hour; uncover and bake 30 minutes longer or until meat and potatoes are tender. If desired, sprinkle with paprika and parsley.

bake at 375° for 60-70 minutes or until heated through. Uncover; bake 10 minutes longer or until bubbly. Let stand for 10 minutes before cutting.

Parsnips & Ham au Gratin

Parsnips, thyme and a little hint of roasted garlic give this entree a hearty harvesttime feel. The crumb topping makes it rustic and special.
—*TASTE OF HOME* TEST KITCHEN

PREP: 20 MIN. • **BAKE:** 1 HOUR
MAKES: 6 SERVINGS

- 1 **pound parsnips, peeled and sliced**
- 1 **pound Yukon Gold potatoes, peeled and sliced**
- 2 **cups cubed fully cooked ham**
- 1 **can (10¾ ounces) condensed cream of mushroom with roasted garlic soup, undiluted**
- ⅔ **cup 2% milk**
- ½ **cup grated Parmesan cheese, divided**
- ½ **teaspoon dried thyme**
- ¼ **teaspoon pepper**
- ¼ **cup dry bread crumbs**
- 2 **tablespoons butter, melted**

1. Arrange the parsnips, potatoes and ham in a greased 9x13-in. baking dish. Combine the soup, milk, ¼ cup cheese, thyme and pepper; pour over parsnip mixture.
2. In a small bowl, combine the bread crumbs, butter and remaining cheese. Sprinkle over top.
3. Cover and bake at 375° for 40 minutes. Uncover; bake 20-25 minutes longer or until potatoes are tender.

FREEZE IT
Make Once, Eat Twice Lasagna

Our family loves this recipe with a green salad and garlic bread. It is so handy on lazy days to have an extra pan, already made, in the freezer.
—**GERI DAVIS** PRESCOTT, AZ

PREP: 35 MIN.
BAKE: 55 MIN. + STANDING
MAKES: 2 LASAGNAS
(12 SERVINGS EACH)

- 1 **package (16 ounces) lasagna noodles**
- 3 **pounds ground beef**
- 3 **jars (26 ounces each) spaghetti sauce**
- 2 **eggs, lightly beaten**
- 1½ **pounds ricotta cheese**
- 6 **cups (24 ounces) shredded part-skim mozzarella cheese, divided**
- 1 **tablespoon dried parsley flakes**
- 1 **teaspoon salt**
- ½ **teaspoon pepper**
- 1 **cup grated Parmesan cheese**

1. Cook noodles according to package directions. Meanwhile, in a Dutch oven, cook beef over medium heat until no longer pink; drain. Remove from the heat; stir in spaghetti sauce. In a large bowl, combine the eggs, ricotta, 4½ cups mozzarella cheese, parsley, salt and pepper.
2. Drain noodles. Spread 1 cup of the meat sauce in each of two greased 9x13-in. baking dishes. Layer each with three noodles, 1 cup ricotta mixture and 1½ cups meat sauce. Repeat layers twice. Top with Parmesan cheese and remaining mozzarella.
3. Cover and freeze one lasagna for up to 3 months. Cover and bake remaining lasagna at 375° for 45 minutes. Uncover; bake 10 minutes longer or until bubbly. Let stand for 10 minutes before cutting.
TO USE FROZEN LASAGNA
Thaw in the refrigerator overnight. Remove from the refrigerator 30 minutes before baking. Cover and

Pizza Noodle Bake

Here's a family-pleasing casserole that comes together in a snap. It's perfect for weeknights. Double the recipe and freeze one for later!

—BERNICE KNUTSON SOLDIER, IA

PREP: 25 MIN. • **BAKE:** 15 MIN.
MAKES: 6 SERVINGS

- 10 **ounces uncooked egg noodles**
- 1½ **pounds ground beef**
- ½ **cup finely chopped onion**
- ¼ **cup chopped green pepper**
- 1 **jar (14 ounces) pizza sauce**
- 1 **can (4 ounces) mushroom stems and pieces, drained**
- 1 **cup (4 ounces) shredded cheddar cheese**
- 1 **cup (4 ounces) shredded part-skim mozzarella cheese**
- 1 **package (3½ ounces) sliced pepperoni**

1. Cook noodles according to package directions. Meanwhile, in a large skillet, cook beef, onion and green pepper over medium heat until meat is no longer pink; drain. Add the pizza sauce and mushrooms; heat through.

2. Drain noodles. In a greased 9x13-in. baking dish, layer half of the noodles, beef mixture, cheeses and pepperoni. Repeat layers. Cover and bake at 350° for 15-20 minutes or until heated through.

FREEZE OPTION *Cover and freeze unbaked casserole for up to 3 months. Remove from the freezer 30 minutes before baking (do not thaw). Cover and bake at 350° for 45-50 minutes. Uncover; bake 15-20 minutes longer or until heated through.*

Ham with Apple-Raisin Sauce

Since running across this recipe several years ago, I've used it often for special dinners. What I really like is the ease of preparation. You don't have a lot of cleanup to worry about because everything is done right there in the bag.

—SANDY OLBERDING SPENCER, IA

PREP: 10 MIN. • **BAKE:** 2 HOURS
MAKES: 16 SERVINGS

- 1 tablespoon all-purpose flour
- 1 large oven roasting bag
- 4 medium tart apples, peeled and chopped
- 2 cups apple juice
- 1 cup raisins
- ½ cup packed brown sugar
- 1 teaspoon ground cinnamon
- 1 boneless fully cooked ham (about 6 pounds)

1. Shake flour in the oven roasting bag. Place bag in an ungreased 9x13-in. baking pan.

Place the apples, apple juice, raisins, brown sugar and cinnamon in the bag; mix well. Place ham in bag. Close bag. Cut six ½-in. slits in top of bag.
2. Bake at 350° for 2 -2¼ hours or until a thermometer reads 140°. Serve with sauce.

FREEZE IT

Cheesy Kielbasa Bake

PREP: 55 MIN. • **BAKE:** 30 MIN.
MAKES: 2 CASSEROLES (8-10 SERVINGS EACH)

- 12 ounces uncooked elbow macaroni
- 2 pounds kielbasa or Polish sausage, halved lengthwise and sliced
- 1 tablespoon olive oil
- 2 medium onions, chopped
- 2 medium zucchini, quartered and sliced
- 2 medium carrots, grated
- ½ teaspoon minced garlic
- 1 jar (26 ounces) spaghetti sauce
- 1 can (14½ ounces) stewed tomatoes
- 1 egg, lightly beaten
- 1 carton (15 ounces) ricotta cheese
- 2 cups (8 ounces) shredded cheddar cheese
- 2 cups (8 ounces) part-skim shredded mozzarella cheese
- 2 green onions, chopped

1. Cook macaroni according to package directions. Meanwhile, in a large skillet, brown sausage in oil over medium heat; drain. Add the onions, zucchini, carrots and garlic; cook and stir for 5-6 minutes or until vegetables are crisp-tender.
2. Stir in spaghetti sauce and tomatoes. Bring to a boil. Reduce heat; simmer, uncovered, for 15 minutes. Drain macaroni.
3. In a small bowl, combine egg and ricotta cheese. In each of two greased 13x9-in. baking dishes, layer a fourth of each of the following: macaroni, meat sauce, ricotta mixture, cheddar and mozzarella cheeses. Repeat layers. Top with green onions.
4. Cool one casserole; cover and freeze for up to 2 months. Cover and bake the remaining casserole at 350° for 15 minutes. Uncover; bake 15 minutes longer or until cheese is melted.

TO USE FROZEN CASSEROLE
Thaw in the refrigerator for 24 hours. Remove from the refrigerator 30 minutes before baking. Cover and bake at 350° for 35-40 minutes or until heated through.

My aunt originally made this hearty casserole for family gatherings. Now I enjoy fixing it for my family any night of the week. What a great way to sneak in some garden veggies.
—**KATE BECKMAN** HEMET, CA

3. Drain ribs; remove rack and return ribs to pan. Cover with sauce. Bake ribs, uncovered, 30 minutes or until meat is tender, basting occasionally. Sprinkle with sesame seeds just before serving.

Orange Pork Tenderloin

This fuss-free pork dish adds flair to any meal. Served with a succulent orange sauce, these tender slices will impress your family and friends.

—*TASTE OF HOME* TEST KITCHEN

PREP: 15 MIN. • **BAKE:** 20 MIN.
MAKES: 3-4 SERVINGS

- 1 **pound pork tenderloin, sliced**
- 1 **tablespoon butter, softened**
- ¼ **teaspoon dried thyme**
  Dash cayenne pepper
- 1 **cup orange juice, divided**
- 1 **tablespoon all-purpose flour**
- 1½ **teaspoons sugar**

1. Place pork in an ungreased 9x13-in. baking dish. Combine butter, thyme and cayenne; spread over pork. Pour ¾ cup orange juice over meat. Bake pork, uncovered, at 425° for 20-25 minutes or until meat is no longer pink, basting it occasionally with pan juices.

2. Remove pork and keep warm. Pour the drippings into a measuring cup; add enough remaining orange juice to measure ¾ cup. Pour into a saucepan. Stir in flour and sugar until smooth.

3. Bring mixture to a boil over medium heat; cook and stir for 2 minutes or until thickened. Serve with pork.

Maple-Glazed Ribs

I love maple syrup and so does my family, so I gave this recipe a try. It's well worth the effort! I make these ribs often, and I never have leftovers. With two teenage boys who like to eat, this main dish is a real winner.

—LINDA KOBELUCK ARDROSSAN, AB

PREP: 30 MIN. • **BAKE:** 1¾ HOURS
MAKES: 6 SERVINGS

- 3 **pounds pork spareribs, cut into serving-size pieces**
- 1 **cup maple syrup**
- 3 **tablespoons orange juice concentrate**
- 3 **tablespoons ketchup**
- 2 **tablespoons soy sauce**
- 1 **tablespoon Dijon mustard**
- 1 **tablespoon Worcestershire sauce**
- 1 **teaspoon curry powder**
- 1 **garlic clove, minced**
- 2 **green onions, minced**
- 1 **tablespoon sesame seeds, toasted**

1. Preheat oven to 350°. Place ribs, meaty side up, on a rack in a greased 9x13-in. baking pan. Cover pan tightly with foil. Bake 1¼ hours.

2. Meanwhile, combine the next nine ingredients in a saucepan. Bring to a boil over medium heat. Reduce heat; simmer 15 minutes, stirring occasionally.

Baked Spaghetti

Wherever I take this spaghetti, people enjoy it. I use whatever cheese I happen to have on hand, so try your favorite.

—**PAT WALTER** PINE ISLAND, MN

PREP: 20 MIN. • **BAKE:** 40 MIN.
MAKES: 12 SERVINGS

- 1 package (16 ounces) spaghetti
- 1½ pounds ground beef
- 1 medium onion, chopped
- ½ cup chopped green pepper
- 1 can (10¾ ounces) condensed cream of mushroom soup, undiluted
- 1 can (10¾ ounces) condensed tomato soup, undiluted
- 1 can (8 ounces) tomato sauce
- 1 cup water
- 2 tablespoons brown sugar
- 1 teaspoon salt
- 1 teaspoon dried basil
- 1 teaspoon dried oregano
- ½ teaspoon dried marjoram
- ½ teaspoon dried rosemary, crushed
- ⅛ teaspoon garlic salt
- 1 cup (4 ounces) shredded part-skim mozzarella cheese, divided

1. Break spaghetti in half; cook according to package directions. Meanwhile, in a Dutch oven, cook the beef, onion and green pepper over medium heat until meat is no longer pink; drain. Stir in the soups, tomato sauce, water, brown sugar and the seasonings.
2. Drain spaghetti; stir into meat sauce. Add ½ cup cheese. Transfer to a greased 9x13-in. baking dish.
3. Cover and bake at 350° for 30 minutes. Uncover; sprinkle with remaining cheese. Bake 10-15 minutes longer or until cheese is melted.

Sunday Chops and Stuffing

My family likes these chops for Sunday dinner. The recipe lets us spend more time having fun together and less time cooking.

—**GEORGIANN FRANKLIN**
CANFIELD, OH

PREP: 30 MIN. • **BAKE:** 25 MIN.
MAKES: 6 SERVINGS

- 2 cups water
- 2 celery ribs, chopped
- 7 tablespoons butter, divided
- ¼ cup dried minced onion
- 1 tablespoon canola oil
- 6 cups seasoned stuffing cubes
- 6 bone-in pork loin chops (7 ounces each)
- ¼ teaspoon salt
- ¼ teaspoon pepper
- 2 medium tart apples, sliced
- ¼ cup packed brown sugar
- ⅛ teaspoon pumpkin pie spice

1. Preheat oven to 350°. In a large saucepan, bring water, celery, 6 tablespoons butter and onion to a boil. Remove from heat; stir in stuffing. Spoon into a greased 9x13-in. baking dish.
2. In a large skillet over medium heat, brown pork chops in oil on both sides. Arrange over stuffing. Sprinkle with salt and pepper.
3. In a small bowl, toss the apples with brown sugar and pie spice; place over pork chops. Dot with remaining butter.
4. Bake casserole, uncovered, for 25-30 minutes or until a thermometer inserted in a pork chop reads 145°. Let the dish stand for 5 minutes before serving.

1. In a large skillet, combine ¾ cup queso dip, ½ cup enchilada sauce, green chilies, water and taco seasoning. Bring to a boil. Reduce heat; simmer, uncovered, for 3 minutes.

2. Spread ⅔ cup sauce mixture into a greased 9x13-in. baking dish. Stir pork into remaining sauce mixture. Place ⅓ cup pork mixture down the center of each tortilla; top with 2 tablespoons cheese. Roll up and place seam side down in prepared dish. Combine remaining queso dip and enchilada sauce; pour over enchiladas.

3. Cover and bake at 350° for 20 minutes. Uncover; sprinkle with remaining cheese. Bake 10-15 minutes longer or until heated through. Serve with lettuce and tomatoes if desired.

FREEZE OPTION *Sprinkle remaining cheese over unbaked casserole. Cover and freeze. To use, partially thaw in refrigerator overnight. Remove from the refrigerator 30 minutes before baking. Preheat oven to 350°. Bake casserole as directed, increasing time as necessary to heat through and for a thermometer inserted in center to read 165°.*

FREEZE IT
Queso Pork Enchiladas

My husband took these to work, and now the guys always ask for them. They're restaurant-style, rich and spicy, and you can prepare them with cooked chicken or beef, too.

—**ANNA RODRIGUEZ** BETHPAGE, NY

PREP: 30 MIN. • **BAKE:** 30 MIN.
MAKES: 6 SERVINGS

- 1 jar (15½ ounces) salsa con queso dip, divided
- 1 can (10 ounces) enchilada sauce, divided
- 1 can (4 ounces) chopped green chilies
- ⅓ cup water
- 2 tablespoons reduced-sodium taco seasoning
- 4 cups cubed cooked boneless country-style pork ribs (from 2 pounds boneless ribs)
- 12 flour tortillas (6 inches), warmed
- 2½ cups (10 ounces) shredded Mexican cheese blend, divided
  Shredded lettuce and chopped tomatoes, optional

DID YOU KNOW?

Enchilada sauce is a blend of tomatoes, oil and spices thickened with a little flour or cornstarch. Green enchilada sauce, which is made from tomatillos instead of tomatoes, is also available.

Potluck Spareribs

When I want to bring home an empty pan from a potluck, I turn to this recipe. The ribs always disappear in minutes!

—**SHERI KIRKMAN** LANCASTER, NY

PREP: 15 MIN. • **BAKE:** 1¾ HOURS
MAKES: 12 SERVINGS

- 6 pounds pork spareribs
- 1½ cups ketchup
- ¾ cup packed brown sugar
- ½ cup white vinegar
- ½ cup honey
- ⅓ cup soy sauce
- 1½ teaspoons ground ginger
- 1 teaspoon salt
- ¾ teaspoon ground mustard
- ½ teaspoon garlic powder
- ¼ teaspoon pepper

1. Cut ribs into serving-size pieces; place with the meaty side up on racks in two greased 9x13-in. baking pans. Cover tightly with foil. Bake at 350° for 1¼ hours or until tender.
2. Remove racks; drain and return ribs to pans. Combine the remaining ingredients; pour over ribs. Bake, uncovered, for 30-40 minutes or until sauce coats ribs, basting occasionally. Ribs can also be grilled over medium-hot heat for the last 30-40 minutes instead of baking.

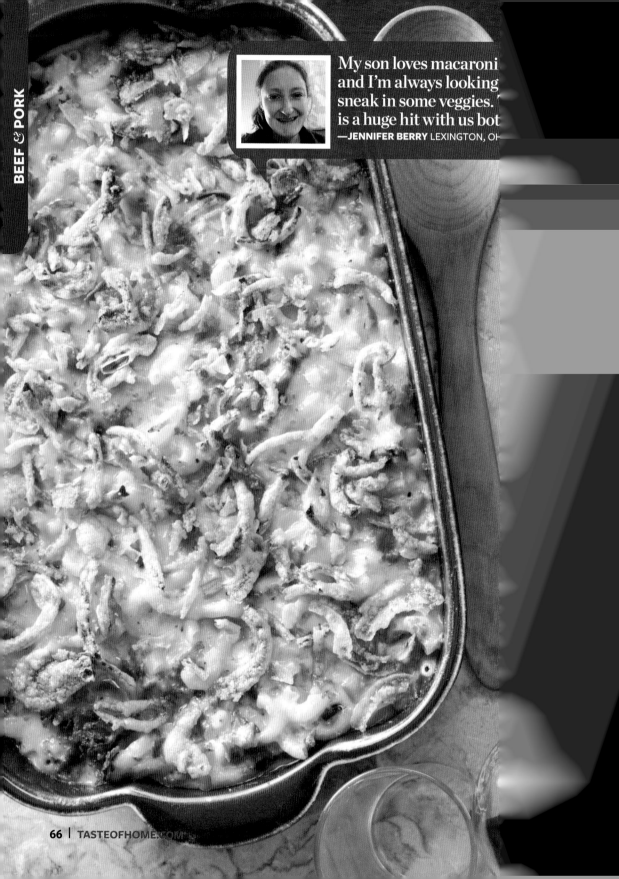

My son loves macaroni
and I'm always looking
sneak in some veggies.
is a huge hit with us bot
—**JENNIFER BERRY** LEXINGTON, OH

Philly-Style Mac and Cheese

PREP: 30 MIN. • **BAKE:** 25 MIN.
MAKES: 6 SERVINGS

- 2 **cups uncooked elbow macaroni**
- ½ **pound sliced fresh mushrooms**
- 1 **medium onion, chopped**
- 1 **medium green pepper, chopped**
- ¼ **cup butter, cubed**
- ¼ **cup all-purpose flour**
- 1 **cup 2% milk**
- 1 **cup beef broth**
- 2 **cups (8 ounces) shredded provolone cheese**
- 2 **cups (8 ounces) shredded part-skim mozzarella cheese**
- 1 **teaspoon garlic powder**
- 1 **teaspoon Montreal steak seasoning**
- ½ **teaspoon onion powder**
- 1 **package (10½ ounces) frozen Steak-umm sliced steaks, browned**
- ½ **cup French-fried onions**

1. Cook macaroni according to package directions.

2. Meanwhile, in a large skillet, saute the mushrooms, onion and green pepper in butter until tender. Stir in flour until blended; gradually add milk and broth. Bring to a boil; cook and stir for 2 minutes or until thickened. Reduce heat. Stir in the cheeses, garlic powder, steak seasoning and onion powder.

3. Drain macaroni; add to sauce mixture. Stir in steak. Transfer to an ungreased 9x13-in. baking dish; sprinkle fried onions over top. Bake, uncovered, at 350° for 25-30 minutes or until bubbly.

Pot Roast Meat Loaf

Can't decide between the classic comfort food flavors of meat loaf and pot roast? Enjoy them both with this gem of a recipe. It saves on cleanup, too, since the vegetables and meat all cook in the same dish.
—**MAGDALENE FISKE** LA FARGE, WI

PREP: 15 MIN. • **BAKE:** 1½ HOURS
MAKES: 6-8 SERVINGS

- 1 **can (5 ounces) evaporated milk**
- ¼ **cup ketchup**
- ½ **cup crushed saltines**
- 2 **tablespoons Worcestershire sauce**
- ½ **teaspoon salt**
- ¼ **teaspoon pepper**
- 2 **pounds lean ground beef**
- 4 **small onions, quartered**
- 4 **small potatoes, peeled and quartered**
- 4 **medium carrots, quartered**
- 1 **large green pepper, cut into strips**
- 2 **tablespoons minced fresh parsley**

1. In a large bowl, combine the milk, ketchup, cracker crumbs, Worcestershire sauce, salt and pepper. Add ground beef. Shape meat mixture into a 4x8-in. oval; place in a 9x13-in. baking dish. Place onions, potatoes, carrots and green pepper around the meat loaf.

2. Cover and bake at 350° for 1¼ hours. Uncover and bake 15 minutes longer or until a thermometer inserted in meat loaf reads 160°. Garnish the vegetables with parsley.

1. Place tenderloin in a large resealable plastic bag. Combine the wine, soy sauce, rosemary, Dijon mustard, ground mustard and garlic. Pour half of the marinade over tenderloin; seal bag and turn to coat. Refrigerate for 4-12 hours, turning several times. Cover and refrigerate remaining marinade.

2. Place the potatoes, Brussels sprouts and carrots in a greased 9x13-in. baking dish; add the reserved marinade and toss to coat. Cover and bake at 425° for 20 minutes; stir.

3. Drain and discard marinade from tenderloin. Place the tenderloin over vegetables. Bake, uncovered, for 40-50 minutes or until meat reaches desired doneness (for medium-rare, a thermometer should read 145°; medium, 160°; well-done, 170°).

4. Remove beef and let stand for 15 minutes. Check vegetables for doneness. If additional roasting is needed, cover with foil and bake for 10-15 minutes or until tender. Slice beef and serve with vegetables.

Beef Tenderloin with Roasted Vegetables

I appreciate this recipe because it includes a side dish of roasted potatoes, Brussels sprouts and carrots. I prepare the entree for celebrations throughout the year.
—**JANET SINGLETON** BELLEVUE, OH

PREP: 20 MIN. + MARINATING
BAKE: 1 HOUR + STANDING
MAKES: 8-10 SERVINGS

- 1 beef tenderloin roast (3 pounds)
- ¾ cup dry white wine or beef broth
- ¾ cup reduced-sodium soy sauce
- 4 teaspoons minced fresh rosemary
- 4 teaspoons Dijon mustard
- 1½ teaspoons ground mustard
- 3 garlic cloves, peeled and sliced
- 1 pound Yukon Gold potatoes, cut into 1-inch wedges
- 1 pound Brussels sprouts, halved
- 1 pound fresh baby carrots

TOP TIP

For best results, allow large cuts of meat to stand before cutting. This allows the meat juices to settle after cooking. Cut in too soon, and the juices will escape, resulting in a drier cut of meat. Standing also finishes the cooking. Large cuts typically rise a few degrees as they stand.

Argentine Lasagna

My family is from Argentina, which has a strong Italian heritage and large cattle ranches. This all-in-one lasagna is packed with meat, cheese and veggies.

—**SYLVIA MAENENR** OMAHA, NE

PREP: 30 MIN.
BAKE: 55 MIN. + STANDING
MAKES: 12 SERVINGS

- 1 **pound ground beef**
- 1 **large sweet onion, chopped**
- ½ **pound sliced fresh mushrooms**
- 1 **garlic clove, minced**
- 1 **can (15 ounces) tomato sauce**
- 1 **can (6 ounces) tomato paste**
- ¼ **teaspoon pepper**
- 4 **cups (16 ounces) shredded part-skim mozzarella cheese, divided**
- 1 **jar (15 ounces) Alfredo sauce**
- 1 **carton (15 ounces) ricotta cheese**
- 2½ **cups frozen peas, thawed**
- 1 **package (10 ounces) frozen chopped spinach, thawed and squeezed dry**
- 1 **package (9 ounces) no-cook lasagna noodles**
  Fresh basil leaves and grated Parmesan cheese, optional

1. In a Dutch oven, cook the beef, onion, mushrooms and garlic over medium heat until meat is no longer pink; drain. Stir in the tomato sauce, tomato paste, pepper and 2 cups mozzarella cheese; set aside.

2. In a large bowl, combine the Alfredo sauce, ricotta cheese, peas and spinach.

3. Spread 1 cup meat sauce into a greased 9x13-in. baking dish. Layer with four noodles, 1¼ cups meat sauce and 1¼ cups spinach mixture. Repeat layers three times. Sprinkle with remaining mozzarella cheese. (Dish will be full.)

4. Cover and bake at 350° for 45 minutes. Uncover; bake 10 minutes longer or until cheese is melted. Let stand 10 minutes before cutting. Garnish with basil and serve with Parmesan cheese if desired.

JOSEPHINE PIRO'S
BERRY-PORT GAME HENS
PAGE 84

Chicken & Turkey

LAUNA SHOEMAKER'S BREADED RANCH CHICKEN *PAGE 74*

BERNICE JANOWSKI'S CHICKEN SPAGHETTI CASSEROLE *PAGE 81*

JOYCE MUMMAU'S PHYLLO CHICKEN *PAGE 91*

Turkey Meat Loaf

For a lighter meat loaf, try making it with ground turkey instead of beef. This one's sure to be a favorite.

—*TASTE OF HOME* TEST KITCHEN

PREP: 15 MIN.
COOK: 70 MIN. + STANDING
MAKES: 8 SERVINGS

- 1 cup chopped onion
- 1 cup shredded carrots
- ½ cup chopped celery
- 1 tablespoon vegetable oil
- 1½ cups crushed saltines (about 45 crackers)
- ¾ cup ketchup, divided
- ¼ cup minced fresh parsley
- 1 egg, lightly beaten
- 4 teaspoons ground mustard, divided
- 2 teaspoons salt
- 2 teaspoons minced garlic
- 1 teaspoon pepper
- 2½ pounds lean ground turkey
- 2 tablespoons brown sugar

1. In a large skillet, saute the onion, carrots and celery in oil until tender. In a large bowl, combine the onion mixture, cracker crumbs, ½ cup ketchup, parsley, egg, 2 teaspoons mustard, salt, garlic and pepper. Crumble turkey over mixture and mix well.

2. Shape into a loaf. Place in a greased 9x13-in. baking dish. Bake, uncovered, at 350° for 1 hour.

3. Combine brown sugar with remaining ketchup and mustard until smooth. Spoon over meat loaf. Bake 10-20 minutes longer or until meat is no longer pink and a meat thermometer reads 160°; drain. Let stand 10 minutes before slicing.

Zippy Turkey and Rice

Hearty and healthful, this tasty casserole is full of rice, beans, tomatoes and cheese. Serve it with fresh fruit or a side salad for a satisfying meal.

—THOMAS LINDGREN
HACKENSACK, MN

PREP: 45 MIN. • **BAKE:** 35 MIN.
MAKES: 8 SERVINGS

- 1 **cup uncooked brown rice**
- 1 **pound lean ground turkey**
- 1 **large onion, chopped**
- 1 **can (14½ ounces) diced tomatoes with mild green chilies, undrained**
- ⅔ **cup picante sauce**
- 2 **teaspoons chili powder**
- 2 **teaspoons ground cumin**
- 1 **can (16 ounces) kidney beans, rinsed and drained**
- 1 **cup (4 ounces) shredded reduced-fat cheddar cheese, divided**

1. Cook rice according to package directions.
2. Meanwhile, in a large nonstick skillet, cook turkey and onion over medium heat until meat is no longer pink; drain. Stir in the tomatoes, picante sauce, chili powder and cumin; heat though. Remove from the heat, stir in kidney beans, ½ cup cheese and cooked rice.
3. Transfer to a 9x13-in. baking dish coated with cooking spray.
4. Cover and bake at 350° for 30 minutes. Uncover; sprinkle with remaining cheese. Bake 5-10 minutes longer or until cheese is melted.

⑤ INGREDIENTS

Savory Chicken Dinner

No one would guess that this flavorful dinner is seasoned with soup mix. The meal is quick to assemble, and it all bakes in one dish so there's little cleanup.

—LESLIE ADAMS SPRINGFIELD, MO

PREP: 10 MIN. • **BAKE:** 45 MIN.
MAKES: 4 SERVINGS

- 1 **envelope savory herb with garlic soup mix**
- 3 **tablespoons water**
- 4 **boneless skinless chicken breast halves (6 ounces each)**
- 2 **large red potatoes, cubed**
- 1 **large onion, halved and cut into small wedges**

1. In a large bowl, combine the soup mix and water. Add the chicken, potatoes and onion; toss to coat.
2. Transfer to a greased 9x13-in. baking dish. Pour potato mixture over chicken.
3. Bake, uncovered, at 350° for 40-45 minutes or until vegetables are tender and a thermometer reads 170°, stirring occasionally.

Paprika Chicken Thighs

This is one of my favorite family meals, and the gravy is perfect over rice, grits or mashed potatoes.

—JUDY ARMSTRONG PRAIRIEVILLE, LA

PREP: 15 MIN. • **BAKE:** 50 MIN.
MAKES: 8 SERVINGS

- ¼ **cup butter**
- 3 **tablespoons all-purpose flour**
- 2 **tablespoons paprika**
- 1 **teaspoon poultry seasoning**
- 8 **bone-in chicken thighs, skin removed**
- ½ **teaspoon salt**
- ½ **teaspoon pepper**
- 1 **can (10¾ ounces) condensed cream of mushroom soup, undiluted**
- 1 **cup 2% milk**
- 8 **ounces sliced fresh mushrooms**
- 2 **tablespoons minced fresh parsley**
  Hot cooked rice, optional

1. In a small saucepan, melt butter. Remove from heat; stir in flour, paprika and poultry seasoning. Sprinkle chicken with salt and pepper; place in an ungreased 9x13-in. baking dish. Spread with butter mixture.
2. In a bowl, whisk soup and milk; stir in mushrooms. Pour over chicken. Bake, covered, at 350° for 35 minutes. Uncover; bake 15-20 minutes longer or until a thermometer inserted in chicken reads 180°. Sprinkle with parsley. If desired, serve with rice.

Breaded Ranch Chicken

A crunchy coating of cornflakes and Parmesan cheese adds delectable flavor to zesty ranch chicken. This golden, crispy chicken is a mainstay I can always count on.

—LAUNA SHOEMAKER LANDRUM, SC

PREP: 10 MIN. • **BAKE:** 45 MIN.
MAKES: 8 SERVINGS

- ½ **cup butter, melted**
- ¾ **cup crushed cornflakes**
- ¾ **cup grated Parmesan cheese**
- 1 **envelope ranch salad dressing mix**
- 8 **boneless skinless chicken breast halves (4 ounces each)**

1. Place butter in a shallow bowl. In another shallow bowl, combine the cornflakes, cheese and salad dressing mix. Dip chicken in butter, then roll in cornflake mixture to coat.
2. Place in a greased 9x13-in. baking dish. Bake, uncovered, at 350° for 45 minutes or until a thermometer reads 170°.

Turkey Cordon Bleu with Alfredo Sauce

For our annual Kentucky Derby party, I wanted to create a twist on a traditional Kentucky Hot Brown sandwich. The turkey is tender and flavorful, filled with smoky ham and melted cheese, but the crispy bacon really sets the dish off.

—SANDY KOMISAREK SWANTON, OH

PREP: 30 MIN. • **BAKE:** 20 MIN.
MAKES: 8 SERVINGS

- 8 **slices part-skim mozzarella cheese**
- 8 **thin slices deli honey ham**
- 8 **turkey breast cutlets**

- 2 **cups panko (Japanese) bread crumbs**
- 2 **eggs, lightly beaten**
- ½ **cup all-purpose flour**
- ½ **teaspoon salt**
- ¼ **teaspoon pepper**
- ¼ **cup canola oil**
- 1 **jar (15 ounces) Alfredo sauce, warmed**
- 8 **bacon strips, cooked and crumbled**
- ¼ **cup grated Parmesan cheese**

1. Preheat oven to 350°. Place mozzarella and ham on cutlets. Roll up each from a short side and secure with toothpicks.

2. Place bread crumbs and eggs in separate shallow bowls. In another shallow bowl, combine flour, salt and pepper. Dip turkey in flour mixture, eggs, then bread crumbs.

3. In a large skillet, brown turkey in oil in batches. Place in a greased 9x13-in. baking dish. Bake, uncovered, 20-25 minutes or until turkey juices run clear. Discard toothpicks.

4. Spoon Alfredo sauce over turkey. Sprinkle with bacon and Parmesan cheese.

Chicken Kiev

This is one of my most popular dishes at holiday suppers and potlucks. Folks love these mildly seasoned chicken rolls.

—**KARIN ERICKSON** BURNEY, CA

PREP: 15 MIN. + FREEZING
BAKE: 35 MIN. • **MAKES:** 6 SERVINGS

- ¼ **cup butter, softened**
- 1 **tablespoon minced chives**
- 1 **garlic clove, minced**
- 6 **boneless skinless chicken breast halves (8 ounces each)**
- ¾ **cup crushed cornflakes**
- 2 **tablespoons minced fresh parsley**
- ½ **teaspoon paprika**
- ⅓ **cup buttermilk**

1. In a small bowl, combine the butter, chives and garlic. Shape into a 3x2-in. rectangle. Cover and freeze until firm, about 30 minutes.

2. Flatten each chicken breast to ¼-in. thickness. Cut butter mixture into six 1-in. pieces; place one piece in center of each chicken breast. Roll up chicken from a long side; tuck ends under. Secure with toothpicks..

3. In a shallow bowl, combine the cornflakes, parsley and paprika. Place buttermilk in another shallow bowl. Dip the chicken into buttermilk, then coat evenly with cornflake mixture.

4. Place chicken seam side down in a greased 9x13-in. baking dish. Bake, uncovered, at 425° for 35-40 minutes or until no longer pink. Discard toothpicks.

Chicken Potpie with Cheddar Biscuit Topping

With chicken, veggies and a golden biscuit topping, this potpie is a hearty, comforting meal.

—SALA HOUTZER GOLDSBORO, NC

PREP: 20 MIN. • **BAKE:** 45 MIN.
MAKES: 9 SERVINGS

- 4 cups cubed cooked chicken
- 1 package (12 ounces) frozen broccoli with cheese sauce
- 1 can (10¾ ounces) condensed cream of chicken and mushroom soup, undiluted
- 1 can (10¾ ounces) condensed cream of chicken soup, undiluted
- 2 medium potatoes, cubed
- ¾ cup chicken broth
- ⅔ cup sour cream
- ½ cup frozen peas
- ¼ teaspoon pepper

TOPPING

- 1½ cups biscuit/baking mix
- ¾ cup shredded sharp cheddar cheese
- ¾ cup 2% milk
- 3 tablespoons butter, melted

1. In a Dutch oven, combine the first nine ingredients; bring to a boil. Transfer to a greased 9x13-in. baking dish.
2. In a small bowl, combine the topping ingredients; spoon over top. Bake, uncovered, at 350° for 40-45 minutes or until bubbly and topping is golden brown. Let stand for 10 minutes before serving.

Club-Style Turkey Enchiladas

Bacon, turkey and Swiss cheese make up these unique, delightful enchiladas. You will need about 1½ cups of leftover turkey meat for this recipe.

—ANNA GINSBERG AUSTIN, TX

PREP: 25 MIN. • **BAKE:** 30 MIN.
MAKES: 4 SERVINGS

- 8 bacon strips, chopped
- ½ cup chopped sweet red pepper
- ⅓ cup chopped onion
- 10 ounces thinly sliced cooked turkey, shredded
- 1½ cups (6 ounces) shredded Swiss cheese, divided
- ¼ teaspoon salt
- ¼ teaspoon pepper
- 8 yellow corn tortillas (6 inches), warmed
- 1 carton (10 ounces) refrigerated Alfredo sauce
- ¼ cup milk
- 2 cups shredded lettuce
- 1 can (14½ ounces) diced tomatoes, well drained

1. In a large skillet, saute bacon, red pepper and onion until bacon is crisp and vegetables are tender; drain. Cool slightly.
2. In a large bowl, combine the turkey, bacon mixture, 1 cup cheese, salt and pepper. Place ½ cup turkey mixture down the center of each tortilla. Roll up and place seam side down in a greased 9x13-in. baking dish. In a small bowl, combine Alfredo sauce and milk; pour over top.
3. Cover and bake at 350° for 25 minutes. Uncover; sprinkle with remaining cheese. Bake 5-10 minutes longer or until cheese is melted. Garnish with lettuce and tomatoes.

Chicken Stuffing Bake

At my bridal shower a few years ago, each guest brought a recipe card for her best dish. We've tried everyone's recipe, but this is a favorite.

—NICOLE VOGL HARDING
SPOKANE, WA

PREP: 5 MIN. • **BAKE:** 45 MIN.
MAKES: 6 SERVINGS

- 6 boneless skinless chicken breast halves (6 ounces each)
- 6 slices Swiss cheese
- 1 can (10¾ ounces) condensed cream of chicken soup, undiluted
- ⅓ cup white wine or chicken broth
- 3 cups seasoned stuffing cubes
- ½ cup butter, melted

1. Place chicken in a greased 9x13-in. baking dish; top with cheese. Combine soup and wine; spoon over the top.
2. In a small bowl, combine the stuffing cubes and butter; sprinkle over soup. Bake casserole, uncovered, at 350° for 45-55 minutes or until a thermometer reads 170°.

FREEZE IT

Cheddar Chicken Mostaccioli

While growing up, I enjoyed cooking for the whole family. So it's no surprise that I'm now a dietitian. This casserole was popular in a cafeteria where I once worked.

—MRS. TROY HAWK SHERIDAN, MO

PREP: 15 MIN. • **BAKE:** 55 MIN.
MAKES: 6-8 SERVINGS

- ½ cup chopped onion
- ½ cup chopped celery
- 1 tablespoon butter
- 1 can (10¾ ounces) condensed cream of mushroom soup, undiluted
- 1 can (10¾ ounces) condensed cream of chicken soup, undiluted
- ½ cup milk
- 1 can (4 ounces) mushroom stems and pieces, drained
- 1 jar (2 ounces) diced pimientos, drained
- ¼ cup sliced pimiento-stuffed olives
- 1 tablespoon Worcestershire sauce
- 1¼ teaspoons garlic salt
- ½ teaspoon each dried basil, oregano and ground pepper
- 4 cups diced cooked chicken
- 3 cups mostaccioli, cooked and drained
- 1¼ cups shredded cheddar cheese, divided
- 1 cup (4 ounces) shredded Swiss cheese

1. In a saucepan, saute onion and celery in butter until tender. Stir in soups, milk, mushrooms, pimientos, olives, Worcestershire sauce and seasonings. Add the chicken, mostaccioli, ¾ cup cheddar cheese and the Swiss cheese; toss to mix.
2. Pour into a greased 9x13-in. baking dish. Cover and bake at 350° for 40 minutes. Uncover; sprinkle with remaining cheddar cheese and bake 15-20 minutes longer or until bubbly and cheese is melted.

Turkey Cabbage Bake

I revised this old recipe by using turkey instead of beef to make it healthier, finely chopping the cabbage for an improved texture, and adding thyme for flavor.

—IRENE GUTZ FORT DODGE, IA

PREP: 30 MIN. • **BAKE:** 15 MIN.
MAKES: 6 SERVINGS

- 2 **tubes (8 ounces each) refrigerated crescent rolls**
- 1½ **pounds ground turkey**
- ½ **cup chopped onion**
- ½ **cup finely chopped carrot**
- 1 **teaspoon minced garlic**
- 2 **cups finely chopped cabbage**
- 1 **can (10¾ ounces) condensed cream of mushroom soup, undiluted**
- ½ **teaspoon dried thyme**
- 1 **cup (4 ounces) shredded part-skim mozzarella cheese**

1. Unroll one tube of crescent dough into one long rectangle; seal seams and perforations. Press onto the bottom of a greased 9x13-in. baking dish. Bake at 425° for 6-8 minutes or until golden brown.

2. Meanwhile, in a large skillet, cook the turkey, onion, carrot and garlic over medium heat until meat is no longer pink. Drain. Add cabbage, soup and thyme. Pour over crust; sprinkle with cheese.

3. On a lightly floured surface, press second tube of crescent dough into a 9x13-in. rectangle, sealing seams and perforations. Place over casserole.

4. Bake, uncovered, at 375° for 14-16 minutes or until crust is golden brown.

Lasagna Roll-Ups

This crowd-pleasing take on lasagna offers up a new way to enjoy a classic dish in individual portions. And it only requires 5 ingredients.

—**SUSAN SABIA** WINDSOR, CA

PREP: 25 MIN. • **BAKE:** 30 MIN.
MAKES: 10 SERVINGS

- 10 uncooked lasagna noodles
- 1 package (19½ ounces) Italian turkey sausage links, casings removed
- 1 package (8 ounces) cream cheese, softened
- 1 jar (26 ounces) spaghetti sauce, divided
- 1¾ cups shredded cheddar cheese, divided

1. Cook noodles according to package directions. Meanwhile, in a large skillet, cook sausage over medium heat until no longer pink; drain. Stir in cream cheese and ⅓ cup spaghetti sauce.

2. Drain noodles; spread ¼ cup meat mixture on each noodle. Sprinkle each with 2 tablespoons cheese; carefully roll up.

3. Spread ⅔ cup spaghetti sauce into an ungreased 9x13-in. baking dish. Place roll-ups seam side down over sauce. Top with remaining sauce and cheese.

4. Cover and bake at 350° for 20 minutes. Uncover; bake 10-15 minutes longer or until bubbly.

Chicken Parmesan

With two small children, I like meals that I can assemble easily and pop in the oven. I always keep the ingredients for this dish on hand.

—**SYLVIA DIRKS** CLEARBROOK, BC

PREP: 10 MIN. • **BAKE:** 1 HOUR
MAKES: 4 SERVINGS

- ¾ cup grated Parmesan cheese
- ¾ cup toasted wheat germ
- 1¼ teaspoons salt
- ½ teaspoon each garlic powder, onion powder and dried oregano
- ½ teaspoon dried rosemary, crushed
- ¼ teaspoon pepper
- 1 broiler/fryer chicken (3½ to 4 pounds), cut up
- 1 cup buttermilk

1. In a large resealable plastic bag, combine the cheese, wheat germ and seasonings. Dip chicken pieces in buttermilk, then add to bag, a few pieces at a time, and shake to coat.

2. Place in a greased 9x13-in. baking dish. Bake, uncovered, at 350° for 1 hour or until juices run clear.

Chicken Spaghetti Casserole

I first made this meal in one when I had unexpected dinner guests. I like it because it takes just minutes to assemble when I'm in a hurry.

—BERNICE JANOWSKI
STEVENS POINT, WI

PREP: 20 MIN. • **BAKE:** 40 MIN.
MAKES: 4 SERVINGS

- **8** ounces uncooked spaghetti
- **1** cup ricotta cheese
- **1** cup (4 ounces) shredded part-skim mozzarella cheese, divided
- **2** tablespoons grated Parmesan cheese
- **½** teaspoon Italian seasoning
- **½** teaspoon garlic powder
- **1** jar (26 ounces) meatless spaghetti sauce
- **1** can (14½ ounces) Italian diced tomatoes, undrained
- **1** jar (4½ ounces) sliced mushrooms, drained
- **4** breaded fully cooked chicken patties (10 to 14 ounces)

1. Cook spaghetti according to package directions. Meanwhile, in a large bowl, combine the ricotta, ½ cup of mozzarella, Parmesan, Italian seasoning and garlic powder; set aside. In another bowl, combine the spaghetti sauce, tomatoes and mushrooms.

2. Drain spaghetti; add 2 cups spaghetti sauce mixture and toss to coat. Transfer to a greased 9x13-in. baking dish; top with cheese mixture.

3. Arrange chicken patties over the top; drizzle with the remaining spaghetti sauce mixture. Sprinkle with the remaining mozzarella. Bake, uncovered, at 350° for 40-45 minutes or until bubbly.

Orange-Soy Chicken

Orange slices add a refreshing twist to tender and juicy baked chicken. This is a wonderful meal for company. The appealing glaze coats the poultry with tangy sweetness.
—**LORRI CLEVELAND** KINGSVILLE, OH

PREP: 20 MIN. • **BAKE:** 65 MIN.
MAKES: 6 SERVINGS

- 6 **bone-in chicken breast halves (7 ounces each), skin removed**
- 1 **tablespoon butter, melted**
- 1 **garlic clove, minced**
- 1 **teaspoon dried basil**
- ½ **teaspoon salt**
- ⅛ **teaspoon pepper**
- 1 **medium onion, thinly sliced**
- 1 **medium navel orange, thinly sliced**
- 3 **tablespoons brown sugar**
- 2 **teaspoons cornstarch**
- ½ **cup orange juice**
- 3 **tablespoons soy sauce**

1. Preheat oven to 350°. Place chicken in a 9x13-in. baking dish coated with cooking spray. Combine butter, garlic, basil, salt and pepper; drizzle over chicken. Arrange onion and orange slices on top. Bake, uncovered, 50 minutes.
2. In a small saucepan, combine brown sugar, cornstarch, orange juice and soy sauce until smooth. Bring to a boil; cook and stir for 1-2 minutes or until thickened.
3. Drain chicken; brush with orange juice mixture. Bake 15-20 minutes or until a thermometer reads 170°.

TLC (Thanksgiving Leftover Casserole)

PREP: 20 MIN. + STANDING
BAKE: 65 MIN.
MAKES: 8 SERVINGS

- 4 **cups seasoned stuffing cubes**
- 4 **cups cubed cooked turkey**
- 2 **celery ribs, finely chopped**
- 1 **cup frozen peas**
- 1 **cup fresh or frozen cranberries**
- ½ **cup chopped sweet onion**
- ¼ **cup all-purpose flour**
- 4 **eggs**
- 3 **cups 2% milk**
- 1 **can (8¼ ounces) cream-style corn**
- ½ **teaspoon salt**
- ½ **teaspoon pepper**
- 2 **tablespoons butter**
- ⅓ **cup chopped pecans**

1. Preheat oven to 350°. Layer first six ingredients in a greased 9x13-in. baking dish. In a large bowl, whisk flour, eggs and milk until smooth. Add corn, salt and pepper; mix well. Pour over top; let stand 15 minutes. Dot with butter and sprinkle with pecans.
2. Cover and bake for 35 minutes. Uncover and bake 30-35 minutes or until a knife inserted near the center comes out clean.

DID YOU KNOW?

Depending on your region, sweet onions may only be available during the warmer months of the year. You can use red onion or yellow onion in the TLC recipe.

Turkey, stuffing and veggies come together in a fabulous casserole made out of leftovers. There's comfort in every bite. —BARBARA LENTO HOUSTON, PA

⑤INGREDIENTS

Berry-Port Game Hens

This recipe uses only five ingredients to create a simple and elegant entree.

—JOSEPHINE PIRO EASTON, PA

PREP: 20 MIN. • **BAKE:** 50 MIN.
MAKES: 2 SERVINGS

- 1 large orange
- 2 Cornish game hens (20 to 24 ounces each)
- ½ teaspoon salt
- ½ teaspoon pepper
- 1 cup ruby port wine or grape juice
- ¼ cup seedless strawberry jam
- 5 teaspoons stone-ground mustard

1. Finely grate peel from orange to measure 1 teaspoon. Cut orange in half widthwise; cut a thin slice from each half. Quarter slices and set aside. Juice the orange to measure ¼ cup.
2. Loosen skin around hen breasts and thighs; place orange slices under the skin.
3. Place hens in a greased 9x13-in. baking dish. Sprinkle with salt and pepper. Bake, uncovered, at 350° for 40 minutes. Meanwhile, in a small pan, bring wine, jam and orange juice to a boil. Reduce heat; simmer, uncovered, 6-8 minutes or until slightly thickened. Stir in mustard and orange peel.
4. Set aside ½ cup sauce for serving; brush remaining sauce over hens. Bake hens for 10-20 minutes longer or until a thermometer reads 180°, basting occasionally. Warm reserved sauce; serve with hens.

Corn Tortilla Chicken Lasagna

This Southwest-style lasagna will satisfy a hungry crowd. It can be stretched with extra beans, and it's super-easy to put together. People love it!

—SUSAN SEYMOUR VALATIE, NY

PREP: 40 MIN.
BAKE: 35 MIN. + STANDING
MAKES: 2 CASSEROLES (12 SERVINGS EACH)

- 36 corn tortillas (6 inches)
- 6 cups shredded or cubed cooked chicken breast
- 2 cans (one 28 ounces, one 16 ounces) kidney beans, rinsed and drained
- 3 jars (16 ounces each) salsa
- 3 cups (24 ounces) sour cream
- 3 large green peppers, chopped
- 3 cans (3.8 ounces each) sliced ripe olives, drained
- 3 cups (12 ounces) shredded Monterey Jack cheese
- 3 cups (12 ounces) shredded cheddar cheese

1. In each of two greased 9x13-in. baking dishes, arrange six tortillas. Layer each with 1 cup chicken, ⅔ cup kidney beans, 1 cup salsa, ½ cup sour cream, ½ cup green pepper, about ⅓ cup olives, ½ cup Monterey Jack cheese and ½ cup cheddar cheese. Repeat layers twice.
2. Cover and bake at 350° for 25 minutes. Uncover; bake 10-15 minutes longer or until cheese is melted. Let stand for 10 minutes before serving.

Turkey Enchiladas Verdes

Planning a fiesta night? These authentic-tasting enchiladas in spicy green sauce are guaranteed to please the whole gang.

—KARYN "KIKI" POWER
ARLINGTON, TX

PREP: 45 MIN. • **BAKE:** 30 MIN.
MAKES: 16 SERVINGS

- 32 **corn tortillas (6 inches)**
- ⅓ **cup plus 1 tablespoon canola oil, divided**
- 1 **medium onion, chopped**
- 3 **cups cubed cooked turkey**
- 1 **can (14½ ounces) Mexican diced tomatoes, undrained**
- 1 **tablespoon chopped pickled jalapeno slices**
- 1 **envelope taco seasoning**
- 1 **teaspoon ground cumin**
- ½ **teaspoon dried oregano**
- ½ **teaspoon dried basil**
- 3 **cans (10 ounces each) green enchilada sauce**
- 1 **can (10¾ ounces) condensed cream of chicken soup, undiluted**
- 3 **cups (12 ounces) shredded Monterey Jack cheese, divided**

1. In a large skillet, fry tortillas in batches, using ⅓ cup oil, for 5 seconds on each side or until golden. Drain on paper towels.
2. In the same skillet, saute onion in remaining oil until tender. Stir in the turkey, tomatoes, jalapenos, taco seasoning, cumin, oregano and basil; heat through.
3. Combine enchilada sauce and soup. Spread ½ cup mixture into each of two 9x13-in. baking dishes. Place 2 tablespoons turkey mixture down the center of each tortilla; top with 1 tablespoon cheese. Roll up and place seam side down in prepared dishes.
4. Pour remaining sauce over the top.
5. Cover and bake at 350° for 25-30 minutes or until heated through. Uncover and sprinkle with remaining cheese. Bake for 5 minutes longer or until cheese is melted.

Mushroom Chicken with Wild Rice

Fix chicken dinner in a snap with this simple recipe. It warms you up.

—CINDY COTHERN NAMPA, ID

PREP: 10 MIN. • **BAKE:** 35 MIN.
MAKES: 6 SERVINGS

- 2 **packages (8.8 ounces each) ready-to-serve long grain and wild rice**
- 6 **boneless skinless chicken breast halves (4 ounces each)**
- 1 **can (10¾ ounces) condensed cream of mushroom soup, undiluted**
- 1 **cup (8 ounces) sour cream**
- ½ **cup water**
- 2 **tablespoons sherry or chicken broth**
- 1 **can (7 ounces) mushroom stems and pieces, drained**
- ½ **cup grated Parmesan cheese**

1. Preheat oven to 375°. Spread rice in a greased 9x13-in. baking dish. Place chicken over rice.
2. In a small bowl, whisk soup, sour cream, water and sherry until blended; stir in mushrooms. Pour over chicken. Bake, covered, 30 minutes.
3. Sprinkle cheese over top. Bake, uncovered, 5-10 minutes longer or until light golden brown and a thermometer inserted in chicken reads 165°.

2. Drain linguine; add 2 cups sauce and toss to coat. Transfer to a greased 9x13-in. baking dish. Make a well in center of pasta, making a space about 6 in. x 4 in.
3. To the remaining sauce, add the turkey, mushrooms, pimientos, parsley and pepper sauce; mix well. Pour into center of dish. Sprinkle with cheese.
4. Cover and bake at 350° for 30 minutes. Uncover; bake 20-30 minutes longer or until bubbly and heated through.

(5) INGREDIENTS
Roasted Turkey Breast

My family always enjoys this turkey at gatherings. The Italian dressing adds zip that you don't find in other recipes. If you like gravy, you can make a flavorful one from the pan drippings.
—**CINDY CARLSON** INGLESIDE, TX

PREP: 10 MIN.
BAKE: 2 HOURS + STANDING
MAKES: 12-14 SERVINGS

- 1 bone-in turkey breast (about 7 pounds)
- 1 teaspoon garlic powder
- ½ teaspoon onion powder
- ½ teaspoon salt
- ¼ teaspoon pepper
- 1½ cups Italian dressing

1. Place turkey breast in a greased 9x13-in. baking dish. Combine the seasonings; sprinkle over turkey. Pour dressing over the top.
2. Cover and bake at 325° for 2 to 2½ hours or until a thermometer reads 170°, basting occasionally with pan drippings. Let stand for 10 minutes before slicing.

Turkey Tetrazzini

What a great way to use up leftover turkey! This casserole bakes up delicious and bubbly for a wonderful main course.
—**AUDREY THIBODEAU** GILBERT, AZ

PREP: 25 MIN. • **BAKE:** 50 MIN.
MAKES: 8-10 SERVINGS

- 1 package (1 pound) linguine
- 6 tablespoons butter
- 6 tablespoons all-purpose flour
- ½ teaspoon salt
- ¼ teaspoon pepper
- ⅛ teaspoon cayenne pepper
- 3 cups chicken broth
- 1 cup heavy whipping cream
- 4 cups cubed cooked turkey
- 1 cup sliced fresh mushrooms
- 1 jar (4 ounces) diced pimientos, drained
- ¼ cup chopped fresh parsley
- 4 to 5 drops hot pepper sauce
- ⅓ cup grated Parmesan cheese

1. Cook linguine according to package directions. In a large saucepan, melt butter over medium heat. Stir in flour and seasonings until smooth. Gradually add broth. Bring to a boil; cook and stir for 2 minutes or until thickened. Remove from the heat; stir in cream.

⑤ INGREDIENTS

Honey-Glazed Chicken

When I was a young girl, this was my oldest sister's Sunday dinner. The tradition has continued, as I make this dish twice a month and my four daughters serve their families this favorite dish. It has an old-fashioned flavor, and the chicken is crisp and golden brown.

—**PAT DUBE** PHOENIX, AZ

PREP: 5 MIN. • **BAKE:** 1 HOUR
MAKES: 6 SERVINGS

- ¼ **cup butter, melted**
- ¼ **cup orange juice**
- ¼ **cup honey**
- ½ **teaspoon salt**
- 1 **broiler/fryer chicken (3 to 4 pounds), cut up**

1. In a shallow bowl, combine the butter, orange juice, honey and salt. Remove ⅓ cup and set aside for basting. Dip chicken pieces in remaining butter mixture; place in a well-greased 9x13-in. baking dish.

2. Bake, uncovered, at 350° for 1 hour or until juices run clear, basting occasionally with reserved butter mixture.

I'm big on spicy food, but the creamy topping makes these enchiladas easy to love for all sorts of eaters.
—**CRYSTAL SCHLUETER** NORTHGLENN, CO

Creamy Buffalo Chicken Enchiladas

PREP: 15 MIN. • **BAKE:** 25 MIN.
MAKES: 6 SERVINGS

- 3 cups shredded rotisserie chicken
- 1 can (10 ounces) enchilada sauce
- ¼ cup Buffalo wing sauce
- 1¼ cups (5 ounces) shredded Monterey Jack or cheddar cheese, divided
- 12 corn tortillas (6 inches), warmed
- 1 can (10¾ ounces) condensed cream of celery soup, undiluted
- ½ cup blue cheese salad dressing
- ¼ cup 2% milk
- ¼ teaspoon chili powder
  Optional toppings: sour cream, thinly sliced green onions and additional Buffalo wing sauce

1. Preheat oven to 350°. In a large bowl, mix chicken, enchilada sauce and wing sauce. Stir in ¾ cup cheese.

2. Place ¼ cup chicken mixture off center on each tortilla. Roll up and place in a greased 9x13-in. baking dish, seam side down.

3. In a small bowl, mix soup, salad dressing and milk; pour over enchiladas. Sprinkle with remaining cheese; top with chili powder.

4. Bake, uncovered, 25-30 minutes or until heated through and cheese is melted. Add toppings as desired.

FREEZE OPTION *Cover and freeze unbaked casserole. To use, partially thaw in refrigerator overnight. Remove from refrigerator 30 minutes before baking. Bake casserole as directed, increasing time as necessary for a thermometer inserted in center to read 165°.*

Indian Baked Chicken

Cumin and turmeric give this hearty entree just the right amount of Indian flavor, but it's subtle enough to appeal to a variety of palates.
—**STEPHANIE KURIN** MUNCIE, IN

PREP: 15 MIN. • **BAKE:** 1 HOUR
MAKES: 6 SERVINGS

- 1 pound small red potatoes, quartered
- 4 medium carrots, cut into 1-inch pieces
- 1 large onion, cut into 1-inch pieces
- 6 boneless skinless chicken thighs (about 1½ pounds)
- 1 can (14½ ounces) chicken broth
- 1 can (6 ounces) tomato paste
- 2 tablespoons olive oil
- 1 tablespoon ground turmeric
- 1 teaspoon chili powder
- 1 teaspoon ground cumin
- ½ teaspoon salt
- ½ teaspoon garlic powder
- ½ teaspoon pepper

1. Place the potatoes, carrots and onion in a greased 9x13-in. baking dish; add chicken. In a small bowl, combine the remaining ingredients and pour over top.

2. Cover and bake at 400° for 1 to 1¼ hours or until a thermometer inserted in chicken reads 180° and vegetables are tender.

Orange Chicken

I found this recipe several years ago while looking for a new way to prepare chicken. It's become our favorite dinner entree.

—**BETTY SEXTON** BLAIRSVILLE, GA

PREP: 15 MIN. • **BAKE:** 45 MIN.
MAKES: 8 SERVINGS

- 1 egg
- ⅓ cup orange juice
- 1 to 1½ cups herb-seasoned stuffing mix, crushed
- 1½ teaspoons paprika
- 1 tablespoon grated orange peel
- 1 teaspoon salt
- 8 boneless skinless chicken breast halves
- 6 tablespoons butter, melted

1. In a shallow bowl, beat egg and orange juice. In another bowl, combine stuffing mix, paprika, orange peel and salt.
2. Dip chicken in egg mixture, then in crumbs, turning to coat well. Pour butter into a 9x13-in. baking dish. Place chicken in baking dish, turning once to butter both sides.
3. Bake, uncovered, at 375° for 45 minutes or until a thermometer reads 170°.

TOP TIP

The outer peel of a citrus fruit has the best flavor. Be careful not to grate too deeply into the peel, as the light colored inner part, the pith, tastes bitter.

FREEZE IT

Penne Chicken with Sun-Dried Tomatoes

The sun-dried tomatoes give this cheesy casserole a sophisticated feel. It's great for company.

—**ROBIN KLAWINSKI** EAGLE, ID

PREP: 20 MIN. • **BAKE:** 50 MIN.
MAKES: 8 SERVINGS

- 3¾ cups uncooked penne pasta
- 2 jars (15 ounces each) sun-dried tomato Alfredo sauce
- 2 packages (9 ounces each) ready-to-use Southwestern chicken strips
- 2 cups oil-packed sun-dried tomatoes, drained and chopped
- 1 jar (6 ounces) sliced mushrooms, drained
- 4 green onions, sliced
- ⅛ teaspoon pepper
- 1½ cups shredded Parmesan cheese

1. Cook pasta according to package directions.
2. In a large bowl, combine the Alfredo sauce, chicken, tomatoes, green onions, pepper and mushrooms. Drain pasta; stir into chicken mixture. Spoon into a greased 9x13-in. baking dish.
3. Cover and bake at 350° for 45-50 minutes or until heated through. Uncover; sprinkle with cheese. Bake 5-8 minutes longer or until cheese is melted.
FREEZE OPTION *Before baking, cover and freeze casserole for up to 3 months. Thaw in the refrigerator overnight. Remove from the refrigerator 30 minutes before baking. Bake, uncovered, at 350° for 50-60 minutes or until bubbly.*

Phyllo Chicken

Phyllo dough is fun to work with. Its flakiness turns everyday ingredients into a special entree.

—JOYCE MUMMAU MOUNT AIRY, MD

PREP: 15 MIN. • **BAKE:** 35 MIN.
MAKES: 12 SERVINGS

- ½ cup butter, melted, divided
- 12 sheets phyllo dough (14 inches x 9 inches)
- 3 cups diced cooked chicken
- ½ pound sliced bacon, cooked and crumbled
- 3 cups frozen chopped broccoli, thawed and drained
- 2 cups (8 ounces) shredded cheddar or Swiss cheese
- 6 eggs
- 1 cup half-and-half cream or evaporated milk
- ½ cup milk
- 1 teaspoon salt
- ½ teaspoon pepper

1. Brush sides and bottom of a 9x13-in. baking dish with some of the melted butter. Place one sheet of phyllo dough in bottom of baking dish; lightly brush with butter.

2. Repeat with five more sheets of phyllo. Keep remaining phyllo covered with plastic wrap and a damp towel to prevent it from drying out.

3. In a large bowl, combine the chicken, bacon, broccoli and cheese; spread evenly over phyllo in baking dish. In a small bowl, whisk the eggs, cream, milk, salt and pepper; pour over chicken mixture. Cover filling with one sheet of phyllo; brush with butter. Repeat with remaining phyllo dough. Brush top with remaining butter.

4. Bake, uncovered, at 375° for 35-40 minutes or until a thermometer reaches 160°. Let stand for 5-10 minutes before cutting.

Caprese Chicken with Bacon

I add smoky bacon to the classic Caprese combo of basil, tomatoes and mozzarella. I like to finish the chicken under the broiler, which gives the cheese a bit of color. Watch it carefully, though: The cheese browns quickly!

—**TAMMY HAYDEN** QUINCY, MI

PREP: 20 MIN. • **BAKE:** 20 MIN.
MAKES: 4 SERVINGS

- 8 **bacon strips**
- 4 **boneless skinless chicken breast halves (6 ounces each)**
- 1 **tablespoon olive oil**
- ½ **teaspoon salt**
- ¼ **teaspoon pepper**
- 2 **plum tomatoes, sliced**
- 6 **fresh basil leaves, thinly sliced**
- 4 **slices part-skim mozzarella cheese**

1. Place bacon in an ungreased 15-in. x 10-in. x 1-in. baking pan. Bake at 400° for 8-10 minutes or until partially cooked but not crisp. Remove to paper towels to drain.
2. Place chicken in an ungreased 9x13-in. baking pan; brush with oil and sprinkle with salt and pepper. Top with tomatoes and basil. Wrap each in two bacon strips, arranging bacon in a crisscross.
3. Bake, uncovered, at 400° for 20-25 minutes or until a meat thermometer reads 170°. Top with cheese; bake 1 minute longer or until melted.

Sausage & Pepper Pizza

All pizza should satisfy a craving. This one easily beats delivery service to your table.

—**JAMES SCHEND**
PLEASANT PRAIRIE, WI

PREP: 25 MIN. • **BAKE:** 20 MIN.
MAKES: 6 SERVINGS

- 1 **package (6½ ounces) pizza crust mix**
- 1 **can (8 ounces) pizza sauce**
- 1¼ **cups (5 ounces) shredded pizza cheese blend, divided**
- 1 **medium onion, sliced**
- 1 **medium green pepper, sliced**
- 2 **fully cooked Italian chicken sausage links, sliced**
  Grated Parmesan cheese, optional

1. Preheat oven to 425°. Prepare pizza dough according to package directions. Press dough onto bottom and ½ in. up sides of a greased 9x13-in. baking pan.
2. Spread with pizza sauce. Top with 1 cup cheese blend, onion, pepper and sausage; sprinkle with remaining cheese blend.
3. Bake 17-20 minutes or until crust is golden brown. If desired, sprinkle with Parmesan cheese.

Cornmeal Oven-Fried Chicken

A crunchy coating of cornmeal and Parmesan really perks up fried chicken. It's a crisp, tasty, mess-free variation on regular fried chicken.

—DEBORAH WILLIAMS PEORIA, AZ

PREP: 20 MIN. • **BAKE:** 40 MIN.
MAKES: 6 SERVINGS

½ cup dry bread crumbs
½ cup cornmeal
⅓ cup grated Parmesan cheese
¼ cup minced fresh parsley or
   4 teaspoons dried parsley
   flakes
¾ teaspoon garlic powder
½ teaspoon salt
½ teaspoon onion powder
½ teaspoon dried thyme
½ teaspoon pepper
½ cup buttermilk
1 broiler/fryer chicken
   (3 to 4 pounds), cut up,
   skin removed
1 tablespoon butter, melted

1. In a large resealable plastic bag, combine the first nine ingredients. Place the buttermilk in a shallow bowl. Dip chicken in buttermilk, then add to bag, a few pieces at a time, and shake to coat.

2. Place in a 9x13-in. baking pan coated with cooking spray. Bake at 375° for 10 minutes; drizzle with butter. Bake 30-40 minutes longer or until juices run clear.

LANA GERMAN'S
HONEY-PECAN BAKED
COD *PAGE 110*

Seafood & Meatless

JULIE LOWER'S CHEESE SPINACH MANICOTTI *PAGE 98*

BARBARA COLUCCI'S CREAMY CAVATAPPI & CHEESE *PAGE 97*

SHARON SEMPH'S BAKED DILL HALIBUT *PAGE 110*

Seafood Tortilla Lasagna

My husband and I enjoy lasagna, seafood and Mexican fare. One evening I combined all three into this deliciously different entree. It certainly is a tempting, memorable change of pace from traditional Italian-style lasagna.

—SHARON SAWICKI

CAROL STREAM, IL

PREP: 40 MIN.
BAKE: 30 MIN. + STANDING
MAKES: 12 SERVINGS

- 1 jar (20 ounces) picante sauce
- 1½ pounds uncooked medium shrimp, peeled and deveined
- ⅛ teaspoon cayenne pepper
- 1 tablespoon olive oil
- 4 to 6 garlic cloves, minced
- ⅓ cup butter, cubed
- ⅓ cup all-purpose flour
- 1 can (14½ ounces) chicken broth
- ½ cup heavy whipping cream
- 15 corn tortillas (6 inches), warmed
- 1 package (16 ounces) imitation crabmeat, flaked
- 3 cups (12 ounces) shredded Colby-Monterey Jack cheese
  Sour cream and minced fresh cilantro, optional

1. Place picante sauce in a blender; cover and process until smooth. Set aside. In a large skillet cook shrimp and cayenne in oil for about 3 minutes or until shrimp turn pink. Add garlic; cook 1 minute longer. Remove and set aside.

2. In the same skillet, melt butter. Stir in flour until smooth. Gradually add broth. Bring to a boil; cook and stir for 2 minutes or until thickened. Reduce heat. Stir in cream and picante sauce; heat through.

3. Spread ½ cup of sauce in a greased 9x13-in. baking dish. Layer with six tortillas, half of the shrimp, crab and sauce and 1¼ cups cheese. Repeat layers. Tear or cut remaining tortillas; arrange over cheese. Sprinkle with remaining cheese.

4. Bake, uncovered, at 375° for 30-35 minutes or until bubbly. Let stand 15 minutes before cutting. Garnish with sour cream and minced cilantro if desired.

HOW TO

PREPARE SHRIMP

1 To peel, pull the largest section of shell and the swimmerets to one side. Continue pulling to remove shell. Pull off tail shell if desired.

2 To devein, make a shallow slit down entire back of shrimp, from head area to tail. Rinse under cold water to remove the vein.

Trout Baked in Cream

Here's a quick and delicious way to serve fish. It's definitely one of our family's all-time favorites.

—ANN NACE PERKASIE, PA

START TO FINISH: 20 MIN.
MAKES: 4-6 SERVINGS

- 6 trout fillets (about 3½ ounces each)
- 2 tablespoons lemon juice
- 1 teaspoon dill weed
- ½ teaspoon salt
- ⅛ teaspoon pepper
- 1 cup heavy whipping cream
- 2 tablespoons seasoned bread crumbs

Place trout in a greased 9x13-in. baking dish. Sprinkle with lemon juice, dill, salt and pepper. Pour cream over all. Sprinkle with bread crumbs. Bake, uncovered, at 350° for 11-15 minutes or until fish flakes easily with a fork.

Creamy Cavatappi & Cheese

Dive fork-first into oodles of noodles baked to bubbly perfection and coated with a to-die-for sharp cheddar cheese sauce in this grown-up mac and cheese. Hot sauce lends a mild heat to the crunchy topping.

—BARBARA COLUCCI ROCKLEDGE, FL

PREP: 30 MIN. • **BAKE:** 20 MIN.
MAKES: 10 SERVINGS

- 6 cups uncooked cavatappi or spiral pasta
- 3 garlic cloves, minced
- ⅓ cup butter
- ¼ cup all-purpose flour
- 1 tablespoon hot pepper sauce
- 4 cups 2% milk
- 6 cups (24 ounces) shredded sharp cheddar cheese
- 1 cup cubed process cheese (Velveeta)
- 3 green onions, chopped

TOPPINGS:
- ½ cup panko (Japanese) bread crumbs
- 1 tablespoon butter, melted
- 3 thick-sliced bacon strips, cooked and coarsley crumbled, optional
- 1 green onion, chopped
Coarsely ground pepper, optional

1. Cook cavatappi according to package directions.

2. Meanwhile, saute garlic in butter in a Dutch oven. Stir in flour and pepper sauce until blended; gradually add milk. Bring to a boil; cook and stir for 2 minutes or until thickened.

3. Stir in cheeses until melted; add green onions. Drain the cavatappi; stir into cheese mixture. Transfer to a greased 9x13-in. baking dish. Combine the bread crumbs, butter and, if desired, bacon; sprinkle over the top.

4. Bake, uncovered, at 350° for 20-25 minutes or until bubbly. Sprinkle with green onion and, if desired, pepper.

Cheese Spinach Manicotti

Cream cheese and cottage cheese beef up the filling in the vegetarian version of this classic entree. And since each generous serving size includes 5 grams of fiber and 25 grams of protein, no one will miss the meat.

—JULIE LOWER KATY, TX

PREP: 55 MIN. • **BAKE:** 55 MIN.
MAKES: 7 SERVINGS

- 1 **large onion, chopped**
- 2 **garlic cloves, minced**
- 1 **tablespoon olive oil**
- 3 **cans (8 ounces each) no-salt-added tomato sauce**
- 2 **cans (6 ounces each) tomato paste**
- 1½ **cups water**
- ½ **cup dry red wine or vegetable broth**
- 2 **tablespoons Italian seasoning**
- 2 **teaspoons sugar**
- 2 **teaspoons dried oregano**

FILLING

- 1 **package (8 ounces) fat-free cream cheese**
- 1¼ **cups (10 ounces) 2% cottage cheese**
- 1 **package (10 ounces) frozen chopped spinach, thawed and squeezed dry**
- ¼ **cup grated Parmesan cheese**
- 2 **large eggs, lightly beaten**
- ½ **teaspoon salt**
- 1 **package (8 ounces) manicotti shells**
- 1 **cup (4 ounces) shredded part-skim mozzarella cheese**

1. In a large saucepan, saute onion and garlic in oil until tender. Stir in the tomato sauce, tomato paste, water, wine, Italian seasoning, sugar and oregano. Bring to a boil. Reduce heat; simmer, uncovered, for 15-20 minutes, stirring occasionally.

2. Meanwhile, in a bowl, beat cream cheese until smooth. Stir in the cottage cheese, spinach, Parmesan cheese, eggs and salt.

3. Stuff cream cheese mixture into uncooked manicotti shells.

Spread 1 cup sauce into a 9x13-in. baking dish coated with cooking spay. Arrange manicotti over sauce. Pour remaining sauce over top.

4. Cover and bake at 350° for 50-55 minutes or until the pasta is tender.

5. Uncover the casserole and sprinkle with mozzarella cheese. Bake 5-10 minutes longer or until cheese is melted.

Cozumel Red Snapper Veracruz

A popular dish in Cozumel, Mexico, is Veracruz-style red snapper. It usually features olives, capers and whole tomatoes. You can't bring it home from vacation, so why not create your own?

—BARB MILLER OAKDALE, MN

PREP: 25 MIN. • **BAKE:** 35 MIN.
MAKES: 4 SERVINGS

4 red snapper fillets (6 ounces each)

½ teaspoon salt
¼ teaspoon pepper
¼ cup white wine or chicken stock
2 large tomatoes, seeded and chopped
1 medium onion, chopped
⅓ cup pitted green olives, chopped
1 jalapeno pepper, seeded and minced
2 tablespoons capers, drained
2 garlic cloves, minced
2 tablespoons olive oil
Hot cooked Israeli couscous and chopped fresh cilantro, optional

1. Preheat oven to 375°. Sprinkle fillets with salt and pepper. Place in a greased 9x13-in. baking dish; drizzle with wine. Top with tomatoes, onion, olives, jalapeno, capers and garlic; drizzle with olive oil.
2. Bake 35-40 minutes or until fish flakes easily with a fork. If desired, serve with couscous and sprinkle with cilantro.
NOTE *Wear disposable gloves when cutting hot peppers; the oils can burn skin. Avoid touching your face.*

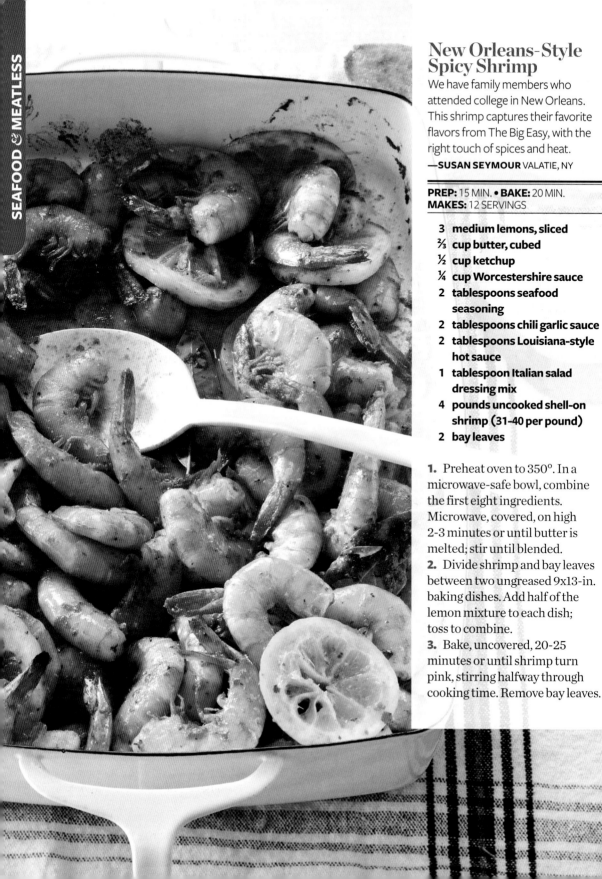

New Orleans-Style Spicy Shrimp

We have family members who attended college in New Orleans. This shrimp captures their favorite flavors from The Big Easy, with the right touch of spices and heat.

—**SUSAN SEYMOUR** VALATIE, NY

PREP: 15 MIN. • **BAKE:** 20 MIN.
MAKES: 12 SERVINGS

- 3 **medium lemons, sliced**
- ⅔ **cup butter, cubed**
- ½ **cup ketchup**
- ¼ **cup Worcestershire sauce**
- 2 **tablespoons seafood seasoning**
- 2 **tablespoons chili garlic sauce**
- 2 **tablespoons Louisiana-style hot sauce**
- 1 **tablespoon Italian salad dressing mix**
- 4 **pounds uncooked shell-on shrimp (31-40 per pound)**
- 2 **bay leaves**

1. Preheat oven to 350°. In a microwave-safe bowl, combine the first eight ingredients. Microwave, covered, on high 2-3 minutes or until butter is melted; stir until blended.

2. Divide shrimp and bay leaves between two ungreased 9x13-in. baking dishes. Add half of the lemon mixture to each dish; toss to combine.

3. Bake, uncovered, 20-25 minutes or until shrimp turn pink, stirring halfway through cooking time. Remove bay leaves.

Crab-Topped Tilapia

I took the crab filling from a stuffed mushroom recipe that's been in my family for many years and served it on tilapia fillets. It's a wonderful special-occasion meal that comes together in just a few minutes.
—LAURA MERKLE DOVER, DE

PREP: 15 MIN. • **BAKE:** 25 MIN.
MAKES: 4 SERVINGS

- 4 tilapia fillets (5 ounces each)
- ¼ teaspoon pepper
- ⅛ teaspoon salt
- ⅓ cup finely chopped celery
- 2 tablespoons finely chopped onion
- 1 garlic clove, minced
- 2½ teaspoons butter, melted, divided
- 2 teaspoons all-purpose flour
- ⅛ teaspoon dried thyme
- ¼ cup fat-free milk
- 1½ teaspoons lemon juice
- ¾ teaspoon marinade for chicken
  Dash hot pepper sauce
- ¼ cup reduced-fat mayonnaise
- 1 cup lump crabmeat, drained
- 4 tablespoons seasoned bread crumbs, divided

1. Sprinkle fish with pepper and salt. Place in a 9x13-in. baking dish coated with cooking spray; set aside.
2. In a small nonstick skillet coated with cooking spray, cook the celery, onion and garlic in 2 teaspoons butter until tender. Stir in flour and thyme until blended. Gradually whisk in milk. Bring to a boil; cook and stir for 1-2 minutes or until thickened. Stir in the lemon juice, marinade for chicken and hot pepper sauce.
3. Remove from the heat; stir in mayonnaise until blended. Stir in crab and 3 tablespoons bread crumbs. Spoon onto fillets. Toss remaining bread crumbs and butter; sprinkle over crab mixture.
4. Cover and bake at 350° for 18 minutes. Uncover; bake 5-10 minutes longer or until fish flakes easily with a fork.
NOTE *This recipe was tested with Lea & Perrins Marinade for Chicken.*

FREEZE IT
Broccoli Tuna Casserole

When I was in the Navy, a friend's wife shared this healthy dish.
—YVONNE COOK HASKINS, OH

PREP: 35 MIN. • **BAKE:** 1 HOUR
MAKES: 8 SERVINGS

- 5 cups uncooked whole wheat egg noodles
- 1 teaspoon butter
- ¼ cup chopped onion
- ¼ cup cornstarch
- 2 cups fat-free milk
- 1 teaspoon dried basil
- 1 teaspoon dried thyme
- ¾ teaspoon salt
- ½ teaspoon pepper
- 1 cup reduced-sodium chicken broth
- 1 cup (4 ounces) shredded Monterey Jack cheese, divided
- 4 cups frozen broccoli florets, thawed
- 2 pouches (6.4 ounces each) albacore white tuna in water
- ⅓ cup panko (Japanese) bread crumbs
- 1 tablespoon butter, melted

1. Preheat oven to 350°. Cook noodles according to package directions; drain. Transfer to a 9x13-in. baking dish coated with cooking spray.
2. Meanwhile, in a large nonstick skillet coated with cooking spray, heat butter over medium-high heat. Add onion; cook and stir until tender.
3. In a small bowl, whisk the cornstarch, milk and seasonings until smooth; stir into pan. Stir in broth. Bring to a boil; cook and stir 2 minutes or until thickened. Stir in ¾ cup of the cheese until melted; stir in broccoli and tuna.
4. Spoon mixture over noodles; mix well. Sprinkle with the remaining cheese. Toss bread crumbs with melted butter; sprinkle over casserole.
5. Bake, covered, 45 minutes. Bake, uncovered, 15-20 minutes longer or until cheese is melted.
FREEZE OPTION *Cool unbaked casserole; cover and freeze. To use, partially thaw in refrigerator overnight. Remove from the refrigerator 30 minutes before baking. Bake casserole as directed, increasing time as necessary for a thermometer inserted in center to read 165°.*

Top with sauce; sprinkle with remaining cheese.

4. Bake, uncovered, 25-30 minutes or until heated through and cheese is melted.

Cajun-Style Catfish

Not terribly spicy, this dish features the green pepper, onion and celery combination common in Cajun mainstays. It's a colorful and flavorful way to serve catfish.

—**IRENE CLIETT** CEDARBLUFF, MS

PREP: 30 MIN. • **BAKE:** 15 MIN.
MAKES: 4 SERVINGS

- ½ **cup chopped onion**
- ½ **cup chopped celery**
- ½ **cup chopped green pepper**
- 1 **tablespoon olive oil**
- 1 **can (14½ ounces) diced tomatoes and green chilies, undrained**
- ½ **cup sliced fresh mushrooms**
- 1 **can (2¼ ounces) sliced ripe olives, drained**
- ½ **teaspoon garlic powder**
- 4 **catfish fillets (6 ounces each)**
- ¼ **cup grated Parmesan cheese**

1. In a large skillet, saute the onion, celery and green pepper in oil until tender. Add the tomatoes, mushrooms, olives and garlic powder. Bring to a boil. Reduce heat; simmer, uncovered, for 10 minutes or until heated through.

2. Place catfish in an ungreased 9x13-in. baking dish. Top with vegetable mixture; sprinkle with cheese. Bake, uncovered, at 400° for 15-20 minutes or until fish flakes easily with a fork.

FREEZE IT

Shrimp Enchiladas with Green Sauce

I started making these enchiladas during Lent. It allows my family to observe Lent and still enjoy Mexican food. At a work potluck, my co-workers couldn't get enough.

—**MARI ACEDO** CHANDLER, AZ

PREP: 35 MIN. • **BAKE:** 25 MIN.
MAKES: 8 SERVINGS

- ½ **cup plus 1 tablespoon olive oil, divided**
- 16 **corn tortillas (6 inches)**
- 2 **medium tomatoes, chopped**
- 2 **medium onions, finely chopped**
- 4 **garlic cloves, minced**
- ½ **teaspoon ground cumin**
- 1½ **pounds uncooked small shrimp, peeled and deveined**
- 2 **packages (10 ounces each) frozen chopped spinach, thawed and squeezed dry**
- 2 **cups (8 ounces) shredded part-skim mozzarella cheese, divided**
- 2 **cans (10 ounces each) green enchilada sauce**

1. Preheat oven to 350°. In a skillet, heat ½ cup oil over medium-high heat. In batches, fry tortillas 10 seconds on each side or until pliable (do not allow to crisp). Drain on paper towels. Cover with foil to keep warm and softened.

2. In a large skillet, heat the remaining oil over medium-high heat. Add tomatoes, onions, garlic and cumin; cook and stir 3-4 minutes or until onions are tender. Add the shrimp; cook 3-4 minutes or until shrimp turn pink, stirring occasionally. Stir in spinach; heat through.

3. Place ¼ cup shrimp mixture off center on each tortilla; top with 1 tablespoon cheese. Roll up and place in a greased 9x13-in. baking dish, seam side down.

Parsley-Crusted Cod

Struggling to add seafood to your family-dinner lineup? You'll appreciate this easy cod entree that takes advantage of kitchen staples. The flavors are mild yet delicious, so even picky eaters will dig in!

—JUDY GREBETZ RACINE, WI

START TO FINISH: 30 MIN.
MAKES: 4 SERVINGS

- ¾ cup dry bread crumbs
- 1 tablespoon minced fresh parsley
- 2 teaspoons grated lemon peel
- 1 garlic clove, minced
- ¼ teaspoon kosher salt
- ¼ teaspoon pepper
- 2 tablespoons olive oil
- 4 cod fillets (6 ounces each)

1. In a shallow bowl, combine the first six ingredients. Brush oil over one side of fillets; gently press into crumb mixture.

2. Place crumb side up in a 9x13-in. baking dish coated with cooking spray. Bake at 400° for 15-20 minutes or until fish flakes easily with a fork.

Flounder with Shrimp Stuffing

The tasty shrimp stuffing makes this flounder main course special enough for company. It's impressive yet easy!

—MARIE FORTE RARITAN, NJ

PREP: 30 MIN. • **BAKE:** 20 MIN.
MAKES: 6 SERVINGS

STUFFING
- 6 tablespoons butter, cubed
- 1 small onion, finely chopped
- ¼ cup finely chopped celery
- ¼ cup finely chopped green pepper
- 1 pound uncooked shrimp, peeled, deveined and chopped
- ¼ cup beef broth
- 1 teaspoon diced pimientos, drained
- 1 teaspoon Worcestershire sauce
- ½ teaspoon dill weed
- ½ teaspoon minced chives
- ⅛ teaspoon salt
- ⅛ teaspoon cayenne pepper
- 1½ cups soft bread crumbs

FISH
- 6 flounder fillets (3 ounces each)
- 5 tablespoons butter, melted
- 2 tablespoons lemon juice
- 1 teaspoon minced fresh parsley
- ½ teaspoon paprika
  Salt and pepper to taste

1. Preheat oven to 375°. In a large skillet, melt butter. Add onion, celery and green pepper; saute until tender. Add shrimp; cook and stir until shrimp turn pink. Add broth, pimientos, Worcestershire sauce, dill, chives, salt and cayenne; heat through. Remove from heat; stir in bread crumbs.

2. Spoon about ½ cup stuffing onto each fillet; roll up. Place seam side down in a greased 9x13-in. baking dish. Drizzle with butter and lemon juice. Sprinkle with seasonings. Bake, uncovered, 20-25 minutes or until the fish flakes easily with a fork.

Artichoke Mushroom Lasagna

White wine adds delightful flavor to this hearty vegetarian entree. No one will miss the meat!

—**BONNIE JOST** MANITOWOC, WI

PREP: 30 MIN.
BAKE: 1 HOUR + STANDING
MAKES: 12 SERVINGS

- 1 **pound sliced baby portobello mushrooms**
- 2 **tablespoons butter**
- 3 **garlic cloves, minced**
- 2 **cans (14 ounces each) water-packed artichoke hearts, rinsed, drained and chopped**
- 1 **cup chardonnay or other white wine**
- ¼ **teaspoon salt**
- ¼ **teaspoon pepper**

SAUCE
- ¼ **cup butter, cubed**
- ¼ **cup all-purpose flour**
- 3½ **cups 2% milk**
- 2½ **cups shredded Parmesan cheese**
- 1 **cup chardonnay or other white wine**

ASSEMBLY
- 9 **no-cook lasagna noodles**
- 4 **cups (16 ounces) shredded part-skim mozzarella cheese, divided**

1. Preheat oven to 350°. In a large skillet, saute mushrooms in butter until tender. Add garlic; cook 1 minute. Add artichokes, wine, salt and pepper; cook over medium heat until liquid is evaporated.

2. For sauce, in a large saucepan over medium heat, melt butter. Stir in the flour until smooth; gradually add milk. Bring to a boil; cook and stir 1 minute or until thickened. Stir in Parmesan cheese and wine.

3. Spread 1 cup sauce into a greased 9x13-in. baking dish. Layer with three noodles, 1⅔ cups sauce, 1 cup mozzarella and 1⅓ cups artichoke mixture. Repeat layers twice.

4. Cover and bake 45 minutes. Sprinkle with remaining mozzarella cheese. Bake, uncovered, 15-20 minutes or until cheese is melted. Let stand 15 minutes before cutting.

Tilapia Florentine

Get a little more heart-healthy fish into your weekly diet with this quick and easy entree. Topped with fresh spinach and a splash of lime, it's sure to become a favorite!

—**MELANIE BACHMAN** ULYSSES, PA

START TO FINISH: 30 MIN.
MAKES: 4 SERVINGS

- 1 **package (6 ounces) fresh baby spinach**
- 6 **teaspoons canola oil, divided**
- 4 **tilapia fillets (4 ounces each)**
- 2 **tablespoons lime juice**
- 2 **teaspoons garlic-herb seasoning blend**
- 1 **egg, lightly beaten**
- ½ **cup part-skim ricotta cheese**
- ¼ **cup grated Parmesan cheese**

1. In a large nonstick skillet, cook spinach in 4 teaspoons oil until wilted; drain. Meanwhile, place tilapia in a greased 9x13-in. baking dish. Drizzle with lime juice and remaining oil. Sprinkle with seasoning blend.

2. Combine the egg, ricotta cheese and spinach; spoon over fillets. Sprinkle with Parmesan.

3. Bake at 375° for 15-20 minutes or until fish flakes easily with a fork.

Company Swordfish

This fantastic entree is so easy to prepare! We're not big fish eaters in my family, but the plates are always scraped clean when this is on the table. Feel free to swap out the swordfish with halibut steaks if you'd like. Serve it alongside hot pasta for a quick side dish.

—CALLIE BERGER
DIAMOND SPRINGS, CA

PREP: 10 MIN. • **BAKE:** 25 MIN.
MAKES: 4 SERVINGS

- 4 swordfish or halibut steaks (7 ounces each)
- 2 jars (7½ ounces each) marinated artichoke hearts, drained and chopped
- ½ cup oil-packed sun-dried tomatoes, drained and chopped
- 4 shallots, chopped
- 2 tablespoons butter, melted
- 1 teaspoon lemon juice

1. Place fish in a greased 9x13-in. baking dish. In a small bowl, combine the artichokes, tomatoes and shallots; spread over fish. Drizzle with the butter and lemon juice.
2. Cover and bake at 425° for 15 minutes. Uncover; bake 6-8 minutes longer or until fish just turns opaque.

TOP TIP

It's easy to mix up Company Swordfish and create a whole new dish. Consider Cheese-Topped Swordfish instead! Start by omitting the topping ingredients altogether.

Next, combine ¼ cup melted butter and 1 cup each shredded Parmesan cheese and mayonnaise. Spread a fourth of the mixture over each fish steak. Bake, uncovered, for 15-20 minutes.

2. Cover and bake at 350° for 15 minutes. Uncover; sprinkle with onions. Bake, uncovered, 12-15 minutes longer or until fish flakes easily with a fork and asparagus is crisp-tender.

3. Meanwhile, in a small saucepan, combine the sauce ingredients. Bring to a boil; cook and stir for 1-2 minutes or until thickened. Discard toothpicks from bundles; serve with sauce.

Lemon-Caper Baked Cod

START TO FINISH: 20 MIN.
MAKES: 4 SERVINGS

- ¼ cup butter, cubed
- 2 tablespoons lemon juice
- ¼ teaspoon garlic pepper blend
- ¼ teaspoon grated lemon peel
- 2 tablespoons capers, drained
- 4 cod or haddock fillets (6 ounces each)
- ½ teaspoon seafood seasoning
- 1 tablespoon crumbled feta cheese

1. In a small microwave-safe bowl, combine the butter, lemon juice, garlic pepper and lemon peel. Microwave, uncovered, on high for 45-60 seconds or until butter is melted. Stir in capers.

2. Place cod in an ungreased 9x13-in. baking dish; sprinkle with seafood seasoning. Spoon butter mixture over fillets. Sprinkle with cheese. Bake, uncovered, at 425° for 10-15 minutes or until fish flakes easily with a fork.

Asparagus Fish Bundles

Low-fat food can be just as appealing as heavy entrees. Wrapped around asparagus bundles, these fish fillets with herb sauce are an ideal example.
—**JANE SHAPTON** IRVINE, CA

PREP: 25 MIN. • **BAKE:** 30 MIN.
MAKES: 4 SERVINGS

- 4 flounder fillets (6 ounces each)
- 20 fresh asparagus spears, trimmed
- ½ teaspoon salt
- ¼ teaspoon pepper
- 2 green onions, chopped

SAUCE
- ⅔ cup white wine or reduced-sodium chicken broth
- 2 tablespoons lemon juice
- 2 teaspoons cornstarch
- 1 teaspoon minced fresh basil or ¼ teaspoon dried basil
- 1 teaspoon minced fresh thyme or ¼ teaspoon dried thyme
- ⅛ teaspoon pepper

1. Wrap each fillet around five asparagus spears; secure with toothpicks. Place in a greased 9x13-in. baking dish. Sprinkle with salt and pepper.

Vacation on a plate is the only way
to describe this buttery and flaky
Lemon-Caper Baked Cod.
—**CAROLYN SCHMELING** BROOKFIELD, WI

Cheese Enchiladas

You won't bring home leftovers when you contribute these easy enchiladas to your next potluck dinner. With an easy homemade tomato sauce and yummy cheese filling, they always go fast! You can substitute any type of cheese you wish and vary the chili powder and cumin to adjust the spice level.

—**ASHLEY SCHACKOW** DEFIANCE, OH

PREP: 25 MIN. • **BAKE:** 25 MIN.
MAKES: 16 ENCHILADAS

- 2 cans (15 ounces each) tomato sauce
- 1⅓ cups water
- 2 tablespoons chili powder
- 2 garlic cloves, minced
- 1 teaspoon dried oregano
- ½ teaspoon ground cumin
- 16 flour tortillas (8 inches)
- 4 cups (16 ounces) shredded Monterey Jack cheese
- 2½ cups (10 ounces) shredded cheddar cheese, divided
- 2 medium onions, finely chopped
- 1 cup (8 ounces) sour cream
- ¼ cup minced fresh parsley
- ½ teaspoon salt
- ½ teaspoon pepper
  Shredded lettuce, sliced ripe olives and additional sour cream, optional

1. In a large saucepan, combine the first six ingredients. Bring to a boil. Reduce heat; simmer, uncovered, for 4-5 minutes or until thickened, stirring mixture occasionally. Spoon 2 tablespoons sauce over each tortilla.

2. In a large bowl, combine the Monterey Jack, 2 cups cheddar cheese, onions, sour cream, parsley, salt and pepper. Place about ⅓ cup down the center of each tortilla. Roll up and place seam side down in two greased 9x13-in. baking dishes.

3. Pour the remaining sauce over top of the enchiladas.

4. Bake, uncovered, at 350° for 20 minutes. Sprinkle with remaining cheddar cheese. Bake 4-5 minutes longer or until cheese is melted. Garnish with lettuce, olives and sour cream if desired.

Southwest Casserole

You won't believe how hearty and delicious this casserole is, and at only 3 grams of fat per serving, it's a healthy choice!

—MELODY DAVIS OVERLAND PARK, KS

PREP: 25 MIN. + SIMMERING
BAKE: 45 MIN. • **MAKES:** 8 SERVINGS

- 1 cup uncooked brown rice
- ⅓ cup uncooked wild rice
- 2¾ cups vegetable broth
- 4 cans (14½ ounces each) diced tomatoes, drained
- 1 can (15 ounces) black beans, rinsed and drained
- 1½ cups frozen corn, thawed
- 1 medium sweet red pepper, finely chopped
- 1 medium onion, finely chopped
- 6 green onions, chopped
- 1 jalapeno pepper, seeded and chopped
- 2 garlic cloves, minced
- 2 teaspoons ground cumin
- ¼ teaspoon cayenne pepper
- ¼ teaspoon pepper
- ½ cup shredded reduced-fat Mexican cheese blend

1. In a saucepan, bring brown rice, wild rice and broth to a boil. Reduce heat; cover and simmer for 50-60 minutes or until liquid is absorbed and rice is tender.
2. Combine the tomatoes, beans, corn, red pepper, onion, green onions, jalapeno, garlic, cumin, cayenne and pepper. Stir in rice.
3. Transfer to a greased 9x13-in. baking dish. Cover and bake at 325° for 40 minutes. Uncover; sprinkle with cheese. Bake 5-10 minutes longer or until heated through and the cheese is melted.

Lasagna Shrimp Roll-Ups

The seasoning and andouille sausage give this dish a nice kick, and seafood fans will appreciate the well-seasoned shrimp.

—MARY BETH HARRIS-MURPHREE
TYLER, TX

PREP: 30 MIN.
BAKE: 25 MIN. + STANDING
MAKES: 6 SERVINGS

- 1¼ pounds uncooked medium shrimp, peeled and deveined
- 1 medium onion, chopped
- 2 tablespoons olive oil
- 4 medium tomatoes, seeded and chopped
- 2 tablespoons Cajun seasoning
- 3 garlic cloves, minced
- ¼ cup butter, cubed
- ¼ cup all-purpose flour
- 2 cups milk
- 1½ cups (6 ounces) shredded cheddar cheese
- 1 cup diced fully cooked andouille sausage
- 12 lasagna noodles, cooked and drained
- 4 ounces pepper Jack cheese, shredded
- 1 teaspoon paprika

1. In a large skillet, saute shrimp and onion in oil until shrimp turn pink. Stir in tomatoes and Cajun seasoning; set aside.
2. In a large saucepan, saute garlic in butter for 1 minute. Stir in flour until blended. Gradually add milk. Bring to a boil over medium heat; cook and stir for 2 minutes or until thickened. Remove from the heat; stir in cheddar cheese until smooth. Add sausage; set aside.
3. Spread ⅓ cup shrimp mixture over each noodle. Carefully roll up; place seam side down in a greased 9x13-in. baking dish. Top with cheese sauce. Sprinkle with pepper Jack cheese and paprika.
4. Cover and bake at 350° for 15 minutes. Uncover roll-ups; bake 10-15 minutes longer or until bubbly. Let stand 15 minutes before serving.

Honey-Pecan Baked Cod

While vacationing in the Blue Ridge Mountains, we tried pecan-crusted fish one night at dinner. We were able to re-create the entree, and now enjoy this tasty version often. You can use fresh or frozen cod.

—**LANA GERMAN** LENOIR, NC

START TO FINISH: 30 MIN.
MAKES: 6 SERVINGS

- 3 **tablespoons honey**
- 2 **tablespoons butter, melted**
- 1 **tablespoon reduced-sodium soy sauce**
- 1½ **teaspoons lemon-pepper seasoning**
- ½ **teaspoon garlic powder**
- ½ **teaspoon paprika**
- ¼ **teaspoon seasoned salt**
- 1½ **cups finely chopped pecans**
- 6 **cod fillets (6 ounces each)**

1. Preheat oven to 400°. In a shallow bowl, combine the honey, butter, soy sauce and seasonings. Place pecans in another shallow bowl. Dip fillets in honey mixture, then coat with the pecans. Place in a greased 9x13-in. baking dish.
2. Bake casserole, uncovered, for 15-20 minutes or until fish flakes easily with a fork.

DID YOU KNOW?

You should always store fish in the coolest part of your refrigerator for no more than one or two days. Thaw frozen fish in its original package in the refrigerator. You should never refreeze fish.

Baked Dill Halibut

This healthy dish goes together in minutes. I make it often for my family because we all enjoy it, and there's never much to clean up!

—**SHARON SEMPH** SALEM, OR

PREP: 15 MIN. • **BAKE:** 25 MIN.
MAKES: 4 SERVINGS

- ⅓ **cup all-purpose flour**
- ½ **teaspoon salt**
- ⅛ **teaspoon pepper**
- 4 **halibut steaks (6 ounces each)**
- ¼ **cup reduced-fat sour cream**
- ¼ **cup reduced-fat mayonnaise**
- 1 **tablespoon chopped dill pickle**
- 1 **tablespoon chopped green onion**
- ½ **teaspoon dill weed**
- ½ **teaspoon lemon juice**
- ⅛ **teaspoon seasoned salt**
- 3 **tablespoons grated Parmesan cheese**

1. In a large resealable plastic bag, combine the flour, salt and pepper. Add halibut, one piece at a time, and shake to coat. Place in a 9x13-in. baking dish coated with cooking spray.
2. In a small bowl, combine the sour cream, mayonnaise, pickle, onion, dill weed, lemon juice and seasoned salt; spread evenly over halibut. Sprinkle with Parmesan cheese. Bake, uncovered, at 350° for 25-30 minutes or until fish flakes easily with a fork.

Seafood Casserole

A family favorite, this rice casserole is stuffed with plenty of seafood and veggies. It's hearty, homey and so easy to assemble!

—**NANCY BILLUPS** PRINCETON, IA

PREP: 20 MIN. • **BAKE:** 40 MIN.
MAKES: 6 SERVINGS

- 1 package (6 ounces) long grain and wild rice
- 1 pound frozen crabmeat, thawed or 2½ cups canned lump crabmeat, drained
- 1 pound cooked medium shrimp, peeled, deveined and cut into ½-inch pieces
- 2 celery ribs, chopped
- 1 medium onion, finely chopped
- ½ cup finely chopped green pepper
- 1 can (4 ounces) mushroom stems and pieces, drained
- 1 jar (2 ounces) diced pimientos, drained
- 1 cup mayonnaise
- 1 cup 2% milk
- ½ teaspoon pepper
  Dash Worcestershire sauce
- ¼ cup dry bread crumbs

1. Cook rice according to package directions. Meanwhile, preheat oven to 375°.

2. In a large bowl, combine the crab, shrimp, celery, onion, green pepper, mushrooms and pimientos. In a small bowl, whisk mayonnaise, milk, pepper and Worcestershire sauce; stir into seafood mixture. Stir in rice.

3. Transfer to a greased 9x13-in. baking dish. Sprinkle with the bread crumbs. Bake, uncovered, 40-50 minutes or until bubbly.

I invented this dish one night when I was having last-minute guests. I ran to a local farm stand, found some amazing produce and created this recipe using fresh portobellos and leftover risotto. My friends still ask for the recipe!

—**RIAN MACDONALD** POWDER SPRINGS, GA

Risotto-Stuffed Portobellos

PREP: 45 MIN. • **BAKE:** 20 MIN.
MAKES: 4 SERVINGS

- 1 **can (14½ ounces) reduced-sodium chicken or vegetable broth**
- 1 **cup water**
- 2 **celery ribs, finely chopped**
- 2 **medium carrots, finely chopped**
- 1 **large onion, finely chopped**
- 1 **tablespoon olive oil**
- 1 **cup uncooked arborio rice**
- ½ **cup chopped shallots**
- 1 **garlic clove, minced**
- 1 **cup dry white wine or additional broth**
- ½ **cup grated Parmesan cheese**
- 4 **green onions, finely chopped**
- 4 **large portobello mushrooms (4 to 4½ inches), stems removed**
- **Cooking spray**
- ¼ **teaspoon salt**
- ⅛ **teaspoon pepper**
- ¼ **cup shredded part-skim mozzarella cheese**

1. In a small saucepan, heat broth and water and keep warm. In a large nonstick skillet coated with cooking spray, saute the celery, carrots and onion in oil until crisp-tender. Add the rice, shallots and garlic; cook and stir for 2-3 minutes. Reduce heat; stir in wine. Cook and stir until all of the liquid is absorbed.

2. Add heated broth mixture, ½ cup at a time, stirring constantly. Allow the liquid to absorb between additions. Cook just until risotto is creamy and rice is almost tender. (Cooking time is about 20 minutes.)

Remove from the heat; add Parmesan cheese and green onions. Stir until cheese is melted.

3. Spritz mushrooms with cooking spray; sprinkle with salt and pepper. Fill each with 1 cup risotto mixture and sprinkle with mozzarella cheese. Place in a 9x13-in. baking dish coated with cooking spray.

4. Bake, uncovered, at 350° for 20-25 minutes or until mushrooms are tender and cheese is melted.

FREEZE IT

Veggie Lasagna

This is my daughter-in-law's recipe. It's tasty and a little different from traditional lasagna recipes—even the meatless ones!

—ALYCE WYMAN PEMBINA, ND

PREP: 30 MIN.
BAKE: 40 MIN. + STANDING
MAKES: 2 CASSEROLES
(9 SERVINGS EACH)

- 18 **uncooked lasagna noodles**
- 2 **eggs, lightly beaten**
- 2 **egg whites**
- 2 **cartons (15 ounces each) reduced-fat ricotta cheese**
- 4 **teaspoons dried parsley flakes**
- 2 **teaspoons dried basil**
- 2 **teaspoons dried oregano**
- 1 **teaspoon pepper**
- 8 **cups garden-style spaghetti sauce**
- 4 **cups (16 ounces) shredded part-skim mozzarella cheese**
- 2 **packages (16 ounces each) frozen cut green beans or 8 cups cut fresh green beans**
- ⅔ **cup grated Parmesan cheese**

1. Cook noodles according to package directions. Meanwhile, in a small bowl, whisk the eggs, egg whites, ricotta cheese, parsley, basil, oregano and pepper; set aside.

2. In each of two 9x13-in. baking dishes coated with cooking spray, spread 1 cup spaghetti sauce. Drain noodles; place three noodles over spaghetti sauce in each dish.

3. Layer each with a quarter of the ricotta mixture, 1 cup spaghetti sauce, 1 cup mozzarella cheese, three lasagna noodles and half of green beans. Top each with the remaining ricotta mixture, 1 cup spaghetti sauce, remaining lasagna noodles, spaghetti sauce and mozzarella cheese. Sprinkle Parmesan cheese over each.

4. Cover and freeze one casserole for up to 3 months. Bake remaining lasagna, uncovered, at 375° for 40-45 minutes or until bubbly and edges are lightly browned. Let stand for 10 minutes before serving.

TO USE FROZEN LASAGNA
Thaw in the refrigerator overnight. Remove from the refrigerator 30 minutes before baking. Cover and bake at 375° for 1¼ to 1½ hours or until bubbly. Let stand for 10 minutes before serving.

**JOANN KOERKENMEIER'S
CREAMY MAKE-AHEAD
MASHED POTATOES** *PAGE 121*

Sides

DONNA FANCHER'S BUTTERMILK MAC 'N' CHEESE *PAGE 120*

NANCY MUELLER'S MAPLE-GLAZED ACORN SQUASH *PAGE 131*

JOE SHERWOOD'S COWBOY BAKED BEANS *PAGE 134*

Durango Potato Casserole

For those who like it spicy, it's easy to turn up the heat on these potatoes by adding a more chili powder or jalapenos for extra kick.

—**PATRICIA HARMON** BADEN, PA

PREP: 35 MIN. • **BAKE:** 25 MIN.
MAKES: 12 SERVINGS (⅔ CUP EACH)

- 2½ pounds potatoes (about 8 medium), peeled and cut into 1-inch cubes
- 8 thick-sliced bacon strips
- 1 can (14½ ounces) diced tomatoes and green chilies, drained
- 3 cups (12 ounces) shredded Mexican cheese blend
- 4 green onions, chopped
- ⅓ cup chopped green pepper
- ⅓ cup chopped sweet red pepper
- 1½ cups reduced-fat mayonnaise
- 2 tablespoons lime juice
- 1 teaspoon seasoned salt
- ¼ teaspoon pepper
- 1½ teaspoons chili powder
- 2 tablespoons minced fresh cilantro

1. Place potatoes in a large saucepan and cover with water. Bring to a boil. Reduce heat; cover and simmer 10-15 minutes or until tender.

2. In a large skillet, cook bacon over medium heat until partially cooked but not crisp. Remove to paper towels to drain; set aside.

3. Drain potatoes and transfer to a large bowl; add tomatoes, cheese, onions and peppers.

4. In a small bowl, whisk the mayonnaise, lime juice, seasoned salt and pepper; add to potatoes and gently stir to coat. Transfer to a greased 9x13-in. baking dish. Coarsely chop bacon; sprinkle over the top. Sprinkle the casserole with chili powder.

5. Bake, uncovered, at 350° for 25-30 minutes or until heated through. Sprinkle with cilantro. Let stand for 5 minutes before serving.

HOW TO

SNIP HERBS

Here's a simple trimming tip. Don't clean up a cutting board! Simply place cilantro or parsley in a small glass container and snip sprigs with kitchen shears until minced.

Seven-Layer Gelatin Salad

By alternating fruity layers of colorful gelatin with sweetened sour cream, I've created one memorable potluck treat. Kids really fall for it, but it's impressive enough to satisfy any adult.

—MELODY MELLINGER
MYERSTOWN, PA

PREP: 20 MIN.
COOK: 10 MIN. + CHILLING
MAKES: 12-15 SERVINGS

- 1 **package (3 ounces) cherry gelatin**
- 4 **cups boiling water, divided**
- 2½ **cups cold water, divided**
- 2 **envelopes unflavored gelatin**
- 2 **cups milk**
- 1 **cup sugar**
- 2 **cups (16 ounces) sour cream**
- 2 **teaspoons vanilla extract**
- 1 **package (3 ounces) lemon gelatin**
- 1 **package (3 ounces) orange gelatin**
- 1 **package (3 ounces) lime gelatin**

1. In a bowl, dissolve cherry gelatin in 1 cup boiling water. Add ½ cup cold water; stir. Pour into a 9x13-in. dish coated with cooking spray; refrigerate until gelatin is set but not firm, about 30 minutes.
2. In a small saucepan, sprinkle unflavored gelatin over ½ cup cold water. Let stand 1 minute. Stir in milk and sugar. Cook and stir over medium heat until gelatin and sugar are dissolved.
3. Remove from the heat. Whisk in sour cream and vanilla until smooth. Spoon 1⅔ cups creamy gelatin mixture over the first

flavored layer. Chill until set but not firm. Prepare remaining flavored gelatins as directed for cherry gelatin. Alternately layer flavored gelatins with creamy gelatin layers, allowing each to set before adding next layer. Top with lime gelatin. Refrigerate overnight. Cut into squares.
NOTE *This recipe takes time to prepare since each layer must be set before the next layer is added.*

Cheddar Cabbage Casserole

The flavors really blend well in this casserole. The crunch of the cornflakes adds just the right texture contrast.

—ALICE JONES DEMOREST, GA

PREP: 10 MIN. • **BAKE:** 45 MIN.
MAKES: 8-10 SERVINGS

- 2½ **cups coarsely crushed cornflakes**
- ½ **cup butter, melted**
- 4½ **cups shredded cabbage**
- ⅓ **cup chopped onion**
- ¼ **to ½ teaspoon salt**
- ¼ **to ½ teaspoon pepper**
- 1 **can (10¾ ounces) condensed cream of celery soup, undiluted**
- 1 **cup milk**
- ½ **cup mayonnaise**
- 2 **cups (8 ounces) shredded cheddar cheese**

1. In a small bowl, toss the cornflakes with butter; sprinkle half into a greased 9x13-in. baking dish. Layer with cabbage, onion, salt and pepper.
2. In a large bowl, combine the soup, milk and mayonnaise until smooth. Spoon over the top; sprinkle with the cheese and remaining cornflake mixture. Bake casserole, uncovered, at 350° for 45-50 minutes or until golden brown.

Christmas Cauliflower Casserole

This creamy casserole is filled with tender cauliflower and topped with a sprinkling of crispy herb stuffing. The holiday classic appeals to both kids and adults.

—**CAROL REX** OCALA, FL

PREP: 20 MIN. • **BAKE:** 20 MIN.
MAKES: 12 SERVINGS (¾ CUP EACH)

- 3 packages (16 ounces each) frozen cauliflower
- 2 cups (16 ounces) sour cream
- 2 cups (8 ounces) shredded cheddar cheese
- 3 teaspoons chicken bouillon granules
- 1½ teaspoons ground mustard
- ¼ cup butter, cubed
- 1 cup stuffing mix
- ¾ cup chopped walnuts

1. Preheat oven to 375°. Cook cauliflower according to package directions; drain.
2. In a large bowl, mix the sour cream, cheese, bouillon and mustard until blended. Stir in cauliflower; transfer to a greased 9x13-in. baking dish.
3. In a large skillet, heat butter over medium heat. Add stuffing mix and walnuts; cook and stir until lightly toasted. Sprinkle over casserole. Bake, uncovered, 17-20 minutes or until heated through and topping is browned.

Cheesy Zucchini Casserole

Whether I'm preparing a sit-down dinner at home or attending a potluck buffet, family and friends have come to expect my signature vegetable dish.

—**EFFIE WANZER** MCDONOUGH, GA

PREP: 25 MIN. • **BAKE:** 40 MIN.
MAKES: 12-16 SERVINGS

- 5 medium zucchini (about 2 pounds), diced
- 2 tablespoons all-purpose flour
- 2 teaspoons baking powder
- 1 teaspoon salt
- ½ cup milk
- 4 eggs, lightly beaten
- 1 can (4 ounces) chopped green chilies
- 4 cups (16 ounces) shredded Colby-Monterey Jack cheese
- ½ cup dry bread crumbs
- 2 tablespoons butter, melted

1. In a large saucepan, cook zucchini in boiling water until crisp-tender, about 4 minutes; drain. Cool for 10 minutes. In a large bowl, combine the flour, baking powder and salt; whisk in milk until smooth. Beat in eggs and chilies. Stir in cheese and zucchini.
2. Transfer to a greased 9x13-in. baking dish. Toss the bread crumbs and butter; sprinkle over the zucchini mixture. Bake casserole, uncovered, at 325° for 40-50 minutes or until a knife inserted near the center comes out clean and edges are lightly browned. Let stand for 5 minutes before cutting.

Savory Mediterranean Orzo

If you like sampling flavors from around the world, you'll love this Mediterranean side. Summer squash, roasted peppers and nutritious spinach make the dish attractive and interesting.
—**KRISTI SILK** FERNDALE, WA

PREP: 25 MIN. • **BAKE:** 20 MIN.
MAKES: 12 SERVINGS (⅔ CUP EACH)

- 4 **cups reduced-sodium chicken broth**
- 1 **package (16 ounces) orzo pasta**
- 1 **medium onion, finely chopped**
- 2 **tablespoons olive oil**
- 4 **garlic cloves, minced**
- 2 **cups (8 ounces) crumbled feta cheese, divided**
- 1 **package (10 ounces) frozen chopped spinach, thawed and squeezed dry**
- 1 **jar (7½ ounces) roasted sweet red peppers, drained and chopped**
- 1 **small yellow summer squash, finely chopped**
- ½ **teaspoon salt**
- ½ **teaspoon pepper**

1. In a large saucepan, bring broth to a boil. Stir in the orzo; cook over medium heat for 6-8 minutes or until tender. Remove from the heat.

2. In a small skillet, saute onion in oil until tender. Add garlic; cook 1 minute longer. Stir into orzo mixture. Stir in 1 cup cheese, spinach, red peppers, squash, salt and pepper.

3. Transfer to a greased 9x13-in. baking dish; sprinkle with the remaining cheese. Bake, uncovered, at 350° for 20-25 minutes or until heated through.

⑤ INGREDIENTS
Buttermilk Mac 'n' Cheese

Once you taste this version of an all-time-favorite comfort food, you may never make the regular kind again. It's my most-requested recipe, and you can serve it with cooked ham for a nice meal.

—**DONNA FANCHER** LAWRENCE, IN

PREP: 15 MIN. • **BAKE:** 45 MIN.
MAKES: 8-10 SERVINGS

- 6 **eggs**
- 3¼ **cups (13 ounces) shredded cheddar cheese**
- 2½ **cups buttermilk**
- ½ **cup butter, melted**
- 1 **teaspoon salt**
- 1 **package (7 ounces) elbow macaroni, cooked and drained**

1. In a large bowl, beat the eggs. Stir in the cheese, buttermilk, butter and salt. Add macaroni; toss to coat.

2. Pour into a greased 9x13-in. baking dish. Bake, uncovered, at 350° for 45-50 minutes or until a thermometer reads 160°.

Creamy Make-Ahead Mashed Potatoes

Can mashed potatoes get any better? My answer is yes—when you top them with a savory trio of cheese, bacon and green onions.

—JOANN KOERKENMEIER

DAMIANSVILLE, IL

PREP: 35 MIN. + CHILLING
BAKE: 40 MIN. • **MAKES:** 10 SERVINGS

- 3 **pounds potatoes (about 9 medium), peeled and cubed**
- 6 **bacon strips, chopped**
- 1 **package (8 ounces) cream cheese, softened**
- ½ **cup sour cream**
- ½ **cup butter, cubed**
- ¼ **cup 2% milk**
- 1½ **teaspoons onion powder**
- 1 **teaspoon salt**
- 1 **teaspoon garlic powder**
- ½ **teaspoon pepper**
- 1 **cup (4 ounces) shredded cheddar cheese**
- 3 **green onions, chopped**

1. Place potatoes in a Dutch oven; add water to cover. Bring to a boil. Reduce heat; cook, uncovered, 10-15 minutes or until tender.
2. Meanwhile, in a skillet, cook bacon over medium heat until crisp. Remove to paper towels with a slotted spoon; drain.
3. Drain potatoes; return to pan. Mash potatoes, gradually adding cream cheese, sour cream and butter. Stir in the milk and seasonings. Transfer to a greased 9x13-in. baking dish; sprinkle with cheese, green onions and bacon. Refrigerate, covered, up to 1 day.
4. Preheat oven to 350°. Remove potatoes from refrigerator and let stand while oven heats. Bake, uncovered, 40-50 minutes or until heated through.

Vegetarian Dressing

Feast your eyes on this two-toned pumpernickel dressing. It's my vegetarian version of the classic Thanksgiving staple.

—THOMAS ROEGER

BLOOMINGTON, IN

PREP: 40 MIN. • **BAKE:** 35 MIN.
MAKES: 12 SERVINGS

- 8 **slices pumpernickel bread, cubed (about 6 cups)**
- 8 **slices whole wheat bread, cubed (about 6 cups)**
- 6 **celery ribs, thinly sliced**
- 1 **large onion, chopped**
- ¼ **cup butter, cubed**
- ½ **cup dried cranberries**
- 1 **teaspoon salt**
- 1 **teaspoon dried rosemary, crushed**
- 1 **teaspoon dried thyme**
- 1 **teaspoon rubbed sage**
- 1 **teaspoon poultry seasoning**
- ½ **teaspoon pepper**
- 2 **cups vegetable stock**

1. Place bread cubes in an ungreased 15x10x1-in. baking pan. Bake at 350° for 15 minutes, stirring twice. Set aside.
2. Meanwhile, in a large skillet, cook celery and onion in butter over medium heat until tender. Stir in the cranberries, salt, rosemary, thyme, sage, poultry seasoning and pepper; cook 2 minutes longer.
3. In a large bowl, combine the bread cubes and celery mixture. Add broth and combine.
4. Transfer to a greased 9x13-in. baking dish. Cover and bake at 350° for 25 minutes. Uncover; bake 10-15 minutes longer or until lightly browned.

Special Herb Dressing

Here's a fabulously satisfying dressing with all the great tastes people crave: satisfying meat, fresh herbs, earthy mushrooms, crunchy apples and water chestnuts, and a zesty burst of tart cranberries.

—TRUDY WILLIAMS

SHANNONVILLE, ON

PREP: 30 MIN. • **BAKE:** 35 MIN.
MAKES: 14-16 SERVINGS

- 1 **pound ground beef**
- 1 **pound bulk pork sausage**
- 1 **pound sliced fresh mushrooms**
- 1 **can (8 ounces) water chestnuts, drained and chopped**
- 2 **cups diced peeled apples**
- 1 **cup chopped onion**
- ¼ **cup minced fresh parsley**
- ¼ **cup chopped fresh celery leaves**
- 1 **cup chopped fresh or frozen cranberries**
- 2 **garlic cloves, minced**
- 1½ **teaspoons salt**
- 1 **teaspoon dried savory**
- 1 **teaspoon dried thyme**
- 1 **teaspoon rubbed sage**
- ¾ **teaspoon pepper**
  Pinch nutmeg
- 12 **cups day-old bread cubes**
- 1 **cup chicken broth**

1. Preheat oven to 350°. In a large skillet, cook the beef and sausage over medium heat until no longer pink; drain. Add the mushrooms, water chestnuts, apples, onion, parsley and celery leaves; cook 6-8 minutes or until the mushrooms and apples are tender. Stir in the cranberries, garlic and seasonings; cook 2 minutes longer.

2. Place bread cubes in large bowl; add meat mixture. Stir in the broth. Spoon into a greased 9x13-in. baking dish. Cover and bake 35-45 minutes.

Rice 'n' Black Bean Bake

When I come home from work, I start cooking rice for this meatless casserole right away. The rest is a breeze, because it's just opening cans and mixing. That's my kind of cooking.

—KATHY PRADO FORT WORTH, TX

START TO FINISH: 30 MIN.
MAKES: 8-10 SERVINGS

- 1 **can (15 ounces) black beans, rinsed and drained**
- 1 **can (10 ounces) diced tomatoes and green chilies, undrained**
- 1 **can (8 ounces) tomato sauce**
- 1 **jar (8 ounces) picante sauce**
- 2 **cups cooked rice**
- 1 **cup (8 ounces) sour cream**
- 2 **cups (8 ounces) shredded cheddar cheese, divided**
  Corn or tortilla chips

1. In a large bowl, combine the first four ingredients. Stir in the rice, sour cream and 1 cup of cheese. Transfer to a greased 9x13-in. baking dish. Sprinkle with the remaining cheese.

2. Bake, uncovered, at 350° for 20 minutes or until the cheese is melted. Serve with corn or tortilla chips.

Parmesan Baked Potatoes

Who knew a simple recipe could make potatoes taste so good? Mom liked to make these for Easter since they were more special than ordinary baked potatoes.

—RUTH SEITZ

COLUMBUS JUNCTION, IA

PREP: 5 MIN. • **BAKE:** 40 MIN.
MAKES: 8 SERVINGS

- 6 **tablespoons butter, melted**
- 3 **tablespoons grated Parmesan cheese**
- 8 **medium unpeeled red potatoes (about 2¾ pounds), halved lengthwise**

Pour butter into a 9x13-in. baking pan. Sprinkle Parmesan cheese over butter. Place potatoes with cut sides down over cheese. Bake, uncovered, at 400° for 40-45 minutes or until tender.

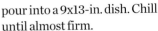

Cherry Pineapple Salad

Dark cherries and cream cheese make a really pretty layered salad. My sister-in-law often brings it to our family get-togethers on holidays and special occasions.

—LEONA LUECKING
WEST BURLINGTON, IA

PREP: 20 MIN. + CHILLING
MAKES: 12-16 SERVINGS

- 3 packages (3 ounces each) cherry gelatin
- 2⅓ cups boiling water
- 2 cans (16½ ounces each) pitted dark sweet cherries
- 1 can (20 ounces) pineapple tidbits
- ⅓ cup lemon juice
- ⅓ cup heavy whipping cream
- ⅓ cup mayonnaise
- 2 packages (3 ounces each) cream cheese, softened
  Dash salt
- ½ cup coarsely chopped nuts

1. In a large bowl, dissolve gelatin in water. Drain and reserve enough cherry and pineapple juices to measure 2½ cups; add to gelatin with lemon juice. Set fruits aside.
2. Divide gelatin in half. Set aside one portion at room temperature; chill the other portion until partially set. Fold pineapple into chilled gelatin; pour into a 9x13-in. dish. Chill until almost firm.
3. In a small bowl, beat cream, mayonnaise, cream cheese and salt until light and fluffy. Spread over the chilled gelatin layer. Refrigerate until firm. Chill reserved gelatin mixture until partially set. Fold in cherries and nuts; spread over cream cheese layer. Chill for at least 3 hours.

Apricot Barley Casserole

My mother was a farm girl who helped feed the threshers during harvesttime. They always asked for seconds of this hearty side dish dotted with dried apricots and golden raisins.

—DIANE SWINK
SIGNAL MOUNTAIN, TN

PREP: 20 MIN. • **BAKE:** 1¼ HOURS
MAKES: 8-10 SERVINGS

- ⅔ cup pine nuts or slivered almonds
- ¼ cup butter, divided
- 2 cups medium pearl barley
- 1 cup sliced green onions
- 7 cups chicken broth
- ⅔ cup diced dried apricots
- ½ cup golden raisins

1. In a large skillet, saute nuts in 2 tablespoons butter until lightly browned; remove and set aside. In the same skillet, saute the barley and onions in remaining butter until onions are tender. Add broth; bring to a boil. Stir in the apricots, raisins and nuts.
2. Pour into a greased 9x13-in. baking dish. Bake, uncovered, at 325° for 1¼ hours or until barley is tender.

Roasted Pepper Salad

Here's a versatile side to go with a summer full of entrees! It's ideal with chicken, steak—even pizza.

—**TRISHA KRUSE** EAGLE, ID

PREP: 15 MIN. • **BAKE:** 25 MIN.
MAKES: 6 SERVINGS

- 2 **cups cherry tomatoes, halved**
- ½ **cup minced fresh basil**
- 8 **garlic cloves, minced**
- 1 **tablespoon balsamic vinegar**
- ½ **teaspoon salt**
- ½ **teaspoon pepper**
- 3 **large sweet yellow peppers, halved and seeded**
- 2 **tablespoons shredded Parmesan cheese**

1. In a small bowl, combine the tomatoes, basil, garlic, vinegar, salt and pepper. Spoon into pepper halves.

2. Transfer to a 9x13-in. baking dish coated with cooking spray. Cover and bake at 400° for 20 minutes. Uncover; sprinkle with cheese. Bake 5-10 minutes longer or until cheese is melted.

DID YOU KNOW?

Balsamic vinegar is made from sweet white grapes and gets its dark color from aging in wooden barrels. The longer it ages, the more thick and sweet it becomes. Highly aged vinegars are expensive and best enjoyed drizzled over cheese or used for dipping with oil and bread. Moderately priced vinegar works fine for most recipes. If desired, add a little sugar to taste.

Smoked Sausage & Potato Dressing

PREP: 30 MIN. • **BAKE:** 20 MIN.
MAKES: 16 SERVINGS (¾ CUP EACH)

- 1 **tablespoon canola oil**
- 1 **medium sweet red pepper, chopped**
- 1 **medium green pepper, chopped**
- 1 **small onion, chopped**
- 4 **garlic cloves, minced**
- 3 **medium red potatoes (about ¾ pound), cubed**
- 3 **cups reduced-sodium chicken broth**
- 1 **tablespoon chicken bouillon granules**
- ½ **teaspoon pepper**
- 1 **package (12 ounces) seasoned stuffing cubes**
- 8 **ounces smoked kielbasa or Polish sausage, chopped**

1. Preheat oven to 350°. In a Dutch oven, heat the oil over medium-high heat. Add peppers and onion; cook and stir until peppers are crisp-tender. Stir in garlic; cook 1 minute longer.
2. Add potatoes, broth, bouillon and pepper. Bring to a boil. Reduce heat; cook, uncovered, 8-10 minutes or just until potatoes are tender. Remove from heat; stir in stuffing cubes and kielbasa.
3. Transfer to a greased 9x13-in. baking dish. Bake 18-22 minutes or until golden brown.

Cheesy Eggplant Bake

Paired with mushrooms and tomatoes, the eggplant stars in this dish.
—**FRANCES SAYRE** CINNAMINSON, NJ

PREP: 25 MIN. + STANDING
BAKE: 50 MIN. • **MAKES:** 6 SERVINGS

- 1 **medium eggplant, peeled**
- 2 **teaspoons salt**
- ¾ **cup dry bread crumbs**
- 3 **teaspoons garlic salt**
- ½ **teaspoon pepper**
- 3 **eggs**
- 3 **tablespoons olive oil, divided**
- 1 **large green pepper, chopped**
- 1 **medium onion, chopped**
- ½ **pound sliced fresh mushrooms**
- 2 **cans (14½ ounces each) stewed tomatoes**
- 1 **package (6 ounces) sliced part-skim mozzarella cheese**

1. Cut eggplant into ¼-in. slices. Place in a colander over a plate; sprinkle with salt. Let stand 30 minutes. Rinse under cold water and pat dry with paper towels.
2. In a shallow bowl, combine bread crumbs, garlic salt and pepper. In another bowl, beat eggs. Dip eggplant into eggs, then coat with crumb mixture.
3. In a large skillet, cook the eggplant in batches in 2 tablespoons oil for 2 minutes on each side or until lightly browned. Transfer to an ungreased 9x13-in. baking dish. In the same skillet, saute green pepper, onion and mushrooms in remaining oil until crisp-tender. Sprinkle over eggplant. Top with tomatoes.
4. Bake, uncovered, at 350° for 25 minutes. Place cheese slices over the top. Bake 25-30 minutes longer or until the cheese is lightly browned.

I tried this recipe for Thanksgiving. My husband is a picky eater, but he ate more of the stuffing than the turkey! Leftovers are good wtih over-easy eggs for breakfast.
—**ADRIANA R. TORRES** EL PASO, TX

Tomatoes Rockefeller

You can serve these tomatoes with a variety of meats, especially beef. The topping freezes well and may be spread thinner to cover more tomato slices, if needed.

—LINDA ROBERSON
COLLIERVILLE, TN

PREP: 20 MIN. • **BAKE:** 35 MIN.
MAKES: 6 SERVINGS

- 3 eggs, lightly beaten
- 1 cup dry bread crumbs
- 3 green onions, chopped
- 1 tablespoon butter, melted
- 1 teaspoon Italian seasoning
- 1 garlic clove, minced
- ½ teaspoon minced fresh thyme
- ¼ teaspoon salt
- ¼ teaspoon pepper
- ⅛ teaspoon Worcestershire sauce
- ⅛ teaspoon hot pepper sauce
- 1 package (10 ounces) frozen creamed spinach
- 2 large tomatoes
- ¼ cup shredded Parmesan cheese

1. In a large bowl, combine the first 11 ingredients. Cook spinach according to package directions; stir into egg mixture.
2. Cut each tomato into six slices; arrange in a single layer in a greased 9x13-in. baking dish. Mound 2 tablespoons of spinach mixture on each slice.
3. Bake, uncovered, at 350° for 30 minutes. Sprinkle with Parmesan cheese. Bake for 5-10 minutes longer or until a thermometer reads 160°.

Three-Cheese Stuffed Onions

These amazing steakhouse-style onions are loaded with Gorgonzola, Romano and rich, tangy cream cheese. They make the meal.

—SONYA LABBE
WEST HOLLYWOOD, CA

PREP: 25 MIN. • **BAKE:** 50 MIN.
MAKES: 8 SERVINGS

- 8 medium onions
- 1 cup crumbled Gorgonzola cheese
- 4 ounces cream cheese, cubed
- 1 tablespoon olive oil
- ½ cup grated Romano cheese
- ½ teaspoon salt
- ½ teaspoon pepper
- 1 can (14½ ounces) vegetable broth

1. Peel onions. Cut a ½-in. slice from top of each onion; remove centers with a melon baller, leaving ½-in. shells.
2. Combine Gorgonzola cheese and cream cheese; stuff into the onion shells. Place in an ungreased 9x13-in. baking dish. Drizzle with oil; sprinkle with Romano cheese, salt and pepper. Pour broth around onions.
3. Bake, uncovered, at 375° for 50-60 minutes or until tender.

Cheesy Broccoli Rice

Looking for a new side dish? Try this hearty recipe that combines rice, broccoli, ground beef and cheese.
—**KAREN WEAVILL** JOHNSTON, RI

PREP: 15 MIN. • **BAKE:** 30 MIN.
MAKES: 6 SERVINGS

- 1 **pound ground beef**
- 1 **medium onion, diced**
- 1 **garlic clove, minced**
- 3 **cups cooked long grain rice**
- 2 **cups fresh or frozen chopped broccoli, thawed**
- 2 **cups (8 ounces) shredded cheddar cheese**
- 2 **tablespoon grated Parmesan cheese**

1. In a skillet, cook beef, onion and garlic over medium heat until the meat is no longer pink; drain. Stir in the rice, broccoli and cheddar cheese.

2. Transfer to a greased 9x13-in. baking dish. Sprinkle with the Parmesan. Bake, uncovered, at 350° for 30-40 minutes or until heated through.

Heavenly Baked Sweet Potatoes

These luscious sweet potatoes taste a little bit like a pumpkin pie. If you like, toss some mini marshmallows on top to make it extra-indulgent.
—**CYNTHIA PETERSON** ROSWELL, NM

PREP: 30 MIN. • **BAKE:** 55 MIN.
MAKES: 10 SERVINGS

- 1 **can (8 ounces) unsweetened pineapple chunks**
- ½ **cup packed brown sugar**
- ¼ **cup apple cider or unsweetened apple juice**
- ¼ **cup maple syrup**
- ¼ **cup butter, cubed**
- ¾ **teaspoon ground cinnamon**
- ⅛ **teaspoon ground cloves**
- 3 **large sweet potatoes, peeled and cut into ¼-inch slices**
- 3 **medium apples, peeled and cut into ¼-inch slices**
- ¾ **teaspoon salt**
- ⅓ **cup chopped pecans**

1. Drain pineapple, reserving juice; set pineapple aside. In a small saucepan, combine brown sugar, apple cider, maple syrup, butter and reserved pineapple juice. Bring to a boil; cook until liquid is reduced to ¾ cup and syrupy, about 20 minutes. Stir in cinnamon and cloves; set aside and keep warm.

2. Preheat oven to 400°. Layer half of the potatoes, apples and pineapple in a 9x13-in. baking dish coated with cooking spray. Repeat layers. Sprinkle with salt. Pour reduced liquid over the top. Cover and bake 40 minutes or just until tender.

3. Sprinkle with pecans. Bake, uncovered, 13-18 minutes longer or until potatoes and apples are tender.

until smooth; gradually add milk. Bring to a boil; cook and stir for 1-2 minutes or until thickened.

3. Stir in 1¼ cups each of the mozzarella and Swiss cheeses until melted. Pour over the vegetables. Bake, uncovered, at 400° for 15-20 minutes or until bubbly. Sprinkle with remaining cheeses. Bake 5 minutes longer or until golden brown.

Mushroom Barley Bake

The first time I tasted this barley was when my daughter made it for a family dinner. Its tempting flavor prompted the whole family to ask for seconds.

—**JEAN SIMONS** WINNIPEG, MB

PREP: 15 MIN. • **BAKE:** 1½ HOURS
MAKES: 8-10 SERVINGS

- ¾ **pound sliced fresh mushrooms**
- 2 **medium onions, chopped**
- ¼ **cup butter**
- 1½ **cups medium pearl barley**
- 1 **jar (2 ounces) diced pimientos, drained**
- 6 **teaspoons chicken bouillon, divided**
- 4 **cups boiling water, divided**

In a skillet, saute mushrooms and onions in butter until tender. Stir in barley and pimientos. Transfer to a greased 9x13-in. baking dish. Dissolve 3 teaspoons bouillon in 2 cups water; stir into barley mixture. Cover and bake at 325° for 1 hour. Dissolve the remaining bouillon in remaining water; stir into barley mixture. Bake, uncovered, 30 minutes longer or until liquid is absorbed and barley is tender.

Broccoli-Cauliflower Cheese Bake

Adding Swiss and mozzarella cheese is a surefire way to get the family to eat more of their vegetables. If you serve this dish to kids, you can leave out the cayenne pepper.

—**JENNIFER TIDWELL** FAIR OAKS, CA

PREP: 35 MIN. • **BAKE:** 20 MIN.
MAKES: 16 SERVINGS

- 7 **cups fresh cauliflowerets**
- 6 **cups fresh broccoli florets**
- 3 **tablespoons butter**
- ⅓ **cup all-purpose flour**
- 1½ **teaspoons spicy brown mustard**
- ¾ **teaspoon salt**
- ¼ **teaspoon ground nutmeg**
- ¼ **teaspoon cayenne pepper**
- ¼ **teaspoon pepper**
- 3¾ **cups fat-free milk**
- 1½ **cups (6 ounces) shredded part-skim mozzarella cheese, divided**
- 1½ **cups (6 ounces) shredded Swiss cheese, divided**

1. Place the cauliflower and broccoli in a Dutch oven; add 1 in. of water. Bring to a boil. Reduce the heat; cover and simmer for 3-5 minutes or until crisp-tender. Drain vegetables; transfer to a 9x13-in. baking dish coated with cooking spray.

2. In small saucepan, melt the butter. Stir in the flour, mustard, salt, nutmeg, cayenne and pepper

Maple-Glazed Acorn Squash

With a maple syrup and brown sugar glaze, winter squash becomes so pleasantly sweet. This dish is true comfort food, easy to prepare and tasty paired with a pork entree.

—NANCY MUELLER
MENOMONEE FALLS, WI

PREP: 10 MIN. • **BAKE:** 55 MIN.
MAKES: 2 SERVINGS

- 1 **medium acorn squash, halved**
- 1½ **cups water**
- ¼ **cup maple syrup**
- 2 **tablespoons brown sugar**
- ½ **teaspoon ground cinnamon**
- ¼ **teaspoon ground ginger**
- ¼ **teaspoon salt**

1. Preheat oven to 350°. Scoop out and discard seeds from squash. Place cut side down in a 9x13-in. baking dish; add water. Bake, uncovered, at 45 minutes.
2. Drain water from pan; turn squash cut side up. Combine syrup, brown sugar, cinnamon, ginger and salt; pour into the squash halves. Bake, uncovered, 10 minutes or until the glaze is heated through.

TOP TIP

Dark brown sugar contains more molasses than light or golden brown sugar. The types are generally interchangeable in recipes. But if you prefer a bolder flavor, choose dark brown sugar.

When I lived in Florida, I went to dinner at a friend's. His wife, who is Greek, served a beautiful side dish called an "eggplant fan" and shared the recipe with me. While I've made her version many times with great success, I was inspired by the movie Ratatouille and created this version.

—JOE SHERWOOD TRYON, NE

Baked Greek Ratatouille

PREP: 30 MIN. + CHILLING
BAKE: 45 MIN.
MAKES: 13 SERVINGS (¾ CUP EACH)

- 1 small eggplant
- 2 small zucchini
- 2 small yellow summer squash
- 4 plum tomatoes
- 1 large sweet onion
- ½ cup butter, melted
- ½ cup minced fresh parsley
- 3 garlic cloves, minced
- ½ teaspoon salt
- ½ teaspoon each dried thyme, oregano, tarragon and basil
- ½ teaspoon dried rosemary, crushed
- ½ teaspoon pepper
- 1 cup (4 ounces) shredded part-skim mozzarella cheese

1. Cut vegetables into ¼-in. slices. In a greased 9x13-in. baking dish, layer the eggplant, zucchini, squash, tomatoes and onion. In a small bowl, combine the butter, parsley, garlic and seasonings; pour over vegetables. Cover and refrigerate overnight.
2. Remove from the refrigerator 30 minutes before baking. Bake casserole, uncovered, at 375° for 35 minutes. Sprinkle with the cheese. Bake 10-15 minutes longer or until cheese is melted. Serve with a slotted spoon.

TOP TIP

For a more distinctly Greek flavor, top the ratatouille with crumbled feta cheese instead of mozzarella.

Brussels Sprouts au Gratin

If you don't typically enjoy Brussels sprouts, this recipe will change your mind. It's creamy, savory, rich and absolutely delicious.

—KEVIN LIEBERMAN

OKLAHOMA CITY, OK

PREP: 45 MIN. • **BAKE:** 10 MIN.
MAKES: 10 SERVINGS

- 2 pounds Brussels sprouts, quartered
- 2 tablespoons butter, melted
- ¾ teaspoon salt
- ⅛ teaspoon pepper

CREAM SAUCE

- 1 large onion, chopped
- 3 tablespoons butter
- 3 tablespoons all-purpose flour
- 1 cup whole milk
- 1 cup heavy whipping cream
- ⅛ teaspoon white pepper
  Dash ground nutmeg

TOPPING

- ½ cup shredded Gruyere cheese
- ¼ cup grated Parmesan cheese

1. In a large bowl, combine the Brussels sprouts, butter, salt and pepper; toss to coat. Transfer to a greased 9x13-in. baking dish. Bake, uncovered, at 425° for 25-30 minutes or until Brussels sprouts are tender, stirring occasionally.
2. Meanwhile, in a large skillet, saute the onion in butter until tender. Stir in flour until blended; gradually add milk and cream. Bring to a boil; cook and stir for 2 minutes or until thickened. Stir in pepper and nutmeg; pour over Brussels sprouts. Sprinkle with cheeses.
3. Reduce heat to 350°. Bake, uncovered, for 10-15 minutes or until heated through and cheeses are melted.

Maple Squash 'n' Apples

I was never a fan of squash. But when I came across this recipe several years ago, I decided to try it. My family and I are so glad I did.
—**SHARON RINK** APPLETON, WI

PREP: 20 MIN. • **BAKE:** 45 MIN.
MAKES: 8-10 SERVINGS

- ¾ cup maple syrup
- ½ cup butter, cubed
- ¼ cup apple juice
- 1 teaspoon ground cinnamon
- ½ teaspoon salt
- ½ teaspoon ground allspice
- 3 small butternut squash (about 1½ pounds each)
- 4 large apples, peeled and sliced

1. In a small saucepan, combine the syrup, butter and apple juice. Bring to a boil over medium heat, stirring occasionally. Cook and stir for 5 minutes or until slightly thickened. Remove from the heat; whisk in the cinnamon, salt and allspice. Set aside.
2. Peel squash and cut in half lengthwise; remove seeds. Cut squash into ¼-inch slices. Place a third of the squash in a greased 9x13-in. baking dish. Layer with half of the apples and a third of the squash. Top with alternating slices of remaining apples and squash. Pour syrup mixture over the top.
3. Cover and bake at 400° for 30-35 minutes or until squash is almost tender. Uncover, bake 15 minutes longer, basting twice.

Cowboy Baked Beans

Baked beans are a perennial favorite at barbecues . My meaty recipe uses molasses, brown sugar and a variety of beans for an unbeatable taste.
—**JOE SHERWOOD** TRYON, NE

PREP: 25 MIN. • **BAKE:** 50 MIN.
MAKES: 12 SERVINGS (¾ CUP EACH)

- 1 pound ground beef
- 1 pound bacon, cooked and crumbled
- 2 cups barbecue sauce
- 1 can (16 ounces) butter beans, rinsed and drained
- 1 can (15¾ ounces) pork and beans
- 1 can (15½ ounces) navy beans, rinsed and drained
- 1 can (15 ounces) black beans, rinsed and drained
- 2 medium onions, chopped
- ¼ cup packed brown sugar
- ¼ cup molasses
- 2 tablespoons balsamic vinegar
- 2 teaspoons ground mustard
- 2 teaspoons Worcestershire sauce
- 1 teaspoon salt
- 1 teaspoon garlic powder
- 1 teaspoon pepper

Preheat oven to 350°. In a Dutch oven, cook beef over medium heat until no longer pink; drain. Stir in the remaining ingredients. Transfer to a greased 9x13-in. baking dish. Bake, uncovered, 50-60 minutes or until heated through.

Cheese & Herb Potato Fans

It's downright fun to make and serve these potatoes—and they taste great, too. The fresh herbs, butter and cheeses are just what a good potato needs.

—SUSAN CURRY WEST HILLS, CA

PREP: 20 MIN. • **BAKE:** 55 MIN.
MAKES: 8 SERVINGS

- 8 **medium potatoes**
- ½ **cup butter, melted**
- 2 **teaspoons salt**
- ½ **teaspoon pepper**
- ⅔ **cup shredded cheddar cheese**
- ⅓ **cup shredded Parmesan cheese**
- 2 **tablespoons each minced fresh chives, sage and thyme**

1. Preheat oven to 425°. With a sharp knife, cut each potato into ⅛-in. slices, leaving the slices attached at the bottom; fan the potatoes slightly and place in a greased 9x13-in. baking dish. In a small bowl, mix butter, salt and pepper; drizzle over potatoes.

2. Bake potatoes, uncovered, for 50-55 minutes or until tender. In a small bowl, toss cheeses with herbs; sprinkle over potatoes. Bake about 5 minutes longer or until cheese is melted.

Triple-Mushroom au Gratin Potatoes

When I started cooking, the only mushrooms I used were the button variety. Now I love experimenting with lots of different types. This is wonderful with grilled steak, or even as a main dish with a green salad.

—NADINE MESCH
MOUNT HEALTHY, OH

PREP: 30 MIN.
BAKE: 1 HOUR + STANDING
MAKES: 10 SERVINGS

- 6 tablespoons butter, divided
- ½ pound each sliced fresh shiitake, baby portobello and button mushrooms
- 1 tablespoon sherry, optional
- 5 tablespoons all-purpose flour
- 3 cups half-and-half cream
- 3 tablespoons minced fresh rosemary
- 1½ teaspoons salt
- 1 teaspoon pepper
- 2 cups (8 ounces) shredded Gruyere cheese
- 2 pounds red potatoes, thinly sliced
- ½ teaspoon paprika

1. Preheat oven to 350°. In a large skillet, heat 1 tablespoon butter over medium-high heat. Add mushrooms; cook and stir until tender. If desired, stir in sherry and cook 1-2 minutes longer or until evaporated. Remove from pan.

2. In same pan, melt remaining butter over medium heat. Stir in flour until smooth; gradually whisk in cream. Bring to a boil, stirring constantly; cook and stir 2 minutes or until thickened. Reduce heat to medium-low. Stir in rosemary, salt and pepper. Gradually add cheese, stirring until melted. Remove from heat.

3. Arrange potatoes in an even layer in a greased 9x13-in. baking dish. Top with mushrooms and sauce mixture; sprinkle with paprika.

4. Bake, covered, 40 minutes. Bake, uncovered, 20-25 minutes longer or until golden brown and bubbly. Let stand 15 minutes before serving.

Parmesan Asparagus

Nothing could be more simple than this tasty side dish. With just four ingredients, it's assembled in no time. Then I pop it in the oven, and it turns out perfect every time.

—MARY ANN MARINO
WEST PITTSBURGH, PA

START TO FINISH: 20 MIN.
MAKES: 10-12 SERVINGS

- 4 pounds fresh asparagus, trimmed
- ¼ pound butter, melted
- 2 cups shredded Parmesan cheese
- ½ teaspoon pepper

1. In a large saucepan, bring ½ in. of water to a boil. Add asparagus; cover and boil for 3 minutes or until crisp-tender.

2. Drain asparagus; place in a greased 9x13-in. baking dish. Drizzle with butter; sprinkle with Parmesan cheese and pepper. Bake, uncovered, at 350° for 10-15 minutes or until cheese is melted.

Four-Cheese Rice Casserole

My husband and I developed this recipe to switch things up from the broccoli and rice casserole we'd been making for years. Now his folks won't let us in the door at the holidays without this dish in hand.

—GRETCHEN KAVANAUGH
OKLAHOMA CITY, OK

PREP: 10 MIN. • **BAKE:** 40 MIN.
MAKES: 12 SERVINGS

- 1 medium sweet onion, chopped
- ¼ cup butter, cubed
- 4 cups cooked long grain rice
- 2 packages (10 ounces each) frozen chopped spinach, thawed and squeezed dry
- 3 cups (12 ounces) shredded part-skim mozzarella cheese, divided
- 1½ cups shredded Parmesan cheese, divided
- 2 packages (8 ounces each) cream cheese, softened
- 1 carton (15 ounces) ricotta cheese
- ¾ cup 2% milk
- ½ teaspoon garlic powder
- ½ teaspoon beau monde seasoning

1. In a small skillet, saute onion in butter until tender. In a large bowl, combine the rice, spinach, 1½ cups mozzarella cheese, 1 cup Parmesan cheese and the onion mixture.

2. In a large bowl, beat cream cheese, ricotta, milk, garlic powder and the beau monde seasoning until smooth. Add to rice mixture and mix well.

3. Spoon into a greased 9x13-in. baking dish. Sprinkle with

remaining mozzarella and Parmesan cheeses. Bake casserole, uncovered, at 325° for 40-45 minutes or until heated through and cheese is melted.

NOTE *This recipe was tested with Spice Islands beau monde seasoning. It is a blend of salt, onion powder and celery seed.*

Three-Cheese Hash Brown Bake

Serve up classic comfort food with this convenient casserole of frozen hash brown potatoes. It takes just 10 minutes of prep work, so it's wonderful when you have company.

—NANCY SIDHU FRANKLIN, WI

PREP: 10 MIN.
BAKE: 55 MIN. + STANDING
MAKES: 12 SERVINGS

- 2 cans (10¾ ounces each) condensed cream of potato soup, undiluted
- 1 cup (8 ounces) sour cream
- 1 teaspoon garlic powder
- ½ teaspoon pepper
- 1 package (32 ounces) frozen cubed hash brown potatoes, thawed
- 2 cups (8 ounces) shredded cheddar cheese
- 1 cup grated Parmesan cheese
- ½ cup shredded Swiss cheese

1. Preheat oven to 350°. In a large bowl, mix the soup, sour cream, garlic powder and pepper until blended. Stir in remaining ingredients.

2. Transfer to a greased 9x13-in. baking dish. Bake, uncovered, 55-65 minutes or until golden brown and potatoes are tender. Let casserole stand 10 minutes before serving.

(5) INGREDIENTS
Mushroom Casserole

When I make this buttery-tasting casserole, my family fights over every last bite. The melted Swiss provides a unique flavor.

—**SUSAN VETTER** CAPE CORAL, FL

PREP: 30 MIN. • **BAKE:** 25 MIN.
MAKES: 8-10 SERVINGS

- 1 package (16 ounces) wide egg noodles
- 2 pounds sliced fresh mushrooms
- ½ cup butter, divided
- 1½ teaspoons salt
- ¾ teaspoon pepper
- 4 cups (16 ounces) shredded Swiss cheese

1. Cook noodles according to package directions; drain. In a large skillet, saute mushrooms in ¼ cup butter for 10-15 minutes or until tender.

2. Place a third of the noodles in a greased 9x13-in. baking dish; sprinkle with ½ teaspoon salt and ¼ teaspoon pepper. Layer with 1⅓ cups cheese and a third of the mushrooms. Repeat layers twice. Dot with remaining butter.

3. Bake, uncovered, at 350° for 25-30 minutes or until bubbly and cheese is melted.

TOP TIP

To give Mushroom Casserole a decadent, crunchy top, melt the remaining ¼ cup of butter. Mix it with some crushed Ritz crackers (and minced parsley, if you have it). Sprinkle over the casserole before baking.

Sweet Potatoes with Pecan-Cinnamon Crunch

This recipe features tender sweet potatoes and tart cranberries topped with a crunchy pecan streusel. Folks won't be able to get enough of this tasty cold-weather side dish.

—**MARY MEEK** TOLEDO, OH

PREP: 25 MIN. • **BAKE:** 55 MIN.
MAKES: 12 SERVINGS

- ½ cup packed brown sugar
- 2 tablespoons orange juice
- 2 teaspoons vanilla extract
- ½ teaspoon salt
- ½ teaspoon ground ginger
- ½ teaspoon ground cinnamon
- 3 pounds sweet potatoes, peeled and cut into 1-inch cubes
- 1 cup dried cranberries
- 2 tablespoons butter

CRUNCH

- ½ cup all-purpose flour
- ¼ cup packed brown sugar
- 1 teaspoon ground cinnamon
- ½ teaspoon ground ginger
- ¼ cup cold butter
- 1 cup chopped pecans

1. In a large bowl, combine the first six ingredients. Add sweet potatoes and cranberries; toss to coat. Transfer to a greased 9x13-in. baking dish and dot with butter.

2. Cover and bake at 400° for 30 minutes; stir. In a small bowl, combine the flour, brown sugar, cinnamon and ginger; cut in butter until mixture resembles coarse crumbs. Stir in pecans.

3. Sprinkle over sweet potato mixture. Bake, uncovered, for 25-30 minutes or until bubbly and sweet potatoes are tender.

Bacon Mac & Cheese

Bacon and jalapeno upgrade ordinary macaroni and cheese, giving it great grown-up taste. I serve this dish throughout the year.

—SHELLY BOEHM SOUTH BEND, IN

PREP: 35 MIN. • **BAKE:** 40 MIN.
MAKES: 16 SERVINGS (¾ CUP EACH)

- 6 **cups uncooked elbow macaroni**
- 1 **pound bacon strips, chopped**
- 1 **jalapeno pepper, seeded and minced**
- 3 **cups 2% milk**
- 2 **cups (8 ounces) shredded pepper Jack cheese**
- 1 **package (8 ounces) process cheese (Velveeta), cubed**
- 1 **cup (4 ounces) shredded Colby-Monterey Jack cheese**
- 1 **cup (4 ounces) shredded cheddar cheese**
- 1 **teaspoon onion powder**
- 1 **teaspoon chili powder**
- ½ **teaspoon salt**
- ½ **teaspoon pepper**
  Dash hot pepper sauce
- 3 **green onions, chopped**

1. Cook macaroni according to package directions.

2. Meanwhile, in a Dutch oven, cook bacon over medium heat until crisp. Using a slotted spoon, remove to paper towels; drain, reserving 1 tablespoon of the drippings. Saute jalapeno in drippings. Add milk and cheeses to pan; cook and stir until blended. Stir in onion powder, chili powder, salt, pepper and pepper sauce.

3. Drain macaroni; add to pan with onions and cooked bacon. Mix well.

4. Transfer to a greased 9x13-in. baking dish. Cover and bake at 350° for 30 minutes. Uncover; bake 10-15 minutes longer or until heated through.

NOTE *Wear disposable gloves when cutting hot peppers; the oils can burn skin. Avoid touching your face.*

with butter; set aside. In a large bowl, beat the eggs, sugar, sour cream and cottage cheese until well blended. Stir in noodles.

2. Transfer to a greased 9x13-in. baking dish. Combine cracker crumbs and butter; sprinkle over top.

3. Bake, uncovered, at 350° for 50-55 minutes or until a thermometer reads 160°. Let stand for 10 minutes before cutting. Serve warm or cold.

Winter Vegetable Medley

Balance out a meaty main dish with this colorful roasted veggie side. I peel and cut the veggies early, then refrigerate them in a resealable storage bag.

—**NANCY BROWN** DAHINDA, IL

PREP: 15 MIN. • **BAKE:** 40 MIN.
MAKES: 8 SERVINGS

- ½ **pound fresh Brussels sprouts, halved**
- ½ **pound parsnips, peeled and cut into ½-inch cubes**
- ½ **pound fresh baby carrots**
- 1 **medium sweet potato, peeled and cut into ½-inch cubes**
- 2 **medium red potatoes, cut into ½-inch cubes**
- 2 **medium white potatoes, peeled and cut into ½-inch cubes**
- ½ **cup butter, melted**
- 1½ **teaspoons rubbed sage**
- 2 **garlic cloves, minced**

1. Place the vegetables in a greased 9x13-in. baking dish. Combine the butter, sage and garlic; drizzle over vegetables.
2. Cover and bake at 375° for 40-50 minutes or until tender.

---

⑤ INGREDIENTS

Pimiento Potato Salad

A neighbor shared the recipe for this easy overnight salad. I love that the recipe uses pantry ingredients and vegetables that are nearly always on hand.

—**DORA LEDFORD** ROCKWALL, TX

PREP: 10 MIN. + CHILLING
MAKES: 12 SERVINGS

- 2 **pounds small red potatoes (about 12), cooked**
- 4 **green onions, thinly sliced**
- 3 **celery ribs, thinly sliced**
- 1 **jar (2 ounces) diced pimientos, drained**
- 1 **bottle (8 ounces) Italian salad dressing**

Cut potatoes into ¼-in. slices. In an ungreased 9x13-in. dish, layer half of the potatoes, onions, celery and pimientos. Repeat layers. Pour dressing over all. Cover and refrigerate overnight. Stir before serving.

Noodle Kugel

I make this traditional dish along with other Jewish specialties for an annual Hanukkah/Christmas party with our friends.

—**LAUREN KARGEN** BUFFALO, NY

PREP: 20 MIN.
BAKE: 50 MIN. + STANDING
MAKES: 12-15 SERVINGS

- 1 **package (1 pound) egg noodles**
- ½ **cup butter, melted**
- 8 **eggs**
- 2 **cups sugar**
- 2 **cups (16 ounces) sour cream**
- 2 **cups (16 ounces) 4% cottage cheese**

TOPPING
- ¾ **cup cinnamon graham cracker crumbs (about 4 whole crackers)**
- 3 **tablespoons butter, melted**

1. Cook noodles according to package directions; drain. Toss

Creamy Blueberry Gelatin Salad

When I was growing up, my mom's blueberry salad was served at every holiday and family celebration. Now my grandchildren look forward to sampling it at every gathering.

—**SHARON HOEFERT** GREENDALE, WI

PREP: 30 MIN. + CHILLING
MAKES: 12-15 SERVINGS

- 2 packages (3 ounces each) grape gelatin
- 2 cups boiling water
- 1 can (21 ounces) blueberry pie filling
- 1 can (20 ounces) unsweetened crushed pineapple, undrained

TOPPING

- 1 package (8 ounces) cream cheese, softened
- 1 cup (8 ounces) sour cream
- ½ cup sugar
- 1 teaspoon vanilla extract
- ½ cup chopped walnuts

1. In a large bowl, dissolve the gelatin in boiling water. Cool for 10 minutes. Stir in the pie filling and the pineapple until blended. Transfer to a 9x13-in. dish. Cover and refrigerate until partially set, about 1 hour.

2. For topping, in a small bowl, combine the cream cheese, sour cream, sugar and vanilla extract. Carefully spread over gelatin; sprinkle with walnuts. Cover and refrigerate until firm.

**NANCY FOUST'S MAPLE-
WALNUT STICKY BUNS**
PAGE 149

Breads, Rolls & Coffee Cakes

**LAURIE FIGONE'S
TOMATO & BRIE FOCACCIA**
PAGE 154

**BRENDA CAUGHELL'S
ONION & GARLIC ROLLS**
PAGE 150

**BLANCHE WHYTSELL'S
GRAHAM STREUSEL
COFFEE CAKE** *PAGE 152*

Raspberry-Rhubarb Coffee Cake

Sweet raspberries and tart rhubarb are perfect partners in this classic coffee cake. It makes a wonderful midmorning snack with a cold glass of milk.

—**CAROL ROSS** ANCHORAGE, AK

PREP: 30 MIN.
BAKE: 1 HOUR + COOLING
MAKES: 12 SERVINGS

- 1 **cup sugar**
- ⅓ **cup cornstarch**
- 3 **cups chopped fresh or frozen rhubarb**
- 1 **cup fresh or frozen raspberries, mashed**
- 2 **teaspoons lemon juice**

BATTER
- ¾ **cup butter-flavored shortening**
- 1½ **cups sugar**
- 3 **eggs**
- 3 **cups all-purpose flour**
- 1½ **teaspoons baking powder**
- ¾ **teaspoon baking soda**
- 1½ **cups (12 ounces) sour cream**

TOPPING
- ½ **cup all-purpose flour**
- ½ **cup sugar**
- ½ **cup quick-cooking oats**
- ½ **teaspoon ground cinnamon**
- ¼ **cup cold butter, cubed**
- ½ **cup flaked coconut**
- ½ **cup chopped walnuts**

1. In a large saucepan, combine sugar and cornstarch; stir in rhubarb and raspberries. Bring to a boil over medium heat; cook 2 minutes or until thickened, stirring constantly. Remove from heat. Stir in lemon juice. Cool slightly.

2. Preheat oven to 350°. In a large bowl, cream shortening and sugar until light and fluffy. Beat in eggs. Combine flour, baking powder and baking soda; add to the creamed mixture alternately with sour cream.

3. Spread two-thirds of the batter into a greased 9x13-in. baking dish. Top with rhubarb mixture. Drop remaining batter by tablespoonfuls over filling.

4. In a small bowl, combine flour, sugar, oats and cinnamon. Cut in butter until crumbly. Stir in coconut and walnuts. Sprinkle over batter.

5. Bake for 60-65 minutes or until a toothpick inserted in the center comes out clean. Cool on a wire rack.

TOP TIP

I like to dress up coffee cake and serve it as dessert with ice cream and a drizzle of caramel or hot fudge topping. I use caramel on my apple and peach coffee cakes and chocolate on my ones with berries.

—**CANDY G.** TUCSON, AZ

Cornmeal Pan Rolls

Nothing rounds out a meal like homemade yeast rolls. My family has been enjoying this tried-and-true recipe for years.

—**VIVIAN ECCLES** GRIDLEY, KS

PREP: 30 MIN. + RISING
BAKE: 15 MIN. • **MAKES:** 1½ DOZEN

- 2½ **cups all-purpose flour**
- ½ **cup cornmeal**
- 2 **tablespoons sugar**
- 1 **package (¼ ounce) active dry yeast**
- 1 **teaspoon salt**
- 1 **cup water**
- 3 **tablespoons butter, divided**
- 1 **egg**

1. In a large bowl, combine the flour, cornmeal, sugar, yeast and salt. In a small saucepan, heat water and 2 tablespoons butter to 120°-130°. Add to the dry ingredients; beat until moistened. Add egg; beat on medium speed for 3 minutes.

2. Turn onto a floured surface; knead until smooth and elastic, about 6-8 minutes. Place in a greased bowl, turning once to grease the top. Cover and let rise in a warm place until doubled, about 1 hour.

3. Punch dough down. Turn onto a lightly floured surface; divide into 18 pieces. Shape each piece into a ball. Place in a greased 9x13-in. baking pan or two 9-in. round baking pans. Cover and let rise in a warm place until doubled, about 30 minutes.

4. Bake rolls at 400° for 15-20 minutes or until golden brown. Melt remaining butter; brush over rolls. Invert onto wire racks.

Overnight Cranberry-Eggnog Coffee Cake

To use up leftover cranberries, eggnog and pecans from the holiday season, I added them to a classic coffee cake recipe. It goes together the night before and bakes in the morning.

—LISA VARNER EL PASO, TX

PREP: 25 MIN. + CHILLING
BAKE: 35 MIN. + COOLING
MAKES: 15 SERVINGS

- ½ cup butter, softened
- 1 cup sugar
- 2 eggs
- 1 cup eggnog
- 1 cup (8 ounces) sour cream
- 1 teaspoon vanilla extract
- 2½ cups all-purpose flour
- 1½ teaspoons baking powder
- 1 teaspoon grated orange peel
- ½ teaspoon baking soda
- ½ teaspoon salt
- ½ cup dried cranberries

STREUSEL

- ⅔ cup sugar
- 2 tablespoons all-purpose flour
- 2 tablespoons butter, softened
- ½ teaspoon ground cinnamon
- ½ cup chopped pecans

GLAZE

- ½ cup confectioners' sugar
- 1 tablespoon eggnog

1. In a large bowl, cream butter and sugar until blended. Add eggs, one at a time, beating well after each addition. In a small bowl, whisk eggnog, sour cream and vanilla. In another bowl, whisk flour, baking powder, orange peel, baking soda and salt; add to the creamed mixture alternately with eggnog mixture, beating well after each addition. Stir in cranberries.

2. Transfer to a greased 9x13-in. baking pan. For streusel, in a small bowl, mix sugar, flour, butter and cinnamon. Stir in pecans; sprinkle over batter. Refrigerate, covered, at least 8 hours or overnight.

3. Preheat oven to 350°. Remove pan from refrigerator while oven heats. Bake 35-40 minutes or until a toothpick inserted in center comes out clean. Cool on a wire rack 20 minutes.

4. For glaze, in a small bowl, mix confectioners' sugar and eggnog until smooth; drizzle over cake. Serve warm.

NOTE *This recipe was tested with commercially prepared eggnog.*

Sour Cream-Pumpkin Coffee Cake

Spiced pumpkin filling is the sweet surprise inside this coffe cake. It's sure to steal the spotlight at a breakfast or brunch.

—RACHEL DODD AVONDALE, AZ

PREP: 30 MIN.
BAKE: 45 MIN. + COOLING
MAKES: 15 SERVINGS

- 1 cup packed brown sugar
- ¼ cup all-purpose flour
- 2 teaspoons pumpkin pie spice
- ⅓ cup cold butter
- 1 cup chopped pecans

BATTER
- ½ cup butter, softened
- ¾ cup sugar
- 3 eggs
- 1 teaspoon vanilla extract
- 2 cups all-purpose flour
- 1 teaspoon baking powder
- 1 teaspoon baking soda
- 1 cup (8 ounces) sour cream

FILLING
- 1 can (15 ounces) solid-pack pumpkin
- 1 egg, lightly beaten
- ⅓ cup sugar
- 1 teaspoon pumpkin pie spice

1. Preheat oven to 325°. For streusel, in a bowl, combine brown sugar, flour and pumpkin pie spice. Cut in butter until crumbly. Stir in pecans; set aside.

2. In a large bowl, cream butter and sugar until light and fluffy. Beat in eggs, one at a time, and vanilla. Combine flour, baking powder and baking soda; add to creamed mixture alternately with sour cream.

3. Spread half of batter into a greased 9x13-in. baking dish. Sprinkle with half of the streusel. Combine filling ingredients; drop by tablespoonfuls over streusel and spread evenly. Top with remaining batter. Sprinkle with remaining streusel.

4. Bake 45-50 minutes or until a toothpick inserted in center comes out clean. Cool coffe cake on a wire rack.

Overnight Cinnamon Rolls

These tender cinnamon rolls are definitely worth the overnight wait.

—CHRIS O'CONNELL

SAN ANTONIO, TX

PREP: 35 MIN. + RISING
BAKE: 20 MIN. • **MAKES:** 2 DOZEN

- 2 **packages (¼ ounce each) active dry yeast**
- 1½ **cups warm water (110° to 115°)**
- 2 **eggs**
- ½ **cup butter, softened**
- ½ **cup sugar**
- 2 **teaspoons salt**
- 5¾ to 6¼ **cups all-purpose flour**

CINNAMON FILLING
- 1 **cup packed brown sugar**
- 4 **teaspoons ground cinnamon**
- ½ **cup softened butter, divided**

GLAZE
- 2 **cups confectioners' sugar**
- ¼ **cup half-and-half cream**
- 2 **teaspoons vanilla extract**

1. In a small bowl, dissolve yeast in warm water. In a large bowl, combine eggs, butter, sugar, salt, yeast mixture and 3 cups flour; beat on medium speed until smooth. Stir in enough of the remaining flour to form a very soft dough (dough will be sticky). Do not knead. Cover with plastic wrap; refrigerate overnight.

2. In a small bowl, mix brown sugar and cinnamon. Turn dough onto a floured surface; divide in half. Roll one portion into an 18x12-in. rectangle. Spread with ¼ cup butter to within ½ in. of edges; sprinkle evenly with half of the brown sugar mixture.

3. Roll up jelly-roll style, starting with a long side; pinch seam to seal. Cut into 12 slices. Place in a greased 9x13-in. baking pan, cut side down. Repeat with the remaining dough and filling.

4. Cover rolls with kitchen towels; let rise in a warm place until doubled, about 1 hour.

5. Bake the rolls at 375° for 20-25 minutes or until lightly browned. Mix the confectioners' sugar, cream and vanilla; spread over warm rolls.

HOW TO

CUT CINNAMON ROLLS

Once dough is rolled into a log, use unflavored dental floss or a serrated knife to slice the cinnamon rolls.

Blackberry Whole Wheat Coffee Cake

This guilt-free coffee cake is loaded with luscious blackberry flavor. Wonderfully moist and tender, it's also good made with fresh or frozen blueberries or raspberries.

—**CAROL FORCUM** MARION, IL

PREP: 20 MIN.
BAKE: 35 MIN. + COOLING
MAKES: 12-16 SERVINGS

- 1½ cups all-purpose flour
- 1⅓ cups packed brown sugar
- 1 cup whole wheat flour
- 2 teaspoons baking powder
- ½ teaspoon baking soda
  Dash salt
- 1 egg
- 1 cup buttermilk
- ⅓ cup canola oil
- ⅓ cup unsweetened applesauce
- 2 teaspoons vanilla extract
- 2 cups fresh or frozen blackberries

1. In a large bowl, combine the first six ingredients. In a small bowl, combine egg, buttermilk, oil, applesauce and vanilla. Stir into dry ingredients just until moistened. Fold in blackberries.

2. Transfer to a 9x13-in. baking pan coated with cooking spray. Bake at 375° for 35-40 minutes or until a toothpick inserted near the center comes out clean. Cool on a wire rack.

Maple-Walnut Sticky Buns

Mmm! These gooey goodies smell just heavenly when they're baking. Everyone will be lining up to get a bite—and grab seconds.

—**NANCY FOUST** STONEBORO, PA

PREP: 45 MIN. + RISING
BAKE: 30 MIN. • **MAKES:** 2 DOZEN

- 1 package (¼ ounce) active dry yeast
- 1 cup warm water (110° to 115°)
- ½ cup mashed potatoes (without added milk and butter)
- 1 egg
- 2 tablespoons shortening
- 2 tablespoons sugar
- 1 teaspoon salt
- 3 to 3½ cups all-purpose flour
TOPPING
- 1 cup maple syrup
- ¾ cup coarsely chopped walnuts
FILLING
- ⅓ cup sugar
- 1½ teaspoons ground cinnamon
- 3 tablespoons butter, softened

1. In a small bowl, dissolve the yeast in warm water. In a large bowl, combine potatoes, egg, shortening, sugar, salt, yeast mixture and 1 cup flour; beat on medium speed until smooth. Stir in enough remaining flour to form a soft dough.

2. Turn dough onto a floured surface; knead until smooth and elastic, about 6-8 minutes. Place in a greased bowl, turning once to grease the top. Cover with plastic wrap and refrigerate overnight.

3. Pour syrup into a greased 9x13-in. baking dish; sprinkle with walnuts. In a small bowl, mix sugar and cinnamon. Punch down dough. Turn onto a lightly floured surface. Roll into a 24x8-in. rectangle. Spread with butter to within ½ in. of edges; sprinkle with cinnamon-sugar. Roll up jelly-roll style, starting with a long side; pinch seam to seal. Cut into 24 slices.

4. Place in prepared pan, cut side down. Cover with a kitchen towel; let rise in a warm place until doubled, about 30 minutes.

5. Bake at 350° for 30-35 minutes or until golden brown. Cool in dish 5 minutes before inverting onto a serving plate.

Onion & Garlic Rolls

I wanted something different from garlic toast, so I made a dough with garlic and onions. The next thing I knew, I had an amazing dinner roll.

—**BRENDA CAUGHELL** DURHAM, NC

PREP: 45 MIN. + RISING
BAKE: 20 MIN. • **MAKES:** 20 ROLLS

- ⅓ **cup dried minced onion**
- ⅓ **cup water**
- 1 **package (¼ ounce) active dry yeast**
- 2 **tablespoons warm water (110° to 115°)**
- 1 **cup warm 2% milk (110° to 115°)**
- ¼ **cup toasted wheat germ**
- 1 **tablespoon canola oil**
- 1 **tablespoon honey**
- 1 **teaspoon garlic powder**
- ¾ **teaspoon salt**
- 3 **to 3¼ cups all-purpose flour**
- 2 **tablespoons butter, melted**

- 1 **cup (4 ounces) shredded part-skim mozzarella cheese**

1. In a small bowl, mix onion and water. Let stand 10 minutes or until onion is softened. In another small bowl, dissolve yeast in warm water.
2. In a large bowl, combine milk, wheat germ, oil, honey, garlic powder, salt, onion mixture, yeast mixture and 1½ cups flour; beat on medium speed until smooth. Stir in enough the remaining flour to form a stiff dough (dough will be sticky).
3. Turn dough onto a floured surface; knead until smooth and elastic, about 6-8 minutes. Place in a greased bowl, turning once to grease the top. Cover with plastic wrap and let rise in a warm place until doubled, about 1 hour.
4. Punch down dough. Turn onto a lightly floured surface; divide and shape into 20 balls. Place in a greased 9x13-in. baking pan. Cover dough with a kitchen towel; let rise in a warm place until almost doubled, about 45 minutes.
5. Preheat oven to 375°. Bake 15-18 minutes or until lightly browned. Brush rolls with butter; sprinkle with cheese. Bake 5-7 minutes longer or until cheese is melted and rolls are golden brown. Serve warm.

Buttery Corn Bread

I got this recipe from a longtime friend, and it's my favorite. I love to serve this corn bread hot from the oven with butter and syrup.

—**NICOLE CALLEN** AUBURN, CA

PREP: 15 MIN. • **BAKE:** 25 MIN.
MAKES: 15 SERVINGS

- ⅔ **cup butter, softened**
- 1 **cup sugar**
- 3 **eggs**
- 1⅔ **cups 2% milk**
- 2⅓ **cups all-purpose flour**
- 1 **cup cornmeal**
- 4½ **teaspoons baking powder**
- 1 **teaspoon salt**

1. In a large bowl, cream butter and sugar until light and fluffy. Combine the eggs and milk. Combine the flour, cornmeal, baking powder and salt; add to creamed mixture alternately with egg mixture.
2. Pour into a greased 9x13-in. baking pan. Bake at 400° for 22-27 minutes or until a toothpick inserted in center comes out clean.

Plum Streusel Kuchen

This recipe is actually called *platz* (flat) in German, and has been in my family since before I was born. The fresh fruits of summer make it a favorite.

—LISA WARKENTIN WINNIPEG, MB

PREP: 25 MIN. • **BAKE:** 35 MIN.
MAKES: 12-15 SERVINGS

- **2 cups all-purpose flour**
- **¼ cup sugar**
- **2 teaspoons baking powder**
- **2 tablespoons shortening**
- **1 egg**
- **1 cup heavy whipping cream**
- **6 fresh plums, sliced**

TOPPING

- **⅔ cup all-purpose flour**
- **⅔ cup sugar**
- **2 tablespoons cold butter**
- **2 tablespoons heavy whipping cream**

1. Preheat oven to 350°. In a large bowl, combine flour, sugar and baking powder; cut in shortening until mixture resembles fine crumbs. In another bowl, whisk egg and cream; add to crumb mixture, tossing gently with a fork until mixture forms a ball.

2. Press dough into a greased 9x13-in. baking dish. Arrange plums over the top.

3. In a small bowl, combine flour and sugar; cut in butter until mixture resembles fine crumbs. Add cream, mixing gently with a fork until moist crumbs form. Sprinkle over plums.

4. Bake 35-40 minutes or until a toothpick inserted in center comes out clean. Cool kuchen on a wire rack.

Graham Streusel Coffee Cake

Quick and easy to make, this simple coffee cake is my go-to sweet.

—BLANCHE WHYTSELL

ARNOLDSBURG, WV

PREP: 20 MIN.
BAKE: 40 MIN. + COOLING
MAKES: 12-16 SERVINGS

- 1½ cups graham cracker crumbs
- ¾ cup packed brown sugar
- ¾ cup chopped pecans
- 1½ teaspoons ground cinnamon
- ⅔ cup butter, melted
- 1 package yellow cake mix (regular size)
- ½ cup confectioners' sugar
- 1 tablespoon milk

1. In a small bowl, combine the cracker crumbs, brown sugar, pecans and cinnamon. Stir in butter; set aside. Prepare the cake mix according to package directions.

2. Pour half of the batter into a greased 9x13-in. baking pan. Sprinkle with half of the graham cracker mixture. Carefully spoon the remaining batter on top. Sprinkle with the remaining graham cracker mixture.

3. Bake at 350° for 40-45 minutes or until a toothpick inserted in the center comes out clean. Cool on a wire rack. Combine the confectioners' sugar and milk; drizzle over coffee cake.

Zucchini & Cheese Drop Biscuits

These surprisingly simple biscuits are packed with Italian flavors. I serve them warm out of the oven.

—KEITH MESCH MOUNT HEALTHY, OH

PREP: 25 MIN. + STANDING
BAKE: 25 MIN. • **MAKES:** 1 DOZEN

- ¾ cup shredded zucchini
- 1¼ teaspoons salt, divided
- 2½ cups all-purpose flour
- 1 tablespoon baking powder
- ½ cup cold butter, cubed
- ½ cup shredded cheddar cheese
- ¼ cup shredded part-skim mozzarella cheese
- ¼ cup shredded Parmesan cheese
- 2 tablespoons finely chopped oil-packed sun-dried tomatoes, patted dry
- 2 tablespoons minced fresh basil or 2 teaspoons dried basil
- 1 cup 2% milk

1. Preheat oven to 425°. Place zucchini in a colander over a plate; sprinkle with ¼ teaspoon salt and toss. Let zucchini stand 10 minutes. Rinse and drain well. Squeeze zucchini to remove excess liquid. Pat dry.

2. In a large bowl, whisk flour, baking powder and remaining salt. Cut in butter until mixture resembles coarse crumbs. Stir in zucchini, cheeses, tomatoes and basil. Add milk; stir just until moistened.

3. Drop by ⅓ cupfuls into a greased 9x13-in. baking pan. Bake 22-26 minutes or until golden brown. Serve warm.

Orange Cheesecake Breakfast Rolls

A good breakfast bun is sticky and sweet, and these orange-infused rolls are both. The cream cheese filling makes these a favorite in my family.

—HANNAH COBB OWINGS MILLS, MD

PREP: 50 MIN. + RISING
BAKE: 25 MIN. • **MAKES:** 2 DOZEN

- 2 packages (¼ ounce each) active dry yeast
- ¾ cup warm water (110° to 115°)
- 1¾ cups warm 2% milk (110° to 115°)
- 1 cup sugar
- 2 eggs
- 3 tablespoons butter, melted
- 1½ teaspoons salt
- 7 to 8 cups all-purpose flour

FILLING
- 1 package (8 ounces) cream cheese, softened
- ½ cup sugar
- 1 tablespoon orange juice concentrate
- ½ teaspoon vanilla extract

GLAZE
- 2 cups confectioners' sugar
- 3 tablespoons orange juice
- 1 teaspoon grated orange peel

1. In a large bowl, dissolve yeast in warm water. Add milk, sugar, eggs, butter, salt and 5 cups flour. Beat until smooth. Stir in enough remaining flour to form a firm dough.

2. Turn onto a floured surface; knead until smooth and elastic, about 6-8 minutes. Place in a greased bowl, turning once to grease the top. Cover and let rise in a warm place until doubled, about 1 hour.

3. In a small bowl, beat cream cheese, sugar, orange juice concentrate and vanilla until smooth. Punch dough down. Turn onto a lightly floured surface; divide in half. Roll one dough portion into an 18x7-in. rectangle. Spread half of the filling to within ½ in. of edges.

4. Roll up jelly-roll style, starting with a long side; pinch seam to seal. Cut into 12 slices; place cut side down in a greased 9x13-in. baking pan. Repeat with the remaining dough and filling. Cover and let rise until doubled, about 30 minutes.

5. Bake breakfast rolls at 350° for 25-30 minutes or until golden brown. Combine confectioners' sugar, orange juice and peel; drizzle glaze over warm rolls. Refrigerate leftovers.

Honey-Oat Pan Rolls

PREP: 45 MIN. + RISING
BAKE: 20 MIN. • **MAKES:** 2 DOZEN

- 2½ to 2¾ cups all-purpose flour
- ¾ cup whole wheat flour
- ½ cup old-fashioned oats
- 2 packages (¼ ounce each) active dry yeast
- 1 teaspoon salt
- 1 cup water
- ¼ cup honey
- 5 tablespoons butter, divided
- 1 egg

1. In a large bowl, mix 1 cup all-purpose flour, whole wheat flour, oats, yeast and salt. In a small saucepan, heat water, honey and 4 tablespoons butter to 120°-130°. Add to the dry ingredients; beat on medium speed 2 minutes. Add egg; beat on high 2 minutes. Stir in enough remaining all-purpose flour to form a soft dough (dough will be sticky).

2. Turn dough onto a floured surface; knead until smooth and elastic, about 6-8 minutes. Place in a greased bowl, turning once to grease the top. Cover with plastic wrap and let rise in a warm place until doubled, about 1 hour.

3. Punch down dough. Turn onto a lightly floured surface; divide and shape into 24 balls. Place in a greased 9x13-in. baking pan. Cover with a kitchen towel; let rise in a warm place until doubled, about 30 minutes.

4. Preheat oven to 375°. Bake 20-22 minutes or until golden brown. Melt remaining butter; brush over rolls. Remove from pan to a wire rack.

Tomato & Brie Focaccia

Combine tender yeast bread with creamy Brie cheese and tomatoes, and you've got an appetizer that guests will line up for. The focaccia is also nice with a bowl of soup.

—LAURIE FIGONE PETALUMA, CA

PREP: 20 MIN. + RISING
BAKE: 25 MIN. • **MAKES:** 12 SERVINGS

- 2½ to 3 cups all-purpose flour
- 2 packages (¼ ounce each) quick-rise yeast
- 1 teaspoon sugar
- 1 teaspoon salt
- 1 cup water
- ¼ cup plus 1 tablespoon olive oil, divided
- 1 can (14½ ounces) diced tomatoes, drained
- 2 garlic cloves, minced
- 1 teaspoon Italian seasoning
- 6 ounces Brie cheese, cut into ½-inch cubes

1. In a large bowl, combine 2 cups flour, yeast, sugar and salt. In a small saucepan, heat the water and ¼ cup oil to 120°-130°. Add to dry ingredients; beat just until moistened. Stir in enough remaining flour to form a soft dough.

2. Turn onto a floured surface; knead until smooth and elastic, about 6-8 minutes. Place in a greased bowl, turning once to grease the top. Cover and let rise for 20 minutes.

3. Preheat oven to 375°. Punch dough down. Press into a greased 9x13-in. baking pan. Cover and let rest 10 minutes.

4. In a small bowl, combine tomatoes, garlic, Italian seasoning and remaining oil. Spread over dough; top with cheese. Bake 25-30 minutes or until golden brown. Place pan on a wire rack.

These tender rolls are a welcome addition to any meal. Whole wheat flour and oats make them nutritious, too. —**ARLENE BUTLER** OGDEN, UT

1 teaspoon poppy seeds
1 teaspoon sesame seeds

PARM-GARLIC DINNER ROLLS

2 tablespoons grated
  Parmesan cheese
½ teaspoon dried minced garlic

ALMOND HERB DINNER ROLLS

2 tablespoons chopped sliced
  almonds
½ teaspoon kosher salt
½ teaspoon dried basil
½ teaspoon dried oregano

1. In a large bowl, mix sugar, yeast, salt and 2 cups flour. In a small saucepan, heat milk, water and butter to 120°-130°. Add to dry ingredients; beat on medium speed 3 minutes. Add 2 eggs; beat on high 2 minutes. Stir in enough remaining flour to form a soft dough (dough will be sticky).

2. Turn dough onto a floured surface; knead until smooth and elastic, about 6-8 minutes. Place in a greased bowl, turning once to grease the top. Cover with plastic wrap and let rise in a warm place until doubled, about 1 hour. Punch down dough. Turn onto a lightly floured surface; divide and shape dough into 24 balls. Place in two greased 9x13-in. baking pans. Cover with kitchen towels; let rise in a warm place until doubled, about 30 minutes. Preheat the oven to 375°.

3. Brush rolls with lightly beaten egg. Sprinkle with toppings for rolls of your choice. Bake rolls for 12-15 minutes or until golden brown. Remove from pans to wire racks; serve warm.

Best Dinner Rolls

If you can't decide which enticing version to bake, just make them all.

—**CHRISTINA PITTMAN**

PARKVILLE, MO

PREP: 35 MIN. + RISING
BAKE: 10 MIN. • **MAKES:** 2 DOZEN

¼ cup sugar
1 package (¼ ounce) active dry
   yeast

1¼ teaspoons salt
4½ to 5 cups all-purpose flour
1 cup milk
½ cup water
2 tablespoons butter
2 eggs
1 egg, lightly beaten

EVERYTHING DINNER ROLLS

1 teaspoon kosher salt
1 teaspoon dried minced garlic
1 teaspoon dried minced onion

Winter Fruit Coffee Cake

Filled with apples, pears and raisins, this spice cake is dressed up with a streusel topping. The heavenly scent of it baking will have your family gathered in the kitchen, waiting for a piece.

—TASTE OF HOME TEST KITCHEN

PREP: 20 MIN. + STANDING
BAKE: 30 MIN. + COOLING
MAKES: 15 SERVINGS

- ½ cup golden raisins
- ¼ cup brandy

TOPPING
- 1 cup packed brown sugar
- 1 teaspoon ground cinnamon
- 2 tablespoons butter, softened
- ½ cup chopped pecans

CAKE
- ½ cup butter, softened
- 1 cup packed brown sugar
- 2 eggs
- 1 teaspoon vanilla extract
- 2 cups all-purpose flour
- 3 teaspoons baking powder
- 1 teaspoon baking soda
- ¾ teaspoon ground cinnamon
- ¼ teaspoon ground nutmeg
- ⅛ teaspoon ground cloves
- ½ teaspoon salt
- 1 cup sour cream
- ¾ cup chopped peeled apple
- ½ cup chopped peeled ripe pear

1. In a small bowl, soak the raisins in brandy for 1 hour.
2. In another bowl, combine brown sugar and cinnamon. With clean hands, work butter into sugar mixture until well combined. Add the pecans. Refrigerate for 15 minutes.
3. Meanwhile, in a large bowl, cream butter and brown sugar until light and fluffy. Beat in the eggs and vanilla. Combine the flour, baking powder, baking soda, spices and salt; add to creamed mixture alternately with sour cream. Fold in the apple, pear and raisins (do not drain raisins). Pour into a greased 9x13-in. baking dish. Sprinkle with topping.
4. Bake at 350° for 28-32 minutes or until a toothpick inserted near the center comes out clean. Cool on a wire rack.

TOP TIP

If you don't have ground cloves or nutmeg for the coffee cake recipe, substitute ground ginger, additional cinnamon or another baking spice. Get creative! You also could substitute apple pie spice for the three spices in the recipe.

Looking for a fantastic brunch item? Then try these ooey-gooey-good sticky buns. They use frozen yeast roll dough and couldn't be simpler to make. The buns rise overnight in the refrigerator, so you just need to bake them the next morning.

—ATHENA RUSSELL FLORENCE, SC

Cranberry-Pistachio Sticky Buns

PREP: 20 MIN. + CHILLING
BAKE: 30 MIN. • **MAKES:** 2 DOZEN

- 1 **cup chopped pistachios**
- ½ **cup dried cranberries**
- 1 **teaspoon ground cinnamon**
- 24 **frozen bread dough dinner rolls, thawed**
- ½ **cup butter, cubed**
- 1 **cup packed brown sugar**
- 1 **package (4.6 ounces) cook-and-serve vanilla pudding mix**
- 2 **tablespoons 2% milk**
- ½ **teaspoon orange extract**

1. Sprinkle nuts, cranberries and cinnamon in a greased 9x13-in. baking dish. Arrange rolls in a single layer on top.
2. In a small saucepan, melt butter. Remove from the heat; stir in remaining ingredients until smooth. Pour over dough. Cover and refrigerate overnight.
3. Remove from the refrigerator 30 minutes before baking. Preheat oven to 350°. Bake 30-35 minutes or until golden brown. (Cover loosely with foil if top browns too quickly.) Cool 1 minute before inverting onto a serving platter.

TOP TIP

To keep parsley fresh, trim the stems and place the bunch in a tumbler of water. Be sure no loose leaves or greenery are in the water. Tie a produce bag over the top to trap humidity; store in the refrigerator.

Herb Potato Rolls

My grandma always made these rolls. She herself enjoyed them as a child in Germany. I practiced for years before I finally perfected the recipe!

—**LONNA SMITH** WOODRUFF, WI

PREP: 30 MIN. + RISING
BAKE: 30 MIN. • **MAKES:** 2 DOZEN

- 5 **to 5½ cups all-purpose flour**
- 1 **cup mashed potato flakes**
- 2 **packages (¼ ounce each) active dry yeast**
- 1 **tablespoon sugar**
- 1 **tablespoon minced chives**
- 2 **teaspoons salt**
- 2 **teaspoons minced fresh parsley**
- 2 **cups 2% milk**
- ½ **cup sour cream**
- 2 **eggs**

1. In a large bowl, combine 3 cups flour, potato flakes, yeast, sugar, chives, salt and parsley. In a small saucepan, heat milk and sour cream to 120°-130°; add to dry ingredients. Beat on medium speed for 2 minutes. Add eggs and ½ cup flour; beat 2 minutes longer. Stir in enough remaining flour to form a soft dough.
2. Turn onto a floured surface; knead until smooth and elastic, about 6-8 minutes. Place in a greased bowl, turning once to grease top. Cover and let rise in a warm place until doubled, about 45 minutes.
3. Punch dough down. Turn onto a lightly floured surface; divide into 24 pieces. Shape each into a roll. Place in a greased 9x13-in. baking pan. Cover and let rise until doubled, about 35 minutes.
4. Bake the rolls at 375° for 30-35 minutes or until golden brown. Remove to wire racks.

Sour Cream Yeast Rolls

These golden brown rolls are the perfect finishing touch for any meal. They represent genuine comfort-food cooking to me.

—CHRISTINE FRAZIER
AUBURNDALE, FL

PREP: 35 MIN. + RISING
BAKE: 25 MIN. • **MAKES:** 1 DOZEN

- 2½ to 3 cups all-purpose flour
- 2 tablespoons sugar
- 1 package (¼ ounce) active dry yeast
- 1 teaspoon salt
- 1 cup (8 ounces) sour cream
- ¼ cup water
- 3 tablespoons butter, divided
- 1 egg

1. In a large bowl, combine 1½ cups flour, sugar, yeast and salt. In a small saucepan, heat the sour cream, water and 2 tablespoons butter to 120°-130°; add to dry ingredients. Beat on medium speed for 2 minutes. Add egg and ½ cup flour; beat 2 minutes longer. Stir in enough of the remaining flour to form a soft dough.

2. Turn onto a floured surface; knead until smooth and elastic, about 6-8 minutes. Place in a greased bowl, turning once to grease the top. Cover and let rise in a warm place until doubled, about 1 hour.

3. Punch dough down. Turn onto a lightly floured surface; divide into 12 pieces. Shape each into a ball. Place in a greased 9x13-in. baking pan. Cover and let rise until doubled, about 30 minutes.

4. Bake the rolls at 375° for 25-30 minutes or until golden brown. Melt remaining butter; brush over rolls. Remove from pan to a wire rack.

Toffee Streusel Coffee Cake

A reminder of my childhood, this coffee cake was one of the many delights my mom often made.

—MEGAN TAYLOR GREENFIELD, WI

PREP: 20 MIN. • **BAKE:** 30 MIN.
MAKES: 12-16 SERVINGS

- 2 cups all-purpose flour
- 1 cup packed brown sugar
- ½ cup sugar
- ⅛ teaspoon salt
- ½ cup cold butter
- 1 teaspoon baking soda
- 1 cup buttermilk
- 1 egg, beaten
- 1 teaspoon vanilla extract
- 1 cup milk chocolate toffee bits or 4 Heath candy bars (1.4 ounces each), chopped

1. In a large bowl, combine the first four ingredients; cut in butter until crumbly. Set aside ½ cup for topping. Stir baking soda into remaining mixture. Combine the buttermilk, egg and vanilla; stir into flour mixture just until moistened.

2. Pour into a greased 9x13-in. baking pan. Add the toffee bits to the reserved crumb topping; sprinkle over batter. Cut through batter with a knife to swirl.

3. Bake at 350° for 30-35 minutes or until a toothpick inserted near the center comes out clean. Cool on a wire rack.

Vegetable & Cheese Focaccia

My family eats up this flavorful bread as fast as I can make it. Sometimes I add different herbs, red onion or crumbled bacon. It's one of my best recipes!

—MARY CASS BALTIMORE, MD

PREP: 20 MIN. + RISING
BAKE: 30 MIN. • **MAKES:** 15 SERVINGS

- 1 cup water (70° to 80°)
- 4½ teaspoons olive oil
- 4½ teaspoons sugar
- 2 teaspoons dried oregano
- 1¼ teaspoons salt
- 3¾ cups bread flour
- 1½ teaspoons active dry yeast

TOPPING

- 1 tablespoon olive oil
- 1 tablespoon dried basil
- 2 medium tomatoes, thinly sliced
- 1 medium onion, thinly sliced
- 1 cup frozen chopped broccoli, thawed
- ¼ teaspoon salt
- ¼ teaspoon pepper
- ¾ cup grated Parmesan cheese
- 1 cup (4 ounces) shredded part-skim mozzarella cheese

1. In bread machine pan, place the first seven ingredients in order suggested by manufacturer. Select dough setting (check dough after 5 minutes of mixing; add 1 to 2 tablespoons of water or flour if needed).

2. When cycle is completed, turn the dough onto a lightly floured surface. Punch dough down. Roll into a 9x13-in. rectangle; transfer to a 9x13-in. baking dish coated with cooking spray.

3. For topping, brush the dough with olive oil; sprinkle with basil. Layer with the tomatoes, onion and broccoli; sprinkle with salt, pepper and Parmesan cheese. Cover and let rise in a warm place until doubled, about 30 minutes.

4. Bake at 350° for 20 minutes. Sprinkle with mozzarella cheese; bake 10-15 minutes longer or until golden brown and cheese is melted.

JILL MORITZ'S
APRICOT BARS *PAGE 183*

Bars & Brownies

**WENDY BAILEY'S COOKIE
DOUGH BROWNIES** *PAGE 169*

**EDEN DRANGER'S GINGERBREAD
BARS** *PAGE 174*

**KEVIN JOHNSON'S
CHERRY OAT BARS** *PAGE 195*

Pumpkin Dessert Bars

Put a twist on traditional pumpkin pie with this recipe. It packs the spicy pumpkin flavor you love, but in a new crowd-size form.

—TENA HUCKLEBY GREENEVILLE, TN

PREP: 35 MIN.
BAKE: 20 MIN. + CHILLING
MAKES: 15 SERVINGS

- 1¾ cups graham cracker crumbs
- 1⅓ cups sugar, divided
- ½ cup butter, melted
- 1 package (8 ounces) cream cheese, softened
- 5 eggs
- 1 can (15 ounces) solid-pack pumpkin
- ½ cup packed brown sugar
- ½ cup milk
- ½ teaspoon salt
- ½ teaspoon ground cinnamon
- 1 envelope unflavored gelatin
- ¼ cup cold water
- Whipped topping and ground nutmeg, optional

1. In a small bowl, combine the graham cracker crumbs and ⅓ cup sugar; stir in butter. Press mixture into a greased 9x13-in. baking dish.

2. In a small bowl, beat cream cheese and ⅔ cup sugar until smooth. Beat in 2 eggs just until blended. Pour over crust. Bake at 350° for 20-25 minutes or until set. Cool on a wire rack.

3. Meanwhile, separate the remaining eggs and set whites aside. In a large saucepan, combine the yolks, pumpkin, brown sugar, milk, salt and cinnamon. Cook and stir over low heat for 10-12 minutes or until mixture is thickened and reaches at least 160°. Remove from the heat.

4. In a small saucepan, sprinkle gelatin over cold water; let stand for 1 minute. Heat mixture over low heat, stirring until gelatin is completely dissolved. Stir into pumpkin mixture; set aside.

5. In a large heavy saucepan, combine the egg whites and remaining sugar. With a portable mixer, beat on low speed for 1 minute. Continue beating over low heat until mixture reaches 160°, about 12 minutes. Remove from the heat; beat until stiff glossy peaks form and the sugar is dissolved.

6. Fold meringue into pumpkin mixture; spread evenly over cream cheese layer. Refrigerate for 4 hours or until set. Garnish with whipped topping and nutmeg if desired.

Double Chocolate Coconut Brownies

Thanks to a head start from brownie mix, it's easy to bake up these decadent treats!

—**BRENDA MELANCON** MCCOMB, MS

PREP: 15 MIN.
BAKE: 40 MIN. + COOLING
MAKES: 2½ DOZEN

- 1 package fudge brownie mix (9x13-inch pan size)
- ½ cup canola oil
- ¼ cup water
- 3 eggs
- ½ cup semisweet chocolate chips
- ½ cup white baking chips
- ½ cup chopped walnuts
- 1 can (14 ounces) sweetened condensed milk
- 2½ cups flaked coconut

FROSTING
- ¼ cup butter, softened
- ¼ cup evaporated milk
- 2 tablespoons baking cocoa
- 2 cups confectioners' sugar
- 1 teaspoon vanilla extract

1. Beat the brownie mix, oil, water and eggs on medium speed in a large bowl until blended; stir in chips and walnuts. Pour into a greased 9x13-in. baking pan.
2. Bake at 350° for 20 minutes. Remove from oven. Combine condensed milk and coconut in a small bowl; spread over top. Bake 20-25 minutes longer or until the center is set. Cool on a wire rack.
3. Place frosting ingredients in a small bowl; beat until smooth. Spread over cooled brownies.

Raspberry Cheesecake Bars

My family's love of raspberries and cheesecake makes this a perfect dessert for us. The creamy, buttery treat is best eaten with a fork.

—**JILL COX** LINCOLN, NE

PREP: 30 MIN.
BAKE: 35 MIN. + CHILLING
MAKES: 2 DOZEN

- 1 cup all-purpose flour
- 1 cup finely chopped pecans
- ⅓ cup packed brown sugar
- ¼ teaspoon ground cinnamon
- ¼ teaspoon salt
- ⅓ cup cold butter
- 1 jar (12 ounces) seedless raspberry jam, divided
- 2 packages (8 ounces each) cream cheese, softened
- ¾ cup sugar
- ½ teaspoon grated lemon peel
- ½ teaspoon vanilla extract
- 3 eggs, lightly beaten

TOPPING
- 1½ cups (12 ounces) sour cream
- 3 tablespoons sugar
- 1 teaspoon vanilla extract

1. In a small bowl, combine the flour, pecans, brown sugar, cinnamon and salt. Cut in butter until crumbly. Press onto the bottom of a greased 9x13-in. baking dish. Bake at 350° for 10-12 minutes or until lightly browned. Cool on a wire rack for 5 minutes.
2. Set aside 3 tablespoons jam; spread remaining jam over crust. In a large bowl, beat cream cheese and sugar until smooth. Beat in lemon peel and vanilla. Add eggs; beat on low speed just until combined. Spread evenly over jam. Bake 20-25 minutes or until almost set.
3. In another bowl, combine the sour cream, sugar and vanilla; gently spread over cheesecake. Warm remaining jam and swirl over top. Bake 5-7 minutes or just until set.
4. Cool on a wire rack for 1 hour. Refrigerate for at least 2 hours. Cut into bars.

Lemony Coconut Bars

These chewy bars with a hint of citrus make a refreshing addition to cookie trays. Try lime juice and zest for a zingy twist.

—NANCY ZIMMERMAN

CAPE MAY COURT HOUSE, NJ

PREP: 25 MIN.
BAKE: 25 MIN. + COOLING
MAKES: 2 DOZEN

- ½ **cup butter, softened**
- ½ **cup packed light brown sugar**
- 1½ **cups all-purpose flour**

FILLING

- 2 **eggs**
- 1 **cup packed light brown sugar**
- ½ **teaspoon grated lemon peel**
- ½ **teaspoon vanilla extract**
- ¼ **teaspoon lemon extract**
- 2 **tablespoons all-purpose flour**
- ½ **teaspoon baking powder**
- ¼ **teaspoon salt**
- 1½ **cups flaked coconut**
- 1 **cup chopped pecans**

GLAZE

- 1 **cup confectioners' sugar**
- 1 **tablespoon butter, melted**
- ½ **teaspoon grated lemon peel**
- 3 **tablespoons lemon juice**

1. Preheat oven to 350°. In a bowl, cream butter and brown sugar until light and fluffy; gradually beat in the flour, mixing well.

2. Press crust onto bottom of a greased 9x13-in. baking pan. Bake 8-10 minutes or until edges are golden brown. Cool crust on a wire rack.

3. For filling, in a large bowl, beat eggs, brown sugar, lemon peel and extracts until blended. In a small bowl, mix flour, baking powder and salt; stir into egg mixture. Stir in coconut and pecans. Spread over crust.

4. Bake 17-20 minutes or until golden brown. Cool 10 minutes on a wire rack. Meanwhile, in a small bowl, mix the glaze ingredients until smooth; drizzle over warm filling. Cool the bars completely before cutting.

⑤INGREDIENTS

Chocolaty S'mores Bars

One night my husband had some friends over to play poker and he requested these s'mores bars. They polished off the pan and asked for more! I shared the recipe, and now his friends make them at home, too.

—REBECCA SHIPP BEEBE, AR

PREP: 15 MIN. + COOLING
MAKES: 1½ DOZEN

- ¼ **cup butter, cubed**
- 1 **package (10 ounces) large marshmallows**
- 1 **package (12 ounces) Golden Grahams**
- ⅓ **cup milk chocolate chips, melted**

1. In a large saucepan, melt butter over low heat. Add marshmallows; cook and stir until blended. Remove from heat. Stir in cereal until coated.

2. Using a buttered spatula, press evenly into a greased 9x13-in. pan. Drizzle with melted chocolate chips. Cool completely. Cut into bars. Store in an airtight container.

Nut-Licious Peanut Butter Bars

My friends were astonished to find that these bars, my favorite go-to treat, are not button-busting. Each one is just 189 calories!

—HANNAH WOLTERS CULLEOKA, TN

PREP: 45 MIN.
BAKE: 15 MIN. + CHILLING
MAKES: 2 DOZEN

CRUST
- 1½ cups reduced-fat graham cracker crumbs (about 10 whole crackers)
- ⅓ cup honey
- 2 tablespoons butter, melted

NUT TOPPING
- ¼ cup chopped pecans
- ¼ cup chopped walnuts
- 2 tablespoons honey
- 1½ teaspoons ground cinnamon

FILLING
- 12 ounces fat-free cream cheese
- ⅔ cup peanut butter
- 3 tablespoons butter, softened
- ½ cup confectioners' sugar
- ½ cup honey
- 1 egg
- 1 teaspoon vanilla extract
- ¼ teaspoon maple flavoring
- ¼ cup all-purpose flour
- ¼ teaspoon baking powder

DRIZZLE
- ⅓ cup semisweet chocolate chips, melted

1. In a bowl, combine crust ingredients. Press onto bottom of a 9x13-in. baking pan coated with cooking spray. Bake at 350° for 8 minutes or until golden brown. Cool on a wire rack. Meanwhile, combine the nuts, honey and cinnamon. Transfer to a baking sheet lined with parchment paper and coated with cooking spray. Bake at 350° for 5-7 minutes or until toasted and fragrant, stirring occasionally. Cool completely. Crumble mixture and set aside.

2. In a small bowl, beat the cream cheese, peanut butter, butter, confectioners' sugar and honey until smooth. Beat in the egg, vanilla and maple flavoring. Combine flour and baking powder; gradually beat into cream cheese mixture. Spread over cooled crust. Bake for 14-16 minutes or until set.

3. Sprinkle nut mixture over warm filling; press in slightly. Drizzle with melted chocolate. Cool completely on a wire rack. Chill for 2 hours or until firm.

Caramel Pecan Bars

This recipe won first place at a cookie contest where I work. The rich bars really capture the flavor of pecan pie.

—EMMA MANNING CROSSETT, AR

PREP: 15 MIN.
BAKE: 20 MIN. + COOLING
MAKES: 4 DOZEN

- 1 **cup butter, cubed**
- 2¼ **cups packed brown sugar**
- 2 **eggs**
- 2 **teaspoons vanilla extract**
- 1½ **cups all-purpose flour**
- 2 **teaspoons baking powder**
- 2 **cups chopped pecans**
  Confectioners' sugar, optional

1. In a large saucepan, stir butter and brown sugar over medium heat until sugar is dissolved. In a small bowl, beat eggs and vanilla. Gradually add hot sugar mixture, stirring constantly. Combine the flour and the baking powder; gradually add to butter mixture and mix well. Stir in pecans.

2. Spread into a greased 9x13-in. baking pan. Bake at 350° for 20-25 minutes or until edges are crisp and a toothpick inserted near the center comes out with moist crumbs. Cool on a wire rack. Dust with confectioners' sugar if desired. Cut into bars.

4. For glaze, in a microwave, melt the chocolate chips and shortening; stir until smooth. Spread over filling. Immediately sprinkle with nuts, pressing down slightly. Let stand until set.

Best Date Bars

These wholesome bars freeze well. Simply cool them in the pan, cut, and then store them in freezer containers or wrap in plastic wrap.

—DOROTHY DELESKE
SCOTTSDALE, AZ

PREP: 25 MIN. • **BAKE:** 35 MIN.
MAKES: 40 BARS

- 2½ cups pitted dates, cut up
- ¼ cup sugar
- 1½ cups water
- ⅓ cup coarsely chopped walnuts, optional
- 1¼ cups all-purpose flour
- 1 teaspoon salt
- ½ teaspoon baking soda
- 1½ cups quick-cooking oats
- 1 cup packed brown sugar
- ½ cup butter, softened
- 1 tablespoon water

1. In a saucepan, combine dates, sugar and water. Cook, stirring frequently, until very thick. Stir in walnuts if desired; cool.
2. Sift the flour, salt and baking soda together in a large bowl; add oats and brown sugar. Cut in butter until mixture is crumbly. Sprinkle water over mixture; stir lightly. Pat half into a greased 9x13-in. baking pan. Spread with the date mixture; cover with the remaining oat mixture and pat lightly.
3. Bake the bars at 350° for 35-40 minutes or until lightly browned. Cool on a wire rack.

Cookie Dough Brownies

When I take these rich brownies to a get-together, I carry the recipe, too, because someone always asks for it. Everyone loves the tempting "cookie dough" filling!

—WENDY BAILEY ELIDA, OH

PREP: 20 MIN. + CHILLING
BAKE: 30 MIN. + COOLING
MAKES: 3 DOZEN

- 4 eggs
- 1 cup canola oil
- 2 cups sugar
- 2 teaspoons vanilla extract
- 1½ cups all-purpose flour
- ½ cup baking cocoa
- ½ teaspoon salt
- ½ cup chopped walnuts, optional

FILLING
- ½ cup butter, softened
- ½ cup packed brown sugar
- ¼ cup sugar
- 2 tablespoons 2% milk
- 1 teaspoon vanilla extract
- 1 cup all-purpose flour

GLAZE
- 1 cup (6 ounces) semisweet chocolate chips
- 1 tablespoon shortening
- ¾ cup chopped walnuts

1. Preheat oven to 350°. In a large bowl, beat eggs, oil, sugar and vanilla until well blended. Combine flour, cocoa and salt; gradually beat into egg mixture. Stir in walnuts if desired.
2. Pour into a greased 9x13-in. baking pan. Bake 30 minutes or until a toothpick inserted in center comes out with moist crumbs. Cool.
3. For filling, in a bowl, cream butter and sugars until light and fluffy. Beat in milk and vanilla. Gradually beat in flour. Spread over brownies; chill until firm.

2 egg yolks
1 teaspoon vanilla extract
1½ cups all-purpose flour
½ teaspoon baking powder
½ teaspoon salt
¼ teaspoon baking soda
3 cups miniature
   marshmallows

TOPPING
⅔ cup corn syrup
¼ cup butter, softened
1 package (10 ounces) peanut
   butter chips
2 teaspoons vanilla extract
2 cups Rice Krispies
1 cup salted peanuts
1 cup milk chocolate M&M's

1. In a large bowl, cream butter and brown sugar until light and fluffy. Beat in egg yolks and vanilla. Combine the flour, baking powder, salt and baking soda; gradually add to the creamed mixture until mixture resembles coarse crumbs (do not overmix).

2. Press into a greased 9x13-in. baking pan. Bake at 350° for 12-14 minutes or until golden brown. Immediately sprinkle with marshmallows; bake 2-3 minutes longer or until marshmallows are puffed. Cool on a wire rack.

3. For topping, in a large saucepan, combine the corn syrup, butter and peanut butter chips. Cook and stir over medium heat until the peanut butter chips are melted and mixture is smooth. Remove from the heat; stir in the vanilla, cereal, nuts and M&M's. Spread over crust. Cool completely before cutting.

⑤ INGREDIENTS
Cherry Crumb Dessert

Here's a sweet treat that's especially good with a dollop of whipped cream or a scoop of ice cream! The crumb topping has a wonderful nutty flavor, and no one will guess this streusel started with a handy cake mix.

—**ANN EASTMAN** SANTA MONICA, CA

PREP: 15 MIN. • **BAKE:** 30 MIN.
MAKES: 12-16 SERVINGS

½ cup cold butter
1 package yellow cake mix
   (regular size)
1 can (21 ounces) cherry or
   blueberry pie filling
½ cup chopped walnuts

1. In a large bowl, cut butter into cake mix until crumbly. Set aside 1 cup for topping. Pat remaining crumbs onto the bottom and ½ in. up the sides of a greased 9x13-in. baking pan.

2. Spread the pie filling over the crust. Combine the walnuts with reserved crumbs; sprinkle over top. Bake at 350° for 30-35 minutes or until golden brown. Cut into bars.

Candy Cereal Treats

These scrumptious bars travel well and are loved by kids of all ages. Terrific for reunions, potlucks—anything, really.

—**JANET SHEARER** JACKSON, MI

PREP: 25 MIN.
BAKE: 15 MIN. + COOLING
MAKES: 2 DOZEN

½ cup butter, softened
⅔ cup packed brown sugar

Banana Squares

When we were first married, my husband was in the Navy, stationed in Puerto Rico. We had banana trees growing in our yard, so I found many ways to use dozens of ripe bananas at a time. I made these banana squares often.

—SUSAN MILLER RALEIGH, NC

PREP: 20 MIN. • **BAKE:** 45 MIN.
MAKES: 12-16 SERVINGS

- 2 eggs, separated
- ⅔ cup shortening
- 1½ cups sugar
- 1 cup mashed ripe bananas (2 to 3 medium)
- 1½ cups all-purpose flour
- 1 teaspoon baking soda
- ¼ cup buttermilk
- ½ teaspoon vanilla extract
- ½ cup chopped walnuts, optional
  Whipped cream and sliced bananas, optional

1. In a small bowl, beat egg whites until soft peaks form; set aside. In a large bowl, cream shortening and sugar. Beat in egg yolks; mix well. Add bananas. Combine flour and baking soda; add to the creamed mixture alternately with buttermilk, beating well after each addition. Add vanilla. Fold in egg whites. Fold in nuts if desired.

2. Pour into a greased 9x13-in. baking dish. Bake at 350° for 45-50 minutes. Cool bars on a wire rack.

3. If desired, garnish the bars with whipped cream and a few banana slices.

Peanut Butter Blondies

The kids I baby-sit love these moist and chewy bars. There's plenty of peanut butter flavor, plus a yummy chocolate frosting and a sprinkling of peanut butter chips.
—**KARLA JOHNSON** TYLER, MN

PREP: 30 MIN.
BAKE: 35 MIN. + COOLING
MAKES: 2 DOZEN

- ¾ cup creamy peanut butter
- ⅔ cup butter, softened
- 1 cup packed brown sugar
- ½ cup sugar
- 2 eggs
- 1 teaspoon vanilla extract
- 1¾ cups all-purpose flour
- 1 teaspoon baking powder
- ⅓ cup milk
- 1 cup peanut butter chips

FROSTING
- ¼ cup butter, softened
- ¼ cup baking cocoa
- 2 tablespoons milk
- 1 tablespoon light corn syrup
- 1 teaspoon vanilla extract
- 1½ cups confectioners' sugar
- ⅓ cup peanut butter chips

1. In a large bowl, cream the peanut butter, butter and sugars until light and fluffy. Beat in eggs and vanilla. Combine the flour and baking powder; add to the creamed mixture alternately with milk, beating well after each addition. Stir in chips.
2. Spread into a greased 9x13-in. baking pan. Bake at 325° for 35-40 minutes or until a toothpick inserted near the center comes out clean (do not overbake). Cool on a wire rack.
3. For frosting, in a small bowl, combine the butter, cocoa, milk, corn syrup and vanilla extract. Gradually add confectioners' sugar; beat until smooth. Frost brownies. Sprinkle with chips. Cut into bars.

Cranberry Shortbread Bars

These bars and a glass of milk make the perfect afternoon treat.
—*TASTE OF HOME* TEST KITCHEN

PREP: 20 MIN.
BAKE: 30 MIN. + COOLING
MAKES: 2 DOZEN

- 1 cup butter, softened
- ½ cup confectioners' sugar
- 1 egg
- 1½ cups all-purpose flour
- ½ cup flaked coconut
- ⅛ teaspoon salt
- ½ cup sugar
- ½ cup packed brown sugar
- 3 tablespoons cornstarch
- 1 package (12 ounces) fresh or frozen cranberries
- 1 cup unsweetened apple juice
- 1 cup chopped walnuts
- 2 ounces white baking chocolate, melted

1. In a large bowl, cream butter and confectioners' sugar until light and fluffy. Beat in egg. Combine the flour, coconut and salt; gradually add to creamed mixture and mix well. Set aside 1 cup for topping. Spread the remaining mixture into a greased 9x13-in. baking dish. Bake at 425° for 10 minutes.
2. Meanwhile, in a small saucepan, combine sugars and cornstarch. Stir in cranberries and apple juice. Bring to a boil. Reduce heat; cook and stir 5 minutes or until thickened. Stir in walnuts. Spread over crust. Sprinkle with reserved crumb mixture.
3. Bake 20-25 minutes or until golden brown. Cool completely. Drizzle with white chocolate.

Glazed Apple-Maple Blondies

My 6-year-old son and I conjured up this recipe to use up the last of the apples we picked at the local orchard. For an extra treat, serve warm with a dollop of sweetened whipped cream.

—**HEATHER BATES** ATHENS, ME

PREP: 25 MIN.
BAKE: 25 MIN. + COOLING
MAKES: 2 DOZEN

- 1⅓ cups packed brown sugar
- ½ cup butter, melted and cooled
- ½ cup maple syrup
- 2 teaspoons vanilla extract
- 2 eggs
- 2 cups all-purpose flour
- ¾ teaspoon salt
- ¼ teaspoon baking soda
- 3 cups chopped peeled apples (about 3 medium)

GLAZE
- ¼ cup butter, cubed
- ½ cup maple syrup
- ¼ cup packed brown sugar

1. Preheat oven to 350°. Line a 9x13-in. baking pan with parchment paper, letting ends extend up sides.

2. In a large bowl, beat brown sugar, melted butter, syrup and vanilla until blended. Beat in eggs. In another bowl, whisk flour, salt and baking soda; gradually beat into brown sugar mixture. Stir in apples (batter will be thick).

3. Transfer to prepared pan. Bake 25-30 minutes or until golden brown and a toothpick inserted in center comes out with moist crumbs.

4. Meanwhile, in a small saucepan, melt butter over medium-low heat; stir in syrup and brown sugar. Bring to a boil over medium heat; cook and stir 2-3 minutes or until slightly thickened. Remove from heat; cool slightly.

5. Pour the glaze over warm blondies. Cool completely in pan on a wire rack. Cut into bars.

Five-Star Brownies

There's a bit of my state's history behind the name and shape of these brownies. In 1990, when I entered them in the state fair, Kansas was celebrating the 100th birthday of a famous native son, Dwight Eisenhower. So I renamed my brownies in honor of his rank and cut them into stars. They ended up winning a blue ribbon!
—**PAM BUERKI ROGERS** VICTORIA, KS

PREP: 15 MIN.
BAKE: 30 MIN. + COOLING
MAKES: 1 DOZEN

- 3 eggs
- 2 cups sugar
- 1½ teaspoons vanilla extract
- ½ cup butter, melted
- ¼ cup shortening, melted
- 1½ cups all-purpose flour
- ¾ cup baking cocoa
- ¾ teaspoon salt
- 1 cup chopped nuts, optional

1. In a bowl, beat eggs, sugar and vanilla until blended. Beat in butter and shortening until smooth. Combine flour, cocoa and salt; gradually beat into egg mixture. Add nuts if desired.
2. Line a 9x13-in. baking pan with foil and grease the foil; pour batter into pan. Bake at 350° for 30 minutes or until a toothpick inserted in center comes out clean. Cool in pan on a wire rack.
3. Using foil, lift brownies out of pan. Discard foil. Cut brownies with a 3-in. star-shaped cookie cutter or into bars.

Gingerbread Meringue Bars

PREP: 20 MIN.
BAKE: 30 MIN. + COOLING
MAKES: 2 DOZEN

- ¼ cup butter, softened
- 1 cup molasses
- 2 egg yolks
- 1 egg
- ¼ cup canned pumpkin
- 1 teaspoon vanilla extract
- 1½ cups whole wheat flour
- 2½ teaspoons ground cinnamon
- 2 teaspoons ground ginger
- 1 teaspoon baking powder
- 1 teaspoon baking soda
- ¾ teaspoon ground allspice
- ¼ teaspoon salt
- 1 cup miniature marshmallows
- ½ cup chopped pecans
- ½ cup semisweet chocolate chips

MERINGUE
- 4 egg whites
- ½ cup packed brown sugar

1. In a large bowl, beat butter and molasses until blended. Add egg yolks and egg, one at a time, beating well after each addition. Beat in pumpkin and vanilla.
2. Combine flour, cinnamon, ginger, baking powder, baking soda, allspice and salt; gradually beat into molasses mixture. Pour into a greased 9x13-in. baking pan. Top with marshmallows, pecans and chocolate chips. Bake at 350° for 20 minutes.
3. Meanwhile, in a small bowl, beat egg whites on medium speed until soft peaks form. Gradually beat in brown sugar, 1 tablespoon at a time, on high until stiff glossy peaks form and sugar is dissolved.
4. Remove gingerbread from oven; spread with meringue. Bake 9-11 minutes longer or until meringue is lightly browned. Cool completely.

For the best of both worlds, I combined my grandmother's gingerbread recipe with my aunt's special brown sugar meringue. The result? These lovable holiday-perfect bars.

—EDEN DRANGER LOS ANGELES, CA

Double Chocolate Orange Brownies

Since we love chocolate and orange together, my husband suggested I create a brownie featuring both of them. These amazing treats do our favorite flavor combination proud.

—ELINOR TOWNSEND

NORTH GRAFTON, MA

PREP: 15 MIN.
BAKE: 30 MIN. + COOLING
MAKES: 2 DOZEN

- ¾ cup butter, cubed
- 4 ounces unsweetened chocolate, chopped
- 3 eggs
- 2 cups sugar
- 1 teaspoon orange extract
- 1 cup all-purpose flour
- 1 cup (6 ounces) semisweet chocolate chips
  Confectioners' sugar

1. In a microwave, melt butter and chocolate; stir until smooth. Cool slightly. In a large bowl, beat eggs and sugar. Stir in the chocolate mixture. Beat in the extract. Gradually add flour to chocolate mixture.

2. Pour into a greased 9x13-in. baking dish. Sprinkle with the chocolate chips. Bake at 350° for 30-35 minutes or until a toothpick inserted near the center comes out clean (do not overbake).

3. Cool completely on a wire rack. Cut into squares. Just before serving, sprinkle with confectioners' sugar.

Raspberry Walnut Bars

This recipe is a Valentine's Day favorite because it's so festive. Here in snowy Maine, the bars are also fun to make on a snow day when our normal routine shifts to a vacation day.

—ABBY KUHN ELLSWORTH, ME

PREP: 20 MIN. + COOLING
BAKE: 25 MIN. • **MAKES:** 3 DOZEN

- ⅓ cup plus ½ cup sugar, divided
- 1½ cups all-purpose flour
- ¾ cup butter, cubed
- 2 eggs, separated
- 1 cup raspberry jam
- 1 cup broken walnuts

1. In a small bowl, combine ⅓ cup sugar, flour, butter and egg yolks. Press into a greased 9x13-in. baking pan. Bake at 350° for 15 minutes or until golden. Cool. Spread jam over crust; sprinkle with nuts.

2. In a small bowl, beat egg whites on medium speed until soft peaks form. Gradually beat in remaining sugar, 1 tablespoon at a time, on high until stiff glossy peaks form and sugar is dissolved. Spread meringue over the nuts.

3. Bake at 350° for 25 minutes or until set and lightly browned. Cool on a wire rack. To cut into bars, use a knife dipped in hot water. Store in the refrigerator.

Million Dollar Pecan Bars

Invest 15 minutes of your time and enjoy a big payoff when you pull these rich bars of golden layered goodness from your oven.

—**LAURA DAVIS** RUSK, TX

PREP: 15 MIN. • **BAKE:** 20 MIN.
MAKES: 2 DOZEN

- ¾ cup butter, softened
- ¾ cup packed brown sugar
- 2 eggs
- 2 teaspoons vanilla extract
- 1 package butter pecan cake mix (regular size)
- 2½ cups quick-cooking oats

FILLING

- 1 can (14 ounces) sweetened condensed milk
- 2 cups milk chocolate chips
- 1 cup butterscotch chips
- 1 tablespoon butter
- 1 teaspoon vanilla extract
- 1½ cups chopped pecans

1. In a large bowl, cream butter and brown sugar until light and fluffy. Add eggs, one at a time, beating well after each addition. Beat in vanilla. Add the cake mix just until blended. Stir in oats. Press 3 cups onto the bottom of a greased 9x13-in. baking pan.
2. In a large microwave-safe bowl, combine milk and chips. Microwave, uncovered, until chips are melted, stirring every 30 seconds. Stir in butter and vanilla until melted. Stir in pecans. Spread over crust.
3. Crumble the remaining oat mixture; sprinkle over top. Bake at 350° for 20-25 minutes or until topping is golden brown. Cool on a wire rack before cutting into bars.

Chocolate Maple Bars

Use real maple syrup for both the bar and chocolate-maple frosting. You won't be able to keep these confections on the table.

—**CATHY SCHUMACHER** ALTO, MI

PREP: 20 MIN.
BAKE: 25 MIN. + COOLING
MAKES: 3 DOZEN

- ½ cup shortening
- ¾ cup maple syrup
- ½ cup sugar
- 3 eggs
- 3 tablespoons milk
- 1 teaspoon vanilla extract
- 1¼ cups all-purpose flour
- ¼ teaspoon baking powder
- ¼ teaspoon salt
- 1½ ounces unsweetened chocolate, melted
- ½ cup chopped pecans
- ½ cup flaked coconut

FROSTING

- ¼ cup butter, softened
- 1 cup confectioners' sugar
- ½ cup baking cocoa
- ½ cup maple syrup
- 1 cup miniature marshmallows

1. In a large bowl, cream the shortening, syrup and sugar until light and fluffy. Beat in the eggs, milk and vanilla. Combine the flour, baking powder and salt; add to creamed mixture and mix well. Remove half of the batter to another bowl.
2. Combine melted chocolate and pecans; stir into one bowl. Spread into a greased 9x13-in. baking pan. Add coconut to the remaining batter. Spread carefully over chocolate batter.
3. Bake at 350° for 25 minutes or until a toothpick inserted near the center comes out clean. Cool completely on a wire rack.
4. For frosting, in a small bowl, beat the butter until smooth. Gradually add the confectioners' sugar and cocoa. Gradually add the syrup, beating until smooth. Fold in the marshmallows. Frost bars.

Peanut Cake Bars

A bakery favorite inspired us to create this recipe. Individual pieces of white cake are coated with a crunchy peanut coating.
—*TASTE OF HOME* TEST KITCHEN

PREP: 1¾ HOURS
BAKE: 30 MIN. + STANDING
MAKES: 20 BARS

- ½ **cup butter, softened**
- 1½ **cups sugar**
- 4 **egg whites**
- 2 **teaspoons vanilla extract**
- 2 **cups all-purpose flour**
- 1 **teaspoon baking powder**
- ½ **teaspoon baking soda**
- ¼ **teaspoon salt**
- 1⅓ **cups buttermilk**

GLAZE

- 7½ **cups confectioners' sugar, divided**
- 1 **cup milk, divided**
- 1 **teaspoon vanilla extract, divided**
- 2 **cans (12 ounces each) salted peanuts, chopped, divided**

1. In a large bowl, cream butter and sugar until light and fluffy. Add egg whites, one at a time, beating well after each addition. Beat in vanilla. Combine the flour, baking powder, baking soda and salt; add to creamed mixture alternately with buttermilk, beating well after each addition.
2. Pour into a greased 9x13-in. baking pan. Bake at 350° for 30-35 minutes or until a toothpick inserted near the center comes out clean. Cool .
3. For glaze, in a shallow bowl, mix 3¾ cups confectioners' sugar, ½ cup of the milk and ½ teaspoon vanilla extract until smooth. Place one can of peanuts in another shallow bowl.
4. Cut cake into 20 bars. Coat the top and sides of each with glaze, then roll in nuts. Place on wire racks over waxed paper; let dry completely.
5. Make a second batch of glaze with remaining confectioners' sugar, milk and vanilla. Coat cake squares a second time, then roll in remaining nuts. Let dry .

Milky Way Crispy Bars

What's not to love about the combination of candy bars and Rice Krispies treats? These give you the crunch of chopped pecans, too.
—**PHYL BROICH-WESSLING**
GARNER, IA

START TO FINISH: 15 MIN.
MAKES: 2 DOZEN

- 6 **cups Rice Krispies**
- 1 **cup chopped pecans**
- 6 **Milky Way candy bars (2.05 ounces each), chopped**
- ¾ **cup butter, cubed**
- ½ **cup white baking chips**
- ½ **teaspoon shortening**

1. In a large bowl, combine cereal and pecans; set aside. In a large microwave-safe bowl, combine candy bars and butter. Microwave, uncovered, on high for 1½ to 2 minutes or until smooth, stirring once. Stir into cereal mixture.
2. Transfer to a greased 9x13-in. pan; press down firmly. In a microwave, melt chips and shortening; stir until smooth. Drizzle over the top. Cool. Cut into bars. Store the bars in an airtight container.

Coconut Graham Bars

My mom called these Out of This World Bars, and I can see why! The chewy coconut base and caramel-rich top really wow.

—PATTY VAN ZYL HOSPERS, IA

PREP: 20 MIN.
BAKE: 15 MIN. + COOLING
MAKES: 4½ DOZEN

- 2 **cups graham cracker crumbs**
- ½ **cup sugar**
- ½ **cup butter, melted**
- 2 **cups flaked coconut**
- 1 **can (14 ounces) sweetened condensed milk**

TOPPING

- 1½ **cups packed brown sugar**
- 6 **tablespoons heavy whipping cream**
- ¼ **cup butter, cubed**
- ¾ **cup semisweet chocolate chips**

1. In a small bowl, combine the cracker crumbs, sugar and butter. Press mixture onto the bottom of a greased 9x13-in. baking pan. Bake at 350° for 8-10 minutes or until lightly browned.

2. Combine the coconut and milk; spread over warm crust. Bake for 12-15 minutes or until edges are lightly browned. Cool on a wire rack.

3. In a large saucepan, combine brown sugar, cream and butter. Bring to a boil over medium heat, stirring constantly. Boil for 1 minute. Remove from the heat; stir in the chocolate chips until melted. Spread over the coconut layer. Cool completely before cutting into bars.

My family can't possibly eat all of the sweets I whip up, so my co-workers are more than happy to sample them. They're especially fond of these rich, chewy brownies, which are full of gooey caramel, chocolate chips and crunchy walnuts.

—**CLARA BAKKE** COON RAPIDS, MN

Caramel Brownies

PREP: 20 MIN.
BAKE: 35 MIN. + COOLING
MAKES: 2 DOZEN

- 2 **cups sugar**
- ¾ **cup baking cocoa**
- 1 **cup canola oil**
- 4 **eggs**
- ¼ **cup 2% milk**
- 1½ **cups all-purpose flour**
- 1 **teaspoon salt**
- 1 **teaspoon baking powder**
- 1 **cup (6 ounces) semisweet chocolate chips**
- 1 **cup chopped walnuts, divided**
- 1 **package (14 ounces) caramels**
- 1 **can (14 ounces) sweetened condensed milk**

1. In a large bowl, beat the sugar, cocoa, oil, eggs and milk. Combine the flour, salt and baking powder; gradually add to egg mixture until well blended. Fold in chips and ½ cup walnuts.
2. Spoon two-thirds of the batter into a greased 9x13-in. baking pan. Bake at 350° for 12 minutes.
3. Meanwhile, in a large saucepan, heat the caramels and condensed milk over low heat until caramels are melted. Pour over baked brownie layer. Sprinkle with the remaining walnuts.
4. Drop remaining batter by teaspoonfuls over caramel layer; carefully swirl brownie batter with a knife.
5. Bake for 35-40 minutes or until a toothpick inserted near the center comes out with moist crumbs (do not overbake). Cool on a wire rack.

Hawaiian Joy Bars

I get rave reviews when I bring these to work or to church. It's like a trip to the islands with the macadamia nuts, coconut and hint of rum.

—JENNIFER NECKERMANN
WENTZVILLE, MO

PREP: 20 MIN.
BAKE: 35 MIN. + COOLING
MAKES: 2 DOZEN

- 1 **cup butter, melted**
- 2 **cups packed brown sugar**
- 2 **eggs, lightly beaten**
- ⅓ **cup rum**
- 3 **teaspoons vanilla extract**
- 2 **cups all-purpose flour**
- 2 **teaspoons baking powder**
- 1 **teaspoon baking soda**
- ½ **teaspoon salt**
- 2¼ **cups semisweet chocolate chips, divided**
- 1 **package (10 to 12 ounces) white baking chips**
- 1½ **cups flaked coconut**
- 1½ **cups macadamia nuts, chopped**
- 1 **teaspoon shortening**
- 1 **ounce white baking chocolate**

1. In a large bowl, stir the butter, brown sugar, eggs, rum and vanilla until well blended. Combine the flour, baking powder, baking soda and salt; gradually add to butter mixture. Stir in 2 cups chocolate chips, white chips, coconut and nuts.
2. Pour into a greased 9x13-in. baking pan. Bake at 350° for 35-40 minutes or until golden brown. Cool on a wire rack.
3. In a microwave, melt the shortening with remaining chocolate chips; drizzle over bars. Melt the white baking chocolate; drizzle over bars. Store in an airtight container.

Super Brownies

Loaded with macadamia nuts, these chunky bite-size treats never fail to catch attention on a buffet table. If you prefer, replace the macadamia nuts with pecans.

—BERNICE MUILENBURG

MOLALLA, OR

PREP: 20 MIN.
BAKE: 55 MIN. + COOLING
MAKES: ABOUT 3½ DOZEN

- ½ **cup butter, cubed**
- 1½ **cups sugar**
- 4⅔ **cups (28 ounces) semisweet chocolate chips, divided**
- 3 **tablespoons hot water**
- 4 **eggs**
- 5 **teaspoons vanilla extract**
- 1½ **cups all-purpose flour**
- ½ **teaspoon baking soda**
- ½ **teaspoon salt**
- 2 **cups coarsely chopped macadamia nuts or pecans, divided**

1. In a large saucepan, melt butter with the sugar over medium heat. Remove from the heat; stir in 2 cups chocolate chips until melted.

2. Pour into a large bowl; beat in water. Add eggs, one at a time, beating well after each addition. Add vanilla. Combine the flour, baking soda and salt; beat into the chocolate mixture until blended. Stir in 2 cups chocolate chips and 1 cup nuts.

3. Pour into a greased 9x13-in. baking pan. Sprinkle with the remaining chips and nuts. Bake at 325° for 55 minutes or until center is set (do not overbake). Cool on a wire rack.

Almond Bars

This fast, delicious dessert always makes an appearance during our Christmas celebrations. Everyone likes the rich almond flavor.

—CHERYL NEWENDORP PELLA, IA

PREP: 15 MIN.
BAKE: 30 MIN. + COOLING
MAKES: 4½ DOZEN

- 1 **cup butter, softened**
- 1 **cup almond paste**
- 2¼ **cups sugar, divided**
- 2 **eggs**
- 1 **teaspoon almond extract**
- 2 **cups all-purpose flour**
- ½ **cup slivered almonds**

1. In a large bowl, cream the butter, almond paste and 2 cups sugar until light and fluffy. Beat in eggs and extract. Gradually add flour just until moistened.

2. Spread into a greased 9x13-in. baking dish. Sprinkle with the remaining sugar; top with the slivered almonds.

3. Bake bars at 350° for 30-35 minutes or until a toothpick inserted near the center comes out clean. Cool on a wire rack. Cut into squares. Store in the refrigerator.

Apricot Bars

This recipe is down-home baking at its best, and it really represents all regions of the country. It's won blue ribbons at county fairs and cookie contests in several states! The treat is easy to make, and it's perfect for potlucks, bake sales, lunch boxes or just plain snacking.

—**JILL MORITZ** IRVINE, CA

PREP: 15 MIN.
BAKE: 30 MIN. + COOLING
MAKES: 2 DOZEN

- ¾ **cup butter, softened**
- 1 **cup sugar**
- 1 **egg**
- ½ **teaspoon vanilla extract**
- 2 **cups all-purpose flour**
- ¼ **teaspoon baking powder**
- 1⅓ **cups flaked coconut**
- ½ **cup chopped walnuts**
- 1 **jar (10 to 12 ounces) apricot preserves**

1. Preheat oven to 350°. In a large bowl, cream butter and sugar until light and fluffy. Beat in egg and vanilla. In a small bowl, whisk flour and baking powder; gradually add to creamed mixture, mixing well. Fold in coconut and walnuts.

2. Press two-thirds of dough onto the bottom of a greased 9x13-in. baking pan. Spread with preserves; crumble remaining dough over preserves. Bake 30-35 minutes or until golden brown. Cool completely in pan on a wire rack. Cut into bars.

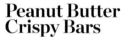

FREEZE IT

Festive Almond Blondies

Short on time? These easy almond blondies get into the oven in a flash. During the holidays, I sprinkle on red and green sugar before baking.

—**ELIZABETH KING** DULUTH, MN

PREP: 20 MIN.
BAKE: 15 MIN. + COOLING
MAKES: 2 DOZEN

- ⅔ cup butter, softened
- 1 cup packed brown sugar
- 2 eggs
- 1 teaspoon almond extract
- 1⅔ cups all-purpose flour
- 1½ teaspoons baking powder
- ½ teaspoon salt
- ½ cup unblanched almonds, finely chopped
- ½ teaspoon ground cinnamon
- 2 teaspoons each red and green colored sugars

1. Preheat oven to 375°. In a large bowl, cream butter and brown sugar until light and fluffy. Beat in eggs and extract. In a small bowl, mix flour, baking powder and salt; gradually add to creamed mixture, mixing well.

2. Spread into a greased 9x13-in. baking pan. Sprinkle with almonds, cinnamon and sugars. Bake 15-20 minutes or until a toothpick inserted in center comes out clean. Cool completely in pan on a wire rack. Cut into bars. Store in an airtight container.

FREEZE OPTION *Freeze bars, layered between waxed paper, in freezer containers. To use, thaw before serving.*

Peanut Butter Crispy Bars

I needed something quick for a gathering and whipped up these bars in no time. The peanut butter, cookie dough and marshmallows were a winning combination.

—**GAIL ANDERSON** JEFFERSON, WI

PREP: 15 MIN.
BAKE: 15 MIN. + COOLING
MAKES: 3 DOZEN

- 1 tube (16½ ounces) refrigerated peanut butter cookie dough
- 4 cups miniature marshmallows
- 2 cups (12 ounces) semisweet chocolate chips
- ½ cup creamy peanut butter
- ¼ cup butter, cubed
- 2 cups Rice Krispies
- ½ cup salted peanuts

1. Preheat oven to 350°. Press cookie dough into an ungreased 9x13-in. baking pan. Bake 10-14 minutes or until edges are lightly browned and center is set. Sprinkle with marshmallows; bake 4-5 minutes or just until marshmallows are puffed. Cool 5 minutes.

2. Meanwhile, in a small saucepan, combine chocolate chips, peanut butter and butter. Cook and stir until chocolate is melted and mixture is smooth. Remove from heat; stir in cereal and peanuts. Drop by spoonfuls over marshmallows; gently spread over the top. Cool and cut into bars.

Layered Chocolate-Raspberry Triangles

My chocolaty triangles layered with raspberry jam are a must during the holiday season. The cakelike bars look festive, and one batch goes a long way.

—**MARY ANN LEE** CLIFTON PARK, NY

PREP: 45 MIN.
BAKE: 15 MIN. + STANDING
MAKES: 4 DOZEN

- 6 **eggs, separated**
- 1½ **cups butter, softened**
- 1½ **cups sugar**
- 2 **teaspoons vanilla extract**
- 2½ **cups all-purpose flour**
- 3 **ounces unsweetened chocolate, melted and cooled slightly**
- 3 **ounces white baking chocolate, melted and cooled slightly**
- ¼ **cup seedless raspberry jam**
- 1 **cup (6 ounces) semisweet chocolate chips, melted**
   White baking chocolate shavings

1. Place egg whites in a large bowl; let whites stand at room temperature for 30 minutes. Preheat oven to 350°. Line the bottoms of two greased matching 9x13-in. baking pans with parchment paper; grease the paper in both pans.

2. In a large bowl, cream butter and sugar until light and fluffy. Add egg yolks, one at a time, beating well after each addition. Add vanilla. Stir in flour.

3. With clean beaters, beat egg whites on medium speed until stiff peaks form. Fold into batter. Transfer half of the batter to another bowl. Fold the melted unsweetened chocolate into one bowl; spread into a prepared pan. Fold melted white chocolate into remaining batter; spread into second prepared pan.

4. Bake 12-16 minutes or until a toothpick inserted in center comes out clean. Cool 5 minutes. Invert cakes onto wire racks. Remove parchment paper; cool cakes completely.

5. Transfer chocolate layer to a baking sheet lined with a large piece of plastic wrap. Spread jam over top; place white chocolate layer over jam. Wrap securely with plastic wrap. Set a cutting board or heavy baking pan over top to flatten layers. Let stand at room temperature 3-4 hours. (Or, refrigerate overnight and return to room temperature before continuing.)

6. Unwrap cake; place on a cutting board. Spread top with melted chocolate chips. Top with white chocolate shavings. Let stand until set. Trim edges with a knife. Cut into 24 squares; cut squares diagonally in half.

Chocolate-Glazed Almond Bars

Moist almond filling, a golden crust and a delectable chocolate drizzle make these bars a triple threat.

—ROBIN HART

NORTH BRUNSWICK, NJ

PREP: 25 MIN.
BAKE: 20 MIN. + COOLING
MAKES: 40 BARS

- 2 **cups all-purpose flour**
- ½ **cup packed brown sugar**
- ½ **teaspoon salt**
- ¾ **cup cold butter, cubed**
- 3 **egg whites**
- 1 **cup sugar**
- 1 **can (12½ ounces) almond cake and pastry filling**
- 2 **cups sliced almonds**
- 4 **ounces bittersweet chocolate, chopped**

1. In a large bowl, combine the flour, brown sugar and salt. Cut in butter until mixture resembles coarse crumbs. Pat into a 9x13-in. baking pan coated with cooking spray. Bake the crust at 350° for 18-22 minutes or until edges are lightly browned.
2. Meanwhile, in a large bowl, whisk the egg whites, sugar and almond filling until blended. Stir in almonds. Pour over crust. Bake for 20-25 minutes or until set. Cool completely on a wire rack.
3. In a microwave, melt the chocolate; stir until smooth. Drizzle over top. Let stand until set. Cut into bars. Store bars in an airtight container in the refrigerator.
NOTE *This recipe was tested with Solo brand cake and pastry filling. Look for it in the baking aisle.*

Blond Butterscotch Brownies

Toffee and chocolate dot the golden brown batter of these delightful brownies. I do a lot of cooking for the police officers I work with, and they always line up for these treats.

—JENNIFER ANN SOPKO

BATTLE CREEK, MI

PREP: 15 MIN.
BAKE: 20 MIN. + COOLING
MAKES: 2 DOZEN

- 2 **cups all-purpose flour**
- 2 **cups packed brown sugar**
- 2 **teaspoons baking powder**
- ¼ **teaspoon salt**
- ½ **cup butter, melted and cooled**
- 2 **eggs**
- 1 **teaspoon vanilla extract**
- 1 **cup semisweet chocolate chunks**
- 4 **Heath candy bars (1.4 ounces each), coarsely chopped**

1. In a large bowl, combine the flour, brown sugar, baking powder and salt. In another bowl, beat the butter, eggs and vanilla until smooth. Stir into the dry ingredients just until combined (batter will be thick).
2. Spread into a 9x13-in. baking pan coated with cooking spray. Sprinkle with chocolate chunks and chopped candy bars; press gently into batter.
3. Bake at 350° for 20-25 minutes or until a toothpick inserted near the center comes out clean. Cool on a wire rack. Cut into bars.

Chocolate Toffee Delights

I combined my best cookie recipe with some ingredients I had on hand and came up with these wonderful bars. The irresistible flavor always reminds me of my favorite Girl Scout cookies.

—**SHANNON KOENE** BLACKSBURG, VA

PREP: 15 MIN.
BAKE: 30 MIN. + COOLING
MAKES: 3 DOZEN

- 1 **cup butter, softened**
- ½ **cup plus 2 tablespoons sugar, divided**
- ¾ **teaspoon almond extract**
- ½ **teaspoon coconut extract**
- 2 **cups all-purpose flour**
- ¼ **teaspoon salt**
- ¼ **teaspoon baking powder**
- ½ **cup flaked coconut**
- ½ **cup sliced almonds, toasted and cooled**
- 1 **jar (12¼ ounces) caramel ice cream topping**
- ¾ **cup dark chocolate chips**

1. Preheat oven to 350°. In a small bowl, cream butter and ½ cup sugar until light and fluffy. Beat in extracts. Combine flour, salt and baking powder; gradually add to the creamed mixture and mix well.

2. Press into a greased 9x13-in. baking pan. Bake 10 minutes. Prick crust with a fork; sprinkle with remaining sugar. Bake for 15 minutes longer or until set.

3. Meanwhile, place coconut and almonds in a food processor; cover and process until finely chopped. Transfer to a small bowl; stir in ice cream topping. Spread over crust. Bake for 5-10 minutes or until edges are bubbly. Cool on a wire rack.

4. In a microwave, melt the chocolate chips; stir until smooth. Drizzle over caramel mixture. Let stand until the chocolate is set. Cut into bars. Store in an airtight container.

TOP TIP

To give Chocolate Toffee Delights a more crunchy and interesting texture, you can process the coconut and almonds to a coarser consistency in the food processor.

3. Bake 30-35 minutes or until a toothpick inserted near the center comes out clean (do not overbake). Cool on a wire rack. Cut into bars. Store in the refrigerator.

Caramel Butter-Pecan Bars

These melt-in-your-mouth bars are simply to die for, and they go together in minutes. Although the chocolate layer takes time to harden, the treats are definitely worth the wait.

—MARY JEAN HLAVAC
MCFARLAND, WI

PREP: 10 MIN.
BAKE: 15 MIN. + COOLING
MAKES: 4 DOZEN

- 2 **cups all-purpose flour**
- 1 **cup packed brown sugar**
- ¾ **cup cold butter, cubed**
- 1½ **cups chopped pecans**
- 1 **jar (12 ounces) caramel ice cream topping, warmed**
- 1 **package (11½ ounces) milk chocolate chips**

1. In a large bowl, combine flour and brown sugar; cut in butter until crumbly. Press into an ungreased 9x13-in. baking dish. Top with pecans. Drizzle caramel topping evenly over pecans.
2. Bake at 350° for 15-20 minutes or until caramel is bubbly. Sprinkle with chocolate chips. Let stand for 5 minutes. Carefully spread chips over caramel layer. Cool at room temperature for at least 6 hours or until the chocolate is set. Cut into bars.

Coconut Meringue Bars

Looking for an ooey-gooey dessert that's deliciously different? This bar combines a shortbread-like crust and a brown sugar meringue with chocolate, coconut and nuts. Put a few on the side for yourself because they disappear fast.

—DIANE BRIDGE CLYMER, PA

PREP: 30 MIN.
BAKE: 30 MIN. + COOLING
MAKES: 3 DOZEN

- ¾ **cup butter, softened**
- 1½ **cups packed brown sugar, divided**
- ½ **cup sugar**
- 3 **eggs, separated**
- 1 **teaspoon vanilla extract**
- 2 **cups all-purpose flour**
- 1 **teaspoon baking powder**
- ¼ **teaspoon baking soda**
- ¼ **teaspoon salt**
- 2 **cups (12 ounces) semisweet chocolate chips**
- 1 **cup flaked coconut**
- ¾ **cup chopped walnuts**

1. Preheat oven to 350°. In a large bowl, cream the butter, ½ cup brown sugar and sugar until light and fluffy. Beat in egg yolks and vanilla. Combine the flour, baking powder, baking soda and salt; gradually add to creamed mixture just until blended (batter will be thick). Spread into a greased 9x13-in. baking pan. Sprinkle with the chocolate chips, coconut and the walnuts.
2. In another large bowl, beat egg whites until soft peaks form. Gradually beat in remaining brown sugar, 1 tablespoon at a time. Beat until stiff peaks form. Spread over the top.

Gooey Butterscotch Bars

With caramels, butterscotch chips and pudding, these luscious bars are a butterscotch lover's dream. And imagine the fun you could have experimenting with different flavors of pudding, chips and cookie mix.

—CAROL BREWER FAIRBORN, OH

PREP: 20 MIN.
BAKE: 20 MIN. + COOLING
MAKES: ABOUT 3 DOZEN

- 1 package (17½ ounces) sugar cookie mix
- 1 package (3.4 ounces) instant butterscotch pudding mix
- ½ cup butter, softened
- 1 egg
- 1 package (14 ounces) caramels
- ½ cup evaporated milk
- 2 cups mixed nuts
- 1 teaspoon vanilla extract
- 1 cup butterscotch chips

1. In a large bowl, combine the sugar cookie mix, pudding mix, butter and egg. Press into an ungreased 9x13-in. baking pan. Bake at 350° for 20-25 minutes or until set.

2. In a large saucepan, combine caramels and milk. Cook and stir over medium-low heat until melted. Remove from the heat. Stir in nuts and vanilla. Pour over crust. Sprinkle with butterscotch chips.

3. Cool completely before cutting into bars. Store in an airtight container.

Peanut Butter-Hazelnut Brownies

Over the years, I'd been adding a bit of this and that to my basic brownie recipe—and then I came up with this amazing combination! It's fudgy and downright delicious.

—**DENISE WHEELER** NEWAYGO, MI

PREP: 20 MIN.
BAKE: 35 MIN. + COOLING
MAKES: 2 DOZEN

- 1 **cup butter, softened**
- 2 **cups sugar**
- 4 **eggs**
- 2 **teaspoons vanilla extract**
- 1 **cup all-purpose flour**
- ¾ **cup baking cocoa**
- ½ **teaspoon baking powder**
  Dash salt
- 1½ **cups coarsely crushed malted milk balls**
- ½ **cup creamy peanut butter**
- ½ **cup Nutella**

1. Preheat oven to 350°. In a large bowl, cream the butter and sugar until light and fluffy. Add eggs, one at a time, beating well after each addition. Beat in vanilla. Combine the flour, cocoa, baking powder and salt; gradually add to creamed mixture. Fold in malted milk balls.
2. Spread into a greased 9x13-in. baking pan. In a microwave-safe bowl, combine peanut butter and Nutella; cover and microwave at 50% power for 1-2 minutes or until smooth, stirring twice. Drizzle over batter; cut through batter with a knife to swirl.
3. Bake 35-40 minutes or until a toothpick inserted near the center comes out clean (do not overbake). Cool on a wire rack.

Coconut-Pecan Brownies

My thick bakery-style brownies are good enough already, but once you top them with cream cheese frosting, they're simply divine! My kids request them for every family gathering.

—**LESLEY PEW** LYNN, MA

PREP: 25 MIN.
BAKE: 35 MIN. + COOLING
MAKES: 2 DOZEN

- 1 **cup butter, cubed**
- 4 **ounces bittersweet chocolate, chopped**
- 4 **eggs**
- 2½ **cups sugar**
- 2 **teaspoons vanilla extract**
- 2 **cups all-purpose flour**
- ½ **teaspoon salt**
- 2 **cups chopped pecans**

FROSTING

- ¾ **cup white baking chips**
- 2 **packages (3 ounces each) cream cheese, softened**
- ½ **cup butter, softened**
- 1½ **cups confectioners' sugar**
- 3 **tablespoons brown sugar**
- ¾ **teaspoon vanilla extract**
- ⅛ **teaspoon salt**
- ¾ **cup flaked coconut**
- ¾ **cup chopped pecans**

1. Melt butter and chocolate; stir until smooth. Cool slightly. In a large bowl, beat eggs, sugar and vanilla. Stir in chocolate mixture. Combine flour and salt; gradually add to chocolate mixture. Fold in the pecans.
2. Transfer brownie batter to a greased 9x13-in. baking pan. Bake at 350° for 35-40 minutes or until a toothpick inserted near the center comes out clean. Cool on a wire rack.
3. For frosting, in a microwave, melt baking chips; stir until smooth. Cool slightly. In a large bowl, beat cream cheese and butter until fluffy. Add the melted chips, sugars, vanilla and salt; beat until smooth. Stir in coconut and pecans. Frost brownies. Store leftovers in the refrigerator.

Honey-Pecan Squares

When we left Texas to head north, a neighbor gave me so many pecans from his trees that my trunk was bulging at the seams! I brought these back for him the next year.

—LORRAINE CALAND

THUNDER BAY, ON

PREP: 15 MIN. • **BAKE:** 30 MIN.
MAKES: 2 DOZEN

- 1 **cup unsalted butter, softened**
- ¾ **cup packed dark brown sugar**
- ½ **teaspoon salt**
- 3 **cups all-purpose flour**

FILLING

- ½ **cup unsalted butter, cubed**
- ½ **cup packed dark brown sugar**
- ⅓ **cup honey**
- 2 **tablespoons sugar**
- 2 **tablespoons heavy whipping cream**
- ¼ **teaspoon salt**
- 2 **cups chopped pecans, toasted**
- ½ **teaspoon maple flavoring or vanilla extract**

1. Preheat oven to 350°. Line a 9x13-in. baking pan with parchment paper, letting ends extend up sides of pan. In a large bowl, cream the butter, brown sugar and salt until light and fluffy. Gradually beat in flour. Press onto bottom of prepared pan. Bake 16-20 minutes or until lightly browned.

2. In a small saucepan, combine the first six filling ingredients; bring to a boil. Cook 1 minute. Remove from the heat; stir in pecans and maple flavoring. Pour over crust.

3. Bake 10-15 minutes or until bubbly. Cool in pan on a wire rack. Lifting with parchment paper, transfer to a cutting board; cut into bars.

Lime Cooler Bars

This favorite is guaranteed to get a thumbs up from your family. Lime juice puts a tangy twist on these tantalizing bars.
—**DOROTHY ANDERSON** OTTAWA, KS

PREP: 15 MIN.
BAKE: 40 MIN. + COOLING
MAKES: 3 DOZEN

- 2½ cups all-purpose flour, divided
- ½ cup confectioners' sugar
- ¾ cup cold butter, cubed
- 4 eggs
- 2 cups sugar
- ⅓ cup lime juice
- ½ teaspoon grated lime peel
- ½ teaspoon baking powder
  Additional confectioners' sugar

1. In a large bowl, combine 2 cups flour and confectioners' sugar; cut in butter until mixture resembles coarse crumbs. Pat into a greased 9x13-in. baking pan. Bake at 350° for 20 minutes or until lightly browned.

2. In a large bowl, whisk eggs, sugar, lime juice and peel until frothy. Combine baking powder and remaining flour; whisk into egg mixture. Pour over crust.

3. Bake for 20-25 minutes or until light golden brown. Cool on a wire rack. Dust with the confectioners' sugar.

Rustic Nut Bars

PREP: 20 MIN.
BAKE: 35 MIN. + COOLING
MAKES: ABOUT 3 DOZEN

- 1 tablespoon plus ¾ cup cold butter, divided
- 2⅓ cups all-purpose flour
- ½ cup sugar
- ½ teaspoon baking powder
- ½ teaspoon salt
- 1 egg, lightly beaten

TOPPING
- ⅔ cup honey
- ½ cup packed brown sugar
- ¼ teaspoon salt
- 6 tablespoons butter, cubed
- 2 tablespoons heavy whipping cream

- 1 cup chopped hazelnuts, toasted
- 1 cup salted cashews
- 1 cup pistachios
- 1 cup salted roasted almonds

1. Line a 9x13-in. baking pan with foil, letting ends extend over sides by 1 inch. Grease the foil with 1 tablespoon butter.

2. In a large bowl, whisk flour, sugar, baking powder and salt. Cut in remaining butter until the mixture resembles coarse crumbs. Stir in egg (the mixture will be dry). Press firmly onto bottom of prepared pan.

3. Bake at 375° for 18-20 minutes or until edges are golden brown. Cool on a wire rack.

4. In a large heavy saucepan, bring honey, brown sugar and salt to a boil over medium heat, stirring frequently to dissolve sugar. Boil 2 minutes without stirring. Stir in butter and cream; return to a boil. Cook and stir 1 minute or until smooth. Stir in nuts. Spread over crust.

5. Bake for 15-20 minutes or until the topping is bubbly. Cool completely in pan on a wire rack. Lifting with foil, remove from pan. Discard foil; cut into bars.

DID YOU KNOW?

You can often use lemon and lime juice and peel interchangeably in recipes to achieve a different flavor. To substitute orange, though, you'll need to keep a little lemon or lime to ensure a bright flavor.

Everyone will enjoy crunching into the shortbread-like crust and wildly nutty topping of these chewy, gooey bars.
—**BARBARA DRISCOLL** WEST ALLIS, WI

Caramel Cashew Chewies

Caramels, cashews and chocolate chunks make any day something special. Let the kids unwrap all those caramels, counting as they go, to see who unwraps the most.

—**AMBER KIEFFER** AURORA, CO

PREP: 30 MIN.
BAKE: 10 MIN. + COOLING
MAKES: ABOUT 3 DOZEN

- ¾ **cup butter, softened**
- ¾ **cup packed brown sugar**
- 1 **egg**
- 1½ **cups all-purpose flour**
- 1 **cup old-fashioned oats**
- 1 **package (14 ounces) caramels**
- ⅓ **cup half-and-half cream**
- 1 **cup semisweet chocolate chunks**
- 1 **cup salted cashew halves, chopped**

1. In a large bowl, cream butter and brown sugar until light and fluffy. Beat in egg. Combine flour and oats; gradually add to creamed mixture.

2. Press into a 9x13-in. baking pan coated with cooking spray. Bake at 350° for 15-18 minutes or until golden brown.

3. Meanwhile, in a small saucepan, combine caramels and cream. Cook over low heat for 4-5 minutes or until the caramels are melted, stirring occasionally. Pour over crust. Sprinkle with chocolate chunks and cashews.

4. Bake for 8-10 minutes or until chocolate is melted. Cool on a wire rack before cutting.

Chocolate Chip Blondies

Folks who love chocolate chip cookies will enjoy that same great flavor in these sweet, easy treats. They're perfect for occasions when company drops by unexpectedly.

—**RHONDA KNIGHT** HECKER, IL

PREP: 10 MIN.
BAKE: 20 MIN. + COOLING
MAKES: 3 DOZEN

1½ cups packed brown sugar
½ cup butter, melted
2 eggs, lightly beaten
1 teaspoon vanilla extract
1½ cups all-purpose flour
½ teaspoon baking powder
½ teaspoon salt
1 cup (6 ounces) semisweet chocolate chips

1. In a large bowl, combine the brown sugar, butter, eggs and vanilla just until blended. Combine flour, baking powder and salt; add to brown sugar mixture. Stir in chocolate chips.
2. Spread into a greased 9x13-in. baking pan. Bake at 350° for 18-20 minutes or until a toothpick inserted near the center comes out clean. Cool on a wire rack. Cut into bars.

TOP TIP

To make cleanup a breeze, spritz your measuring cup with a little cooking spray before measuring sticky ingredients such as honey and molasses.

Cherry Oat Bars

The addition of dried cherries and cherry preserves make these old-fashioned bars a hit at my school's morning staff meetings. Each bar provides both a sweet pick-me-up and lasting energy.

—**KEVIN JOHNSON** GLENDORA, CA

PREP: 30 MIN.
BAKE: 25 MIN. + COOLING
MAKES: 2 DOZEN

2 cups all-purpose flour
2 cups old-fashioned oats
1 cup chopped pecans
½ cup toasted wheat germ
½ cup packed brown sugar
1 teaspoon salt
1 teaspoon baking soda
1 teaspoon ground cinnamon
½ teaspoon ground allspice
1 cup butter, melted
½ cup honey
2 eggs, beaten
1 teaspoon vanilla extract
1 jar (12 ounces) cherry preserves
⅓ cup dried cherries, chopped
½ cup flaked coconut

1. In a large bowl, combine the first nine ingredients. In another bowl, combine the butter, honey, eggs and vanilla. Stir into oat mixture until combined. Set aside 1⅓ cups for topping.
2. Press remaining oat mixture into a greased 9x13-in. baking pan. Combine preserves and dried cherries; spread over crust. Sprinkle with coconut and reserved oat mixture; press down lightly.
3. Bake at 350° for 25-30 minutes or until golden brown. Cool on a wire rack. Cut into bars.

Minty Chocolate Cream Cheese Bars

I always looked forward to my grandma's rich cream cheese bars when I was growing up. This version includes mint, which is one of my favorite flavor add-ins.
—**JILL LUTZ** WOODBURY, MN

PREP: 15 MIN.
BAKE: 30 MIN. + COOLING
MAKES: 2 DOZEN

- 1 **package chocolate cake mix (regular size)**
- ½ **cup butter, softened**
- 1 **teaspoon almond extract**
- 1 **teaspoon vanilla extract**
- 4 **eggs, divided use**
- 1 **package (10 ounces) Andes creme de menthe baking chips, divided**
- 1 **package (8 ounces) cream cheese, softened**
- 1⅔ **cups confectioners' sugar**

1. Preheat oven to 350°. In a large bowl, beat cake mix, butter, extracts and 2 eggs until blended. Spread into a greased 9x13-in. baking pan. Sprinkle with ¾ cup baking chips.
2. In a small bowl, beat cream cheese and confectioners' sugar until smooth. Add remaining eggs; beat on low speed just until blended. Pour over chocolate layer, spreading evenly; sprinkle with remaining baking chips.
3. Bake 30-35 minutes or until edges begin to brown. Cool in pan on a wire rack. Cut into bars. Refrigerate leftovers.

Blondie Nut Bars

Full of nuts and chocolate chips, these blondies definitely have more fun. With a subtle vanilla and coffee flavor, they make a sweet treat for potlucks, office parties and picnics.
—**LORI PHILLIPS** ORANGE, CA

PREP: 15 MIN.
BAKE: 25 MIN. + COOLING
MAKES: 2 DOZEN

- 4 **eggs**
- 2 **tablespoons heavy whipping cream**
- 2 **tablespoons butter, melted**
- 2 **teaspoons instant coffee granules**
- 1 **teaspoon vanilla extract**
- 2 **cups all-purpose flour**
- 2 **cups sugar**
- 2 **teaspoons baking powder**
- ¼ **teaspoon salt**
- 1 **cup chopped almonds**
- 1 **cup chopped walnuts**
- 1 **cup (6 ounces) semisweet chocolate chips**
  Confectioners' sugar

1. In a large bowl, beat the eggs, cream, butter, coffee and vanilla until blended. Combine the flour, sugar, baking powder and salt; gradually add to butter mixture. Stir in the almonds, walnuts and chocolate chips (the batter will be stiff).
2. Spread into a greased 9x13-in. baking pan. Bake at 350° for 25-30 minutes or until lightly browned. Cool on a wire rack. Cut into bars. Dust with the confectioners' sugar.

Swedish Raspberry Almond Bars

When I was a young single mom, my neighbor brought me a batch of these cookies at Christmas. My daughter's 36 now, and I still make these wonderful cookies.

—MARINA CASTLE

CANYON COUNTRY, CA

PREP: 35 MIN.
BAKE: 20 MIN. + COOLING
MAKES: 2 DOZEN

- ¾ **cup butter, softened**
- ¾ **cup confectioners' sugar**
- 1½ **cups all-purpose flour**
- ¾ **cup seedless raspberry jam**
- 3 **egg whites**
- 6 **tablespoons sugar**
- ½ **cup flaked coconut**
- 1 **cup sliced almonds, divided**
  Additional confectioners'
  sugar, optional

1. Preheat oven to 350°. In a large bowl, cream butter and confectioners' sugar until light and fluffy. Gradually add flour and mix well. Press onto the bottom of a greased 9x13-in. baking pan. Bake 18-20 minutes or until lightly browned.

2. Spread jam over crust. In a large bowl, beat egg whites until soft peaks form. Gradually beat in sugar, 1 tablespoon at a time, on high until stiff peaks form. Fold in the coconut and ½ cup almonds. Spread over the jam. Sprinkle with the remaining almonds. Bake 18-22 minutes or until golden brown. Cool completely on a wire rack. Dust with additional confectioners' sugar if desired.

SARA KINGSMORE'S
TRIPLE-BERRY
SHORTCAKE *PAGE 201*

Cakes

Sad Cake

Sad is such a misnomer. This simple-to-make cake—it takes only 10 minutes to mix up—is sweet and yummy!

—**LORI HANLEY** HARTSVILLE, SC

PREP: 10 MIN. • **BAKE:** 30 MIN.
MAKES: 15 SERVINGS

- 2¼ cups packed brown sugar
- 2 cups biscuit/baking mix
- 4 eggs
- ½ cup canola oil
- 1 teaspoon vanilla extract
- 1 cup chopped pecans
- 1 cup flaked coconut

1. Preheat oven to 350°. In a large bowl, mix brown sugar and baking mix. In another bowl, whisk eggs, oil and vanilla until blended. Add to sugar mixture; stir just until moistened. Fold in pecans and coconut.

2. Transfer to a greased 9x13-in. baking pan. Bake 30-35 minutes or until browned and a toothpick inserted in center comes out with moist crumbs. Cool completely in pan on a wire rack.

Bananas & Cream Pound Cake

This dessert got me a date with my future husband. At a church event, he loved it so much, he asked for another piece. The rest is history!

—**COURTNEY MECKLEY**
CARTERSVILLE, GA

PREP: 20 MIN.
BAKE: 40 MIN. + CHILLING
MAKES: 15 SERVINGS

- ½ cup butter, softened
- 1½ cups sugar
- 3 eggs
- 1 teaspoon vanilla extract

- 1½ cups all-purpose flour
- ¼ teaspoon salt
- ⅛ teaspoon baking soda
- ½ cup buttermilk

LAYERS
- 2 cups 2% milk
- 1 package (3.4 ounces) instant French vanilla pudding mix
- 1 package (8 ounces) cream cheese, softened
- ½ cup sweetened condensed milk
- 1 package (12 ounces) frozen whipped topping, thawed, divided
- 5 medium ripe bananas

1. In a large bowl, cream butter and sugar until light and fluffy. Add eggs, one at a time, beating well after each addition. Beat in vanilla. In another bowl, mix the flour, salt and baking soda; add to the creamed mixture alternately with buttermilk, beating after each addition just until mixture is combined.

2. Transfer to a greased and floured 9x5-in. loaf pan. Bake at 325° for 40-45 minutes or until a toothpick inserted in center comes out clean. Cool in pan for 10 minutes before removing to a wire rack to cool completely. In a small bowl, whisk milk and pudding mix for 2 minutes. Let stand for 2 minutes. In a large bowl, beat cream cheese and condensed milk until smooth; fold in pudding. Fold in 3½ cups whipped topping.

3. Cut cake into eight slices; arrange on bottom of an ungreased 9x13-in. dish, trimming to fit as necessary. Slice bananas; arrange over cake. Spread pudding mixture over top. Refrigerate, covered, for 3 hours. Serve with remaining whipped topping.

Triple-Berry Shortcake

My great-great grandmother, who was French, handed down her treasured shortcake recipe. I'm sharing it because why keep the classic dessert a secret when it's so fabulous?

—SARA KINGSMORE
VADNAIS HEIGHTS, MN

PREP: 25 MIN.
BAKE: 25 MIN. + COOLING
MAKES: 15 SERVINGS

- 1 cup butter, softened
- 2 cups sugar
- 4 eggs
- 2 tablespoons vanilla extract
- 3 cups all-purpose flour
- 1 teaspoon baking powder
- ½ teaspoon baking soda
- ½ teaspoon salt
- 1 cup buttermilk

TOPPING

- 1½ cups fresh blueberries
- 1½ cups sliced fresh strawberries
- 1½ cups fresh raspberries
- 2 tablespoons sugar
  Sweetened whipped cream, optional

1. Preheat oven to 350°. In a large bowl, cream butter and sugar until light and fluffy. Add eggs, one at a time, beating well after each addition. Beat in vanilla. In another bowl, whisk flour, baking powder, baking soda and salt; add to creamed mixture alternately with buttermilk, beating well after each addition.

2. Transfer batter to a greased 9x13-in. pan. Bake 25-30 minutes or until a toothpick inserted in center comes out clean. Cool completely in pan on a wire rack.

3. For topping, in a large bowl, combine berries; add sugar and toss gently to coat. Serve with cake; top with whipped cream, if desired.

Yummy S'more Snack Cake

This cake is a close second to s'mores by the campfire. You can adjust the amount of marshmallows and chocolate chips to your liking.

—DEBORAH WILLIAMS PEORIA, AZ

PREP: 20 MIN.
BAKE: 20 MIN. + COOLING
MAKES: 20 SERVINGS

- 2½ cups reduced-fat graham cracker crumbs (about 15 whole crackers)
- ½ cup sugar
- ⅓ cup cake flour
- ⅓ cup whole wheat flour
- 2 teaspoons baking powder
- ¼ teaspoon salt
- 3 egg whites
- 1 cup light soy milk
- ¼ cup unsweetened applesauce
- ¼ cup canola oil
- 2 cups miniature marshmallows
- 1 cup (6 ounces) semisweet chocolate chips

1. In a large bowl, combine the first six ingredients. In a small bowl, whisk the egg whites, soy milk, applesauce and oil. Stir into dry ingredients just until moistened. Transfer to a 9x13-in. baking pan coated with cooking spray.

2. Bake at 350° for 12-15 minutes or until a toothpick inserted near the center comes out clean. Sprinkle with marshmallows. Bake 4-6 minutes longer or until marshmallows are softened. Cool cake for 10 minutes.

3. In a microwave, melt chocolate chips; stir until smooth. Drizzle over cake. Cool completely on a wire rack.

Spiced Pudding Cake

I found this pudding cake years ago and made a few changes. Now it's a popular comfort food in my family. My mom's church group even serves it for dessert quite regularly.

—KELLY KIRBY VICTORIA, BC

PREP: 25 MIN.
BAKE: 35 MIN. + COOLING
MAKES: 15 SERVINGS

- ½ **cup butter, softened**
- ½ **cup sugar**
- 1 **egg**
- 1 **cup molasses**
- 2½ **cups all-purpose flour**
- 1½ **teaspoons baking soda**
- 1½ **teaspoons ground cinnamon**
- 1¼ **teaspoons ground ginger**
- ½ **teaspoon ground allspice**
- ¼ **teaspoon ground nutmeg**
- ¼ **teaspoon salt**
- 2½ **cups water, divided**
- ⅔ **cup packed brown sugar**
- ¼ **cup butter, cubed**
  Whipped cream and ground cinnamon, optional

1. In a large bowl, cream butter and sugar until light and fluffy. Add egg; beat well. Beat in molasses. Combine the flour, baking soda, spices and salt; add to the creamed mixture alternately with 1 cup water, beating well after each addition.
2. Transfer to an ungreased 9x13-in. baking pan; sprinkle with brown sugar. In a microwave, heat butter and remaining water until butter is melted; carefully pour over batter.
3. Bake cake at 350° for 35-40 minutes or until a toothpick inserted near the center comes out clean. Cool on a wire rack. Serve warm. Garnish with whipped cream and cinnamon if desired.

Chocolate Peanut Butter Cake

The original recipe called for a cake made from scratch, but I use cake mix to save time. Our family loves this rich dessert.

—PATRICIA ECKARD

SINGERS GLEN, VA

PREP: 15 MIN.
BAKE: 35 MIN. + COOLING
MAKES: 12-15 SERVINGS

- 1 **package devil's food cake mix (regular size)**
- 1 **cup creamy peanut butter**
- 1 **tablespoon canola oil**
- 1 **can (16 ounces) chocolate frosting**

1. Prepare and bake cake according to the package directions, using a greased 9x13-in. baking pan.
2. In a small bowl, combine peanut butter and oil until smooth; spread over warm cake. Cool completely on a wire rack.
3. In a microwave, heat frosting on high for 25-30 seconds or until pourable; stir until smooth. Carefully pour and spread over peanut butter layer. Let stand until set.
NOTE *Reduced-fat peanut butter is not recommended for this recipe.*

Mrs. Thompson's Carrot Cake

I received this recipe from the mother of a patient I cared for back in 1972 in St. Paul, Minnesota. It was, and is, the best carrot cake I have ever tasted.

—**BECKY WACHOB** KELLY, WY

PREP: 30 MIN. • **BAKE:** 35 MIN.
MAKES: 15 SERVINGS

- 3 **cups shredded carrots**
- 1 **can (20 ounces) crushed pineapple, well-drained**
- 2 **cups sugar**
- 1 **cup canola oil**
- 4 **eggs**
- 2 **cups all-purpose flour**
- 2 **teaspoons baking soda**
- 2 **teaspoons ground cinnamon**

FROSTING

- 1 **package (8 ounces) cream cheese, softened**
- ¼ **cup butter, softened**
- 2 **teaspoons vanilla extract**
- 3¾ **cups confectioners' sugar**

1. In a large bowl, beat the first five ingredients until well blended. In another bowl, mix the flour, baking soda and cinnamon; gradually beat into carrot mixture.

2. Transfer to a greased 9x13-in. baking pan. Bake at 350° for 35-40 minutes or until a toothpick inserted in center comes out clean. Cool completely in pan on a wire rack.

3. For frosting, in a large bowl, beat the cream cheese, butter and vanilla until blended. Gradually beat in confectioners' sugar until smooth. Spread over cake. Refrigerate leftovers.

Pineapple Orange Cake

Here's one of my favorite cakes...it's very satisfying. I've been making healthier swaps into the recipe for years and now it's almost guilt-free.
—**PAM SJOLUND** COLUMBIA, SC

PREP: 15 MIN.
BAKE: 25 MIN. + CHILLING
MAKES: 15 SERVINGS

- 1 package yellow cake mix (regular size)
- 1 can (11 ounces) mandarin oranges, undrained
- 4 egg whites
- ½ cup unsweetened applesauce

TOPPING

- 1 can (20 ounces) crushed pineapple, undrained
- 1 package (1 ounce) sugar-free instant vanilla pudding mix
- 1 carton (8 ounces) reduced-fat whipped topping

1. In a large bowl, beat the cake mix, oranges, egg whites and applesauce on low speed for 2 minutes. Pour into a 9x13-in. baking dish coated with cooking spray.
2. Bake at 350° for 25-30 minutes or until a toothpick inserted near the center comes out clean. Cool on a wire rack.
3. In a bowl, combine the pineapple and pudding mix. Fold in whipped topping just until blended. Spread over cake. Refrigerate for at least 1 hour before serving.

Flourless Chocolate Cake with Peanut Butter Ice Cream

This luscious dessert features a chocolaty cake, peanut butter ice cream and a smooth coffee-flavored sauce. Every element is convenient to make in advance.

—REBEKAH BEYER SABETHA, KS

PREP: 45 MIN. + FREEZING
BAKE: 20 MIN. + COOLING
MAKES: 12 SERVINGS

ICE CREAM
- ½ cup 2% milk
- ¼ cup sugar
- 2 egg yolks, beaten
- ¼ cup creamy peanut butter
- ¾ cup half-and-half cream
- 1 teaspoon vanilla extract

CAKE
- 5 eggs, separated
- 1 pound semisweet chocolate, chopped
- ½ cup plus 2 tablespoons butter, cubed
- ¼ teaspoon cream of tartar
- 1 tablespoon sugar

SAUCE
- 2 egg yolks
- 2 tablespoons sugar
- 1 cup heavy whipping cream
- 2 teaspoons instant espresso powder
- 1½ teaspoons coffee liqueur
  Chopped chocolate

1. In a large heavy saucepan, heat milk and sugar until bubbles form around sides of pan. Whisk a small amount of hot mixture into egg yolks. Return all to the pan, whisking constantly.

2. Cook and stir over low heat until mixture is thickened and coats the back of a spoon. Quickly transfer to a bowl; stir in peanut butter until blended. Place in ice water and stir for 2 minutes. Stir in cream and vanilla. Refrigerate for several hours or overnight.

3. Pour into cylinder of ice cream freezer; freeze according to the manufacturer's directions.

4. For cake, let egg whites stand at room temperature for 30 minutes. In a small heavy saucepan, melt chocolate and butter over medium-low heat. Remove from the heat; whisk in egg yolks.

5. In a large bowl, beat egg whites and cream of tartar on medium speed until soft peaks form. Gradually beat in sugar on high until stiff glossy peaks form and sugar is dissolved. Fold into chocolate mixture.

6. Transfer to a greased and floured 9x13-in. baking pan. Bake at 325° for 20-25 minutes or until set. Cool completely.

7. Meanwhile, for sauce, in a small bowl, whisk egg yolks and sugar. In a small saucepan, heat heavy cream and espresso powder until bubbles form around the sides of pan. Whisk a small amount into yolk mixture. Return all to pan, whisking constantly. Cook until thickened. Remove from the heat; stir in liqueur. Refrigerate until serving.

8. Serve cake with ice cream and sauce. Garnish servings with chopped chocolate.

Chocolate Mallow Cake

Nothing compares to homemade cake, especially when it's topped with sweet marshmallow frosting like this one.

—**EDNA HOFFMAN** HEBRON, IN

PREP: 1 HOUR
BAKE: 30 MIN. + CHILLING
MAKES: 15 SERVINGS

- ⅓ cup shortening
- 1 cup sugar
- ½ cup packed brown sugar
- 2 eggs
- 2 ounces unsweetened chocolate, melted and cooled
- 1 teaspoon vanilla extract
- 1 cup buttermilk
- ¼ cup water
- 1¾ cups cake flour
- 1½ teaspoons baking soda
- ¾ teaspoon salt

FILLING
- 1 cup packed brown sugar
- 3 tablespoons all-purpose flour
- 1 cup milk
- 2 egg yolks, beaten
- 2 tablespoons butter
- 1 teaspoon vanilla extract
- ½ cup chopped pecans

FROSTING
- 1½ cups sugar
- 2 egg whites
- ⅓ cup water
- 1 tablespoon light corn syrup
- ¼ teaspoon cream of tartar
- 2 cups miniature marshmallows
- 1 ounce unsweetened chocolate, melted

1. In a large bowl, cream shortening and sugars. Add eggs, one at a time, beating well after each addition. Beat in chocolate and vanilla. Combine buttermilk and water. Combine the cake flour, baking soda and salt; add to creamed mixture alternately with buttermilk mixture.

2. Pour into a greased and floured 9x13-in. baking pan. Bake at 350° for 30-35 minutes or until a toothpick inserted in center comes out clean. Cool for 10 minutes before removing from pan to a wire rack.

3. For filling, in a small saucepan, combine brown sugar and all-purpose flour. Stir in milk until smooth. Cook and stir over medium-high heat until thickened and bubbly. Reduce heat; cook and stir 2 minutes longer. Remove from heat. Stir a small amount of hot mixture into egg yolks; return all to pan, stirring constantly. Bring to a gentle boil; cook and stir 2 minutes longer.

4. Remove from heat. Gently stir in butter and vanilla. Cool to room temperature without stirring. Spread over cake to within ½ in. of edges; top with pecans. Refrigerate until set.

5. For frosting, in a heavy saucepan over low heat, combine the sugar, egg whites, water, corn syrup and cream of tartar. With a portable mixer, beat on low speed for 1 minute. Continue beating on low over low heat for 8-10 minutes or until frosting reaches 160°.

6. Pour into the large bowl of a heavy-duty stand mixer; add marshmallows. Beat on high for 7-9 minutes or until stiff peaks form. Spread over cake. Pipe thin lines of melted chocolate over cake; pull a toothpick through lines in alternating directions.

Chunky Apple Snack Cake

We enjoy this cake as a snack, in lunches or as a scrumptious dessert when warmed and topped with a scoop of low-fat ice cream. If the batter seems overly thick, don't worry, once you stir in the apples it loosens up.

—**CINDY BEBERMAN** ORLAND PARK, IL

PREP: 30 MIN.
BAKE: 25 MIN. + COOLING
MAKES: 20 SERVINGS

- 2 **eggs**
- ½ **cup packed brown sugar**
- 6 **tablespoons butter, melted**
- ¼ **cup sugar**
- 2 **teaspoons vanilla extract**
- 2 **cups all-purpose flour**
- 2 **teaspoons ground cinnamon**
- 1 **teaspoon baking powder**
- 1 **teaspoon baking soda**
- ¼ **teaspoon salt**
- 4 **medium Gala or Fuji apples, shredded (about 4 cups)**
- ¾ **cup chopped pecans**

1. Preheat oven to 350°. Coat a 9x13-in. baking pan with cooking spray. In a large bowl, beat eggs, brown sugar, melted butter, sugar and vanilla until well blended. In another bowl, whisk flour, cinnamon, baking powder, baking soda and salt; gradually beat into egg mixture. Stir in apples and pecans.

2. Transfer to prepared pan. Bake 25-30 minutes or until a toothpick inserted in center comes out clean. Cool in pan on a wire rack.

Potluck Banana Cake

I found this recipe more than five years ago and have been making it for family gatherings ever since. The coffee-flavored frosting complements the moist banana cake.

—KATHY HOFFMAN TOPTON, PA

PREP: 25 MIN.
BAKE: 35 MIN. + COOLING
MAKES: 12-15 SERVINGS

- ½ cup butter, softened
- 1 cup sugar
- 2 eggs
- 1 teaspoon vanilla extract
- 2 cups all-purpose flour
- 2 teaspoons baking soda
- ½ teaspoon salt
- 1½ cups mashed ripe bananas (about 3 medium)
- 1 cup (8 ounces) sour cream

COFFEE FROSTING

- ⅓ cup butter, softened
- 2½ cups confectioners' sugar
- 2 teaspoons instant coffee granules
- 2 to 3 tablespoons milk

1. In a large bowl, cream butter and sugar until light and fluffy. Add eggs, one at a time, beating well after each addition. Stir in vanilla. Combine the flour, baking soda and salt; add to creamed mixture alternately with bananas and sour cream, beating well after each addition.
2. Pour into a greased 9x13-in. baking dish. Bake at 350° for 35-40 minutes or until a toothpick inserted near the center comes out clean. Cool completely on a wire rack.

3. For frosting, in a small bowl, beat butter and confectioners' sugar until smooth. Dissolve coffee granules in milk; add to butter mixture and beat until smooth. Spread over cake.

⑤ INGREDIENTS

Cherry Cake

A friend brought this pretty pink cake to work for a birthday party. You can use any flavor of yogurt, but I always stick with cherry because it's so delicious!

—JUDY LENTZ EMMETSBURG, IA

PREP: 10 MIN.
BAKE: 30 MIN. + COOLING
MAKES: 15 SERVINGS

- 1 package white cake mix (regular size)
- 1¼ cups water
- 4 egg whites
- ⅓ cup canola oil
- 1½ cups (12 ounces) fat-free cherry yogurt, divided
- 1 carton (8 ounces) frozen fat-free whipped topping, thawed

1. In a large bowl, combine first four ingredients; beat on low speed for 30 seconds. Beat on medium for 2 minutes. Fold in ¾ cup yogurt.
2. Pour into a greased 9x13-in. baking dish. Bake at 350° for 30-35 minutes or until a toothpick inserted near the center comes out clean. Cool.
3. Place remaining yogurt in a small bowl; fold in whipped topping. Spread over cake.

Caramel-Pecan Chocolate Cake

No one will believe this ooey-gooey chocolate cake is actually light. The decadent treat features two layers of chocolate cake with creamy caramel in between.

—**RUTH LEE** TROY, ON

PREP: 35 MIN.
BAKE: 35 MIN. + COOLING
MAKES: 24 SERVINGS

- 1 **package (14 ounces) caramels**
- 1 **can (14 ounces) fat-free sweetened condensed milk**
- ⅓ **cup butter**
- 4 **ounces unsweetened chocolate, chopped**
- ⅓ **cup canola oil**
- 1½ **cups water**

- ⅓ **cup unsweetened applesauce**
- 2 **egg whites**
- 1 **egg**
- 2 **teaspoons vanilla extract**
- 2½ **cups all-purpose flour**
- 1⅓ **cups sugar**
- ⅓ **cup sugar blend**
- 1 **teaspoon baking soda**
- 1 **teaspoon salt**
- ¾ **cup chopped pecans, toasted**
- 1 **teaspoon confectioners' sugar**

1. In a small heavy saucepan, heat the caramels, milk and butter over low heat until caramels are melted and mixture is smooth, stirring frequently; set aside.

2. In a large bowl, combine chocolate and oil. Stir in the water, applesauce, egg whites, egg and vanilla. Combine the flour, sugar, sugar blend, baking soda and salt; gradually add to chocolate mixture until blended.

3. Pour half of the batter into a 9x13-in. baking pan well coated with cooking spray. Bake at 350° for 14-18 minutes or until center is set. Spread caramel mixture evenly over cake; top with remaining batter. Sprinkle with pecans.

4. Bake 18-23 minutes longer or until a toothpick inserted near the center of the top layer comes out clean. Cool on a wire rack. Sprinkle with confectioners' sugar.

NOTE *This recipe was tested with Splenda sugar blend.*

Pear-Cranberry Gingerbread Cake

PREP: 25 MIN.
BAKE: 35 MIN. + COOLING
MAKES: 15 SERVINGS

- ¾ cup butter, melted, divided
- ⅔ cup packed brown sugar, divided
- 3 medium pears, sliced
- 2 cups fresh or frozen cranberries, thawed
- ¾ cup brewed chai tea
- ½ cup sugar
- ½ cup molasses
- 1 egg
- 2 cups all-purpose flour
- 1 teaspoon ground ginger
- 1 teaspoon ground cinnamon
- ½ teaspoon salt
- ½ teaspoon baking soda
- ½ teaspoon ground cloves
- ¼ teaspoon ground nutmeg

1. Pour ¼ cup melted butter into a 9x13-in. baking dish; sprinkle with ⅓ cup brown sugar. Arrange pears and cranberries in a single layer over brown sugar.
2. In a small bowl, beat the brewed tea, sugar, molasses, egg and remaining butter and brown sugar until well blended. Combine the remaining ingredients; gradually beat into tea mixture until blended.
3. Spoon over pears. Bake at 350° for 35-45 minutes or until a toothpick inserted near the center comes out clean. Cool for 10 minutes before inverting onto a serving plate. Serve warm.

Macadamia Toffee Snack Cake

Ever since I worked in a restaurant preparing desserts, I've been collecting recipes that make people happy. This incredible cake is loaded with white chocolate chips, macadamia nuts and coconut.
—**MARIE ZAJDOWICZ** RIVA, MD

PREP: 15 MIN.
BAKE: 30 MIN. + COOLING
MAKES: 20 SERVINGS

- 2 cups all-purpose flour
- 1½ cups packed brown sugar
- ½ cup cold butter, cubed
- 1 teaspoon baking powder
- ½ teaspoon salt
- 1 egg
- 1 cup milk
- 1 teaspoon vanilla extract
- 1 cup white baking chips
- ½ cup chopped macadamia nuts
- ¼ cup flaked coconut

1. In a large bowl, combine flour and brown sugar. Cut in butter until mixture resembles coarse crumbs. Set aside 1 cup for topping. Add baking powder and salt to remaining crumb mixture. In another bowl, whisk egg, milk and vanilla. Stir into crumb mixture just until moistened.
2. Transfer to a greased 9x13-in. baking pan; sprinkle with topping mixture, baking chips, nuts and coconut. Bake at 350° for 30-35 minutes or until golden brown and edges pull away from sides of pan. Cool on a wire rack.

I love the warm, spicy flavors and festive fall fruits in this upside-down gingerbread cake. It has a place at any special-occasion buffet.
—**GLENDA JARBOEK** OROVILLE, CA

Orange-Cola Chocolate Cake

Substituting cola for water, adding a hint of orange flavor and serving each slice with a dipped strawberry turns a simple mix into a spectacular dessert people love!

—**STEPHANIE VOGEL** LINCOLN, NE

PREP: 25 MIN.
BAKE: 30 MIN. + COOLING
MAKES: 12 SERVINGS

- 1 package devil's food cake mix (regular size)
- 3 eggs
- 1⅓ cups cola
- ½ cup canola oil
- 1 tablespoon orange extract

CHOCOLATE-COVERED STRAWBERRIES

- ½ cup semisweet chocolate chips
- 1 teaspoon shortening
- 12 fresh strawberries

FROSTING

- ½ cup butter, softened
- 3¾ cups confectioners' sugar
- 3 tablespoons instant chocolate drink mix

- ¼ cup cola
- ½ teaspoon orange extract

1. In a large bowl, combine the cake mix, eggs, cola, oil and extract. Beat on low speed for 30 seconds; beat on medium for 2 minutes. Pour into a greased 9x13-in. baking pan.

2. Bake at 350° for 30-35 minutes or until a toothpick inserted near the center comes out clean. Cool on a wire rack.

3. In a small microwave-safe bowl, melt chocolate chips and shortening; stir until smooth. Wash strawberries and pat dry. Dip each strawberry into chocolate; allow excess to drip off. Place on a waxed paper-lined baking sheet; refrigerate until set, about 30 minutes.

4. In a small bowl, combine the frosting ingredients; beat until smooth. Frost cake. Garnish each serving with a chocolate-covered strawberry.

NOTE *Diet cola is not recommended for this recipe.*

Poppy Seed Cake

This tender cake is chock-full of poppy seeds. Cream cheese icing adds the sweet final touch.

—**DARLIS WILFER** WEST BEND, WI

PREP: 20 MIN. + STANDING
BAKE: 25 MIN. + COOLING
MAKES: 12-15 SERVINGS

- ⅓ cup poppy seeds
- 1 cup 2% milk
- 4 egg whites
- ¾ cup shortening
- 1½ cups sugar
- 1 teaspoon vanilla extract
- 2 cups all-purpose flour
- 2 teaspoons baking powder

CREAM CHEESE FROSTING

- 1 package (8 ounces) cream cheese, softened
- ½ cup butter, softened
- 1 teaspoon vanilla extract
- 2 cups confectioners' sugar

1. Soak poppy seeds in milk for 30 minutes. Place egg whites in a large bowl; let stand at room temperature for 30 minutes.

2. In a bowl, cream shortening and sugar until light and fluffy. Beat in vanilla. Combine flour and baking powder; add to creamed mixture alternately with poppy seed mixture, beating well after each addition. Beat egg whites until soft peaks form; fold into batter.

3. Pour into a greased 9x13-in. baking dish. Bake at 375° for 25-30 minutes or until a toothpick inserted near the center comes out clean. Cool.

4. For frosting, in a bowl, beat the cream cheese, butter and vanilla until smooth. Gradually beat in confectioners' sugar. Frost cake.

Strawberry-Rhubarb Flip Cake

My friend Dave always brought two strawberry-rhubarb cakes to work to celebrate his birthday. He'd use up rhubarb growing in the yard and treat his co-workers.

—CHARLENE SCHWARTZ

MAPLE PLAIN, MN

PREP: 20 MIN.
BAKE: 40 MIN. + COOLING
MAKES: 12 SERVINGS

- 1 cup packed brown sugar
- 3 tablespoons quick-cooking tapioca
- 6 cups sliced fresh or frozen rhubarb, thawed
- 3 cups sliced fresh or frozen strawberries, thawed
- ½ cup butter, softened
- 1 cup sugar
- 2 eggs
- 1 teaspoon vanilla extract
- 2 cups all-purpose flour
- 2½ teaspoons baking powder
- ¼ teaspoon salt
- 1 cup 2% milk
  Sweetened whipped cream or vanilla ice cream, optional

1. Preheat oven to 350°. In a large bowl, mix brown sugar and tapioca. Add rhubarb and strawberries; toss to coat. Let stand 15 minutes.

2. Meanwhile, in a large bowl, cream butter and sugar until light and fluffy. Add eggs, one at a time, beating well after each addition. Beat in vanilla. In another bowl, whisk flour, baking powder and salt; add to creamed mixture alternately with milk, beating well after each addition.

3. Transfer rhubarb mixture to a greased 9x13-in. baking dish; pour batter over top. Bake 40-45 minutes or until a toothpick inserted in center comes out clean. Cool completely in pan on a wire rack. Invert each piece onto a serving plate.

NOTE *If using frozen rhubarb, measure rhubarb while still frozen, then thaw completely. Drain in a colander, but do not press liquid out.*

Zucchini Chip Chocolate Cake

This moist, chocolaty cake makes good use of zucchini. Serve it alone or with fresh berries.

—WEDA MOSELLIE PHILLIPSBURG, NJ

PREP: 25 MIN.
BAKE: 45 MIN. + COOLING
MAKES: 15 SERVINGS

- ½ cup butter, softened
- 1¾ cups sugar
- ½ cup canola oil
- 2 eggs
- 1 teaspoon vanilla extract
- 1 cup 2% milk
- ½ cup buttermilk
- 2½ cups all-purpose flour
- ¼ cup baking cocoa
- 1 teaspoon baking soda
- ½ teaspoon baking powder
- ½ teaspoon salt
- 2 cups shredded zucchini
- ½ cup semisweet chocolate chips
    Confectioners' sugar

1. Preheat oven to 325°. In a large bowl, beat butter, sugar and oil until smooth. Add eggs, one at a time, beating well after each addition. Beat in vanilla. Combine milk and buttermilk. Combine flour, cocoa, baking soda, baking powder and salt; add to batter alternately with milk mixture, beating well after each addition. Fold in zucchini. Transfer to a greased 9x13-in. baking pan. Sprinkle with chips. Bake 45-50 minutes or until a toothpick inserted in center comes out clean. Cool cake on a wire rack. Dust with confectioners' sugar.

Lemon Crumb Cake

If you like the tangy flavor of lemon, you won't be able to get enough of this citrus delight! The tender crumb-topped cake is the perfect finale to a special springtime brunch or dinner.

—KATHERINE WOLLGAST
FLORISSANT, MO

PREP: 20 MIN.
BAKE: 30 MIN. + COOLING
MAKES: 20 SERVINGS

- 2 cups buttermilk
- 1 cup sugar
- 2 eggs
- 2 tablespoons butter, melted
- 2 teaspoons vanilla extract
- 3 cups all-purpose flour
- 1¼ teaspoons baking powder
- 1 teaspoon salt
- ½ teaspoon baking soda
- 1 can (15¾ ounces) lemon pie filling

TOPPING

- 1 cup all-purpose flour
- ⅔ cup sugar
- ⅓ cup cold butter, cubed
- ¼ cup sliced almonds, toasted
    Reduced-fat vanilla ice cream, optional

1. In a large bowl, beat the first five ingredients until well blended. In a small bowl, combine the flour, baking powder, salt and baking soda; gradually beat into buttermilk mixture until blended. Pour into a 9x13-in. baking pan coated with cooking spray. Drop pie filling by teaspoonfuls over batter.
2. In a small bowl, combine flour and sugar. Cut in butter until crumbly. Stir in almonds; sprinkle over batter. Bake at 350° for 30-35 minutes or until a toothpick inserted near the center comes out clean.
3. Cool for 10 minutes on a wire rack. Serve warm with ice cream if desired.

Cranberry-Walnut Cake with Butter Sauce

The cake is tart, but the warm butter sauce creates the ideal balance of sweet and tangy. Pour the sauce over the cake just before serving.

—KATIE KAHRE DULUTH, MN

PREP: 25 MIN.
BAKE: 30 MIN. + COOLING
MAKES: 15 SERVINGS

- 3 **tablespoons butter, softened**
- 1 **cup sugar**
- ½ **cup water**
- 2 **cups all-purpose flour**
- 3 **teaspoons baking powder**
- 1 **teaspoon salt**
- ½ **cup evaporated milk**
- 1 **package (12 ounces) fresh or frozen cranberries**
- 1 **cup chopped walnuts**

SAUCE

- 2 **cups sugar**
- 1 **cup butter, cubed**
- ¼ **cup evaporated milk**
- 1 **teaspoon vanilla extract.**

1. In a large bowl, beat butter and sugar until crumbly, about 2 minutes. Gradually beat in water. In another bowl, whisk flour, baking powder and salt; add to butter mixture alternately with milk, beating well after each addition. Fold in cranberries and walnuts (batter will be thick).

2. Spread into a greased 9x13-in. baking pan. Bake at 375° for 30-35 minutes or until a toothpick inserted in center comes out clean. Cool.
In a saucepan, bring sauce ingredients to a boil over medium heat; stir constantly to dissolve sugar. Serve with cake.

The perfect combination of sweet and tart, this gorgeous dessert delights kids and grown-ups alike. It'll keep a few days and is actually better the second day, so go ahead and make it a day ahead.
—**SHERRY CONLEY NOEL** HANTS COUNTY, NS

Pineapple Cranberry Upside-Down Cake

PREP: 20 MIN.
BAKE: 50 MIN. + COOLING
MAKES: 15 SERVINGS

- 1 **cup packed brown sugar**
- ½ **cup butter, melted**
- 1 **can (20 ounces) sliced pineapple, drained**
- 1 **cup fresh or frozen cranberries**

CAKE

- 1 **cup butter, softened**
- 1¼ **cups sugar**
- 2 **eggs**
- 1 **teaspoon vanilla extract**
- 2 **cups all-purpose flour**
- 2 **teaspoons baking powder**
- 1 **teaspoon salt**
- 1 **teaspoon ground cinnamon**
- ½ **teaspoon ground allspice**
- ¾ **cup sour cream**
- 1 **cup fresh or frozen cranberries, halved**
  Sweetened whipped cream, optional

1. Preheat oven to 350°. In a small bowl, mix brown sugar and butter; spread onto the bottom of a greased 9x13-in. baking pan. Top with pineapple slices. Place a whole cranberry in the center of each pineapple; sprinkle remaining cranberries around pineapple.

2. For cake, in a large bowl, cream butter and sugar until light and fluffy. Add eggs, one at a time, beating well after each addition. Beat in vanilla. In another bowl, whisk flour, baking powder, salt, cinnamon and allspice; add to creamed mixture alternately with sour cream, beating well after each addition.

Fold in cranberries; spoon over pineapple.

3. Bake 50-60 minutes or until a toothpick inserted in center comes out clean. Cool 10 minutes; invert onto a serving plate. Serve warm; if desired, top with whipped cream.

Toffee Poke Cake

This recipe is a favorite among family and friends. I enjoy making it because it is simple. The caramel tastes wonderful with the smooth chocolate cake.

—**JEANETTE HOFFMAN** OSHKOSH, WI

PREP: 25 MIN.
BAKE: 25 MIN. + CHILLING
MAKES: 15 SERVINGS

- 1 **package chocolate cake mix (regular size)**
- 1 **jar (17 ounces) butterscotch-caramel ice cream topping**
- 1 **carton (12 ounces) frozen whipped topping, thawed**
- 3 **Heath candy bars (1.4 ounces each), chopped**

1. Prepare and bake cake according to package directions, using a greased 9x13-in. baking pan. Cool on a wire rack.

2. Using the handle of a wooden spoon, poke holes in cake. Pour ¾ cup caramel topping into holes. Spoon remaining caramel over cake. Top with whipped topping. Sprinkle with candy. Refrigerate for at least 2 hours before serving.

Sticky Toffee Pudding with Butterscotch Sauce

Sticky toffee pudding is a classic dessert in Britain. I love that I can enjoy the traditional treat with its rich butterscotch sauce at home.
—**AGNES WARD** STRATFORD, ON

PREP: 30 MIN. + COOLING
BAKE: 30 MIN. • **MAKES:** 15 SERVINGS
(2½ CUPS SAUCE)

- 2 **cups coarsely chopped pitted dates (about 12 ounces)**
- 2½ **cups water**
- 2 **teaspoons baking soda**
- 1⅔ **cups sugar**
- ½ **cup butter, softened**
- 4 **eggs**
- 2 **teaspoons vanilla extract**
- 3¾ **cups all-purpose flour**
- 2 **teaspoons baking powder**

BUTTERSCOTCH SAUCE

- 7 **tablespoons butter, cubed**
- 2¼ **cups packed brown sugar**
- 1 **cup half-and-half cream**

- 1 **tablespoon brandy**
- ¼ **teaspoon vanilla extract**
  Whipped cream, optional

1. In a small saucepan, combine dates and water; bring to a boil. Remove from the heat; stir in baking soda. Cool to lukewarm.
2. In a large bowl, cream sugar and butter until light and fluffy. Add eggs, one at a time, beating well after each addition. Beat in vanilla. In another bowl, mix flour and baking powder; gradually add to creamed mixture. Stir in date mixture.
3. Transfer to a greased 9x13-in. baking pan. Bake at 350° for 30-40 minutes or until a toothpick inserted in center comes out clean. Cool slightly in pan on a wire rack.
4. Meanwhile, in a small saucepan, melt butter; add brown sugar and cream. Bring to a boil over medium heat, stirring

constantly. Remove from the heat. Stir in brandy and vanilla. Serve warm with warm cake. If desired, top with whipped cream.

Watergate Cake

The cake was a huge hit the very first time I made it! I wasn't sure I'd like it, but I was hooked immediately. You'll enjoy its light flavor if you're looking for a dessert that's not super sweet.
—**STEPHANIE CURVELO**
NEW BEDFORD, MA

PREP: 10 MIN.
BAKE: 30 MIN. + COOLING
MAKES: 15 SERVINGS

- 1 **package yellow cake mix (regular size)**
- 1 **package (3.4 ounces) instant pistachio pudding mix**
- 1 **cup club soda**
- ½ **cup canola oil**
- 3 **eggs**
- ¾ **cup pistachios**

FROSTING

- 2 **packages (3.4 ounces each) instant pistachio pudding mix**
- 2 **cups heavy whipping cream**
- 1 **cup 2% milk**

1. Preheat oven to 350°. In a large bowl, combine cake mix, pudding mix, club soda, oil and eggs; beat on low speed for 30 seconds. Beat on medium for 2 minutes. Stir in pistachios. Transfer to a greased 9x13-in. baking pan. Bake 30-35 minutes or until a toothpick inserted in center comes out clean. Cool on a wire rack.
2. For frosting, in a small bowl, combine pudding mix, whipping cream and milk; beat until soft peaks form. Spread over cake.

Cuppa Joe Caramel Cake

I get compliments on this cake wherever I take it. It really appeals to adults with its hint of coffee complimented by the warm tastes of brown sugar and caramel.

—**LEIGH DOUTT** PUEBLO WEST, CO

PREP: 30 MIN.
BAKE: 20 MIN. + COOLING
MAKES: 15 SERVINGS

- 1 **cup buttermilk**
- 4 **teaspoons instant coffee granules**
- ½ **cup butter, softened**
- 1 **cup packed brown sugar**
- 2 **eggs**
- 1 **teaspoon vanilla extract**
- 2 **cups all-purpose flour**
- 2 **tablespoons cornstarch**
- 1½ **teaspoons baking powder**
- ½ **teaspoon baking soda**
- ½ **teaspoon salt**
- ¼ **teaspoon ground nutmeg**
- ¾ **cup caramel ice cream topping, divided**

FROSTING
- 1 **tablespoon baking cocoa**
- 2 **teaspoons instant coffee granules**
- ¼ **cup boiling water**
- ½ **cup butter, softened**
- ¼ **cup confectioners' sugar**
- ¾ **cup semisweet chocolate chips, melted**

1. Microwave buttermilk for 30-45 seconds or just until warmed. Stir in coffee granules until dissolved.

2. In a large bowl, cream butter and brown sugar until light and fluffy. Add eggs, one at a time, beating well after each addition. Beat in vanilla. Combine the flour, cornstarch, baking powder, baking soda, salt and nutmeg; add to creamed mixture alternately with buttermilk mixture, beating well after each addition.

3. Transfer to a greased 9x13-in. baking pan. Bake at 350° for 20-25 minutes or until a toothpick inserted near the center comes out clean. Cool on a wire rack for 5 minutes.

4. Using the end of a wooden spoon handle, poke holes in cake 2 in. apart. Pour ½ cup caramel topping into holes. Spoon remaining caramel topping over cake. Cool completely.

5. For frosting, in a small bowl, stir cocoa and coffee granules into boiling water until dissolved; cool to room temperature. In a small bowl, cream butter and confectioners' sugar until light and fluffy. Stir in chocolate and cocoa mixture until well combined. Frost cake.

Devil's Food Cake

My grandmother gave me the recipe for her famous homemade chocolate cake. I remember she often had it when we came over. The creamy chocolate filling makes it delicious, and a fluffy white frosting just puts it over the top.

—BONNIE CAPPER-ECKSTEIN

MAPLE GROVE, MN

PREP: 50 MIN.
BAKE: 30 MIN. + COOLING
MAKES: 12 SERVINGS

- 4 egg whites
- ½ cup butter, softened
- 1¾ cups sugar
- 1 teaspoon vanilla extract
- 2 cups all-purpose flour
- ½ cup baking cocoa
- ½ teaspoon baking soda
- ¼ teaspoon salt
- 1 cup water

PUDDING

- 1 cup sugar
- ¼ cup all-purpose flour
- ½ teaspoon salt
- 2 cups 2% milk
- 2 egg yolks, beaten
- 3 ounces unsweetened chocolate, chopped
- 1 tablespoon butter
- 1 teaspoon vanilla extract

FROSTING

- 1 cup sugar
- 3 egg whites
- 3 tablespoons cold water
- 2 tablespoons light corn syrup
- ½ teaspoon cream of tartar
- ⅛ teaspoon salt
- 1 teaspoon vanilla extract

1. Place egg whites in a large bowl; let stand at room temperature for 30 minutes. Meanwhile, in a large bowl, cream butter and sugar until light and fluffy. Beat in vanilla. Combine the flour, cocoa, baking soda and salt; add to the creamed mixture alternately with water, beating well after each addition.

2. Beat egg whites with clean beaters until stiff peaks form; fold into batter. Transfer to a greased 9x13-in. baking pan. Bake at 350° for 30-35 minutes or until a toothpick inserted near the center comes out clean. Cool on a wire rack.

3. For pudding, in a large heavy saucepan, combine the sugar, flour and salt. Stir in milk until smooth. Cook and stir over medium-high heat until thickened and bubbly. Reduce the heat to low; cook and stir 2 minutes longer. Remove from the heat.

4. Stir a small amount of hot mixture into egg yolks; return all to the pan, stirring constantly. Bring to a gentle boil; cook and stir 2 minutes longer. Remove from the heat. Stir in chocolate until smooth. Stir in the butter and vanilla. Cool to room temperature, stirring occasionally. Spread over cake.

5. In a large heavy saucepan, combine the sugar, egg whites, water, corn syrup, cream of tartar and salt over low heat. With a hand mixer, beat on low speed for 1 minute. Continue beating on low over low heat until frosting reaches 160°, about 8-10 minutes.

6. Pour into a large bowl; add vanilla. Beat on high until stiff peaks form, about 7 minutes. Spread over cake. Store in the refrigerator.

Billie's Southern Sweet Potato Cake

I made this cake for my kids when they were younger and they told me, "Mommy, you're the best baker." Little did they know that their sweet potato dessert was my first attempt at homemade cake!

—BILLIE WILLIAMS-HENDERSON
BOWIE, MD

PREP: 25 MIN.
BAKE: 40 MIN. + COOLING
MAKES: 20 SERVINGS

- 4 **eggs**
- 2 **cups sugar**
- 2 **cups canola oil**
- 2 **teaspoons vanilla extract**
- 2 **cups all-purpose flour**
- 2 **teaspoons baking soda**
- 2 **teaspoons ground cinnamon**
- ½ **teaspoon ground ginger**
- ½ **teaspoon ground allspice**
- ½ **teaspoon salt**
- 3 **cups shredded peeled sweet potatoes (about 2 medium)**
- 1 **cup finely chopped walnuts**

FROSTING
- 1 **package (8 ounces) cream cheese, softened**
- ½ **cup butter, softened**
- 1 **teaspoon vanilla extract**
- 2 **cups confectioners' sugar**

1. Preheat oven to 350°. Grease a 9x13-in. baking pan. In a large bowl, beat eggs, sugar, oil and vanilla until well blended. In another bowl, whisk flour, baking soda, spices and salt; gradually beat into egg mixture. Stir in sweet potatoes and walnuts.

2. Transfer to prepared pan. Bake 40-45 minutes or until a toothpick inserted in center comes out clean. Cool completely in pan on a wire rack.

3. In a small bowl, beat cream cheese, butter and vanilla until blended. Gradually beat in confectioners' sugar until smooth. Spread over cooled cake. Refrigerate leftovers.

Cinnamon-Sugar Rhubarb Cake

A real crowd-pleaser, this tender cake is chock-full of rhubarb and sprinkled with a sweet cinnamon-sugar topping. Everyone will be asking for the recipe...or seconds!

—MARLYS HABER WHITE, SD

PREP: 30 MIN. • **BAKE:** 40 MIN.
MAKES: 12-15 SERVINGS

- ½ **cup shortening**
- 1 **cup packed brown sugar**
- 1 **cup sugar, divided**
- 1 **egg**
- 1 **teaspoon vanilla extract**
- 2 **cups all-purpose flour**
- 1 **teaspoon baking soda**
- ½ **teaspoon salt**
- 1 **cup buttermilk**
- 2 **cups diced fresh or frozen rhubarb**
- 1 **teaspoon ground cinnamon**

1. In a large bowl, cream the shortening, brown sugar and ½ cup sugar until light and fluffy. Add egg and vanilla; beat for 2 minutes. Combine the flour, baking soda and salt; add to creamed mixture alternately with buttermilk, beating well after each addition. Stir in the rhubarb.

2. Pour into a greased 9x13-in. baking dish. Combine the cinnamon and remaining sugar; sprinkle over batter. Bake at 350° for 40-45 minutes or until a toothpick inserted in center comes out clean. Serve warm. **NOTE** *If using frozen rhubarb, measure rhubarb while still frozen, then thaw completely. Drain in a colander, but do not press liquid out.*

Spice Cake with Salted Caramel Icing

As a busy mom, I was always looking for baking shortcuts. When I found this easy snack cake, I knew I'd hit the jackpot. I still make the recipe for my kids and grandkids.

—ELLEN HARTMAN CHICO, CA

PREP: 20 MIN.
BAKE: 15 MIN. + COOLING
MAKES: 2 DOZEN

- 1 **package spice cake mix (regular size)**
- ¾ **cup butter, melted**
- ⅓ **cup evaporated milk**
- 1 **egg**

FROSTING

- ⅓ **cup packed brown sugar**
- ⅓ **cup evaporated milk**
- ¼ **cup butter, cubed**
- 2 **cups confectioners' sugar**
- 1 **teaspoon vanilla extract**
- ½ **teaspoon sea salt**

1. Preheat oven to 350°. Grease a 9x13-in. baking pan. In a large bowl, combine cake mix, butter, milk and egg; beat on low speed 30 seconds. Beat on medium 2 minutes (batter will be thick).
2. Transfer to prepared pan. Bake 15-20 minutes or until a toothpick inserted in center comes out clean. Cool in pan on a wire rack.
3. For frosting, in a large saucepan, combine brown sugar, milk and butter over medium heat; bring to a boil, stirring occasionally. Reduce heat; simmer, uncovered, 3 minutes.
4. Remove from heat. Stir in confectioners' sugar and vanilla. Immediately spread icing over cake; sprinkle with salt. Cool completely before cutting.

Coconut Cream Yummy Cake

I found this recipe as a kid in one of my mother's cookbooks. I didn't make it until I was older, but now it's a mainstay at Christmas. Sometimes I tint the coconut for the holiday.

—ANGELA RENAE FOX GOBER, TX

PREP: 30 MIN.
BAKE: 40 MIN. + CHILLING
MAKES: 15 SERVINGS

- 6 **egg whites**
- ¾ **cup butter, softened**
- 1⅓ **cups sugar**
- 1 **cup coconut milk**
- ½ **cup 2% milk**
- 2 **teaspoons vanilla extract**
- 2¼ **cups cake flour**
- 2½ **teaspoons baking powder**
- 1 **teaspoon salt**

SYRUP

- 1 **can (13.66 ounces) coconut milk**
- 1 **can (14 ounces) sweetened condensed milk**

TOPPING

- 1½ **cups heavy whipping cream**
- 3 **tablespoons confectioners' sugar**
- ¼ **teaspoon vanilla extract**
  Flaked coconut

1. Place the egg whites in a large bowl; let stand at room temperature for 30 minutes. In another large bowl, cream butter and sugar until light and fluffy. Combine the coconut milk, milk and vanilla. Combine the flour, baking powder and salt; add to creamed mixture alternately with milk mixture.
2. With clean beaters, beat egg whites on medium speed until soft peaks form. Gradually fold into batter. Spread into a greased 9x13-in. baking pan.
3. Bake at 350° for 40-45 minutes or until cake springs back when lightly touched. Place pan on a wire rack.
4. Poke holes in cake with a skewer, about ½ in. apart. Combine syrup ingredients; slowly pour over cake, allowing mixture to absorb into cake. Let stand for 30 minutes. Cover and refrigerate for 2 hours.
5. In a large bowl, beat cream until it begins to thicken. Add confectioners' sugar and vanilla; beat until soft peaks form. Spread over cake; sprinkle with coconut.

TOP TIP

Sweetened condensed milk is milk with most of the water cooked off, to which sugar (up to 45% by weight) has been added. It's generally used in candy and dessert recipes. Evaporated milk is concentrated in the same way, but doesn't contain added sugar. It lends rich texture to foods without the fat of cream.

CokeCola Cake

We live in Coca-Cola country, where everyone loves a chocolaty, moist sheet cake made with the iconic soft drink. Our rich version does the tradition proud.

—HEIDI JOBE CARROLLTON, GA

PREP: 25 MIN. • **BAKE:** 25 MIN.
MAKES: 15 SERVINGS

- 2 **cups all-purpose flour**
- 2 **cups sugar**
- 1 **teaspoon baking soda**
- ½ **teaspoon salt**
- ½ **teaspoon ground cinnamon**
- 1 **can (12 ounces) cola**
- 1 **cup butter, cubed**
- ¼ **cup baking cocoa**
- 2 **eggs**
- ½ **cup buttermilk**
- 1 **teaspoon vanilla extract**

GLAZE
- 1 **can (12 ounces) cola**
- ½ **cup butter, cubed**
- ¼ **cup baking cocoa**
- 4 **cups confectioners' sugar, sifted**

1. Preheat oven to 350°. Grease a 9x13-in. baking pan.

2. In a large bowl, whisk the first five ingredients. In a small saucepan, combine cola, butter and cocoa; bring just to a boil, stirring occasionally. Add to the flour mixture, stirring just until moistened. In a small bowl, whisk eggs, buttermilk and vanilla until blended; whisk into flour mixture.

3. Transfer to prepared pan. Bake at 350° for 25-30 minutes or until a toothpick inserted in center comes out clean.

4. About 15 minutes before cake is done, prepare glaze. In a small saucepan, bring cola to a boil; cook 12-15 minutes or until reduced to ½ cup. Stir in butter and cocoa until butter is melted; remove from heat. Stir in confectioner's sugar until smooth. Pour immediately over hot cake.

4. Bake cake at 350° for 40-45 minutes or until a toothpick inserted near the center comes out clean. Cool on a wire rack. Cut into squares and invert onto serving plates.

Grandma's Lemon Poppy Seed Cake

This is from a collection of family recipes. My granddaughter, Riley, likes that it tastes like lemons and is refreshingly sweet. It's always wonderful.

—**PHYLLIS HARMON** NELSON, WI

PREP: 20 MIN.
BAKE: 30 MIN. + COOLING
MAKES: 15 SERVINGS

- 1 package lemon cake mix (regular size)
- 1 package (3.4 ounces) instant vanilla pudding mix
- 4 eggs
- 1 cup water
- ½ cup canola oil
- ¼ cup poppy seeds

DRIZZLE

- 2 cups confectioners' sugar
- 2 tablespoons water
- 2 tablespoons lemon juice

1. In a large bowl, combine the cake mix, pudding mix, eggs, water and oil; beat on low speed for 30 seconds. Beat on medium for 2 minutes. Fold in poppy seeds. Transfer to a greased and floured 9x13-in. baking pan. Bake at 350° for 30-35 minutes or until a toothpick inserted near the center comes out clean. Cool on a wire rack.

2. For drizzle, in a small bowl, combine the confectioners' sugar, water and lemon juice; drizzle over cake.

Upside-Down German Chocolate Cake

This recipe is from my mother, an excellent baker and cook. When my three brothers and I were growing up, there was always something new to try in the kitchen!

—**JULIANN NELSON** MINNEAPOLIS, MN

PREP: 30 MIN. • **BAKE:** 40 MIN.
MAKES: 12-15 SERVINGS

- 1 package (4 ounces) German sweet chocolate
- ½ cup water
- ½ cup butter, softened
- 1½ cups sugar
- 3 eggs
- 1 teaspoon vanilla extract
- 1 cup (8 ounces) sour cream
- 2½ cups sifted all-purpose flour
- 1 teaspoon baking soda
- ½ teaspoon salt

TOPPING

- 1 cup packed brown sugar
- 1 cup flaked coconut
- ¼ cup butter, cubed
- 1¼ cups water
- 2 cups miniature marshmallows
- 1 cup coarsely chopped pecans or walnuts

1. In a large heavy saucepan, melt chocolate in water over low heat, stirring until smooth. Cool.

2. In a large bowl, cream butter and sugar until fluffy. Add eggs, one at a time, beating well after each addition. Add chocolate and vanilla. Beat in sour cream. Combine the flour, baking soda and salt; gradually add to creamed mixture. Beat for 2 minutes (batter will be thick); set aside.

3. For topping, sprinkle brown sugar and coconut into a greased 9x13-in. baking pan. Melt butter in water; add to pan and mix with sugar and coconut. Sprinkle marshmallows and nuts into the pan. Gently spoon batter over the top.

Eggnog Tres Leches Cake

When the holidays roll around, my family eagerly anticipates tasting this dessert. By poking holes in the cake, you ensure that the creamy eggnog sauce is absorbed into every last crumb.

—JAN VALDEZ CHICAGO, IL

PREP: 40 MIN. + STANDING
BAKE: 25 MIN. + CHILLING
MAKES: 15 SERVINGS

- 1 **package white cake mix (regular size)**
- 1⅓ **cups water**
- 2 **tablespoons canola oil**
- 3 **egg whites**
- 2 **cups eggnog**
- 1 **can (14 ounces) sweetened condensed milk**
- ½ **cup 2% milk**
- 1½ **cups heavy whipping cream**
- ¼ **cup sugar**
- ⅛ **teaspoon ground cinnamon**
- ⅛ **teaspoon ground nutmeg**

1. Preheat oven to 350°. In a large bowl, combine cake mix, water, oil and egg whites; beat on low speed 30 seconds. Beat on medium 2 minutes. Pour into a greased and floured 9x13-in. baking pan.

2. Bake 25-30 minutes or until a toothpick inserted in center comes out clean. Cool on a wire rack. Using a skewer, poke holes in cake 1 in. apart.

3. In a large bowl, combine eggnog, sweetened condensed milk and 2% milk. Pour a scant ¾ cup mixture over cake; let stand 20-30 minutes or until liquid is absorbed. Repeat four times. Cover and refrigerate for 8 hours or overnight.

4. In a large bowl, beat cream until it begins to thicken. Add sugar; beat until soft peaks form. Spread over cake. Sprinkle with cinnamon and nutmeg. Refrigerate leftovers.

NOTE *This recipe was tested with commercially prepared eggnog.*

HOW TO

REMOVE CAKE FROM THE PAN

Grease the pan and line the bottom with parchment paper, trimming to fit. Grease the paper. After baking, cool cake in the pan 10 minutes, then run a knife around the edges of the pan. Invert the pan onto a wire rack and lift up. Peel off the parchment paper and discard. Let the cake cool completely before transferring to a serving plate and frosting.

RITA WINTERBERGER'S
PRETZEL DESSERT
PAGE 229

Desserts

FLO BURTNETT'S PATRIOTIC DESSERT
PAGE 234

MARILEE EVENSON'S PEANUT BUTTER CUSTARD BLAST *PAGE 231*

CAROLINE WAMELINK'S BANANA SUNDAE DESSERT
PAGE 235

White Chocolate-Strawberry Tiramisu

Here's a terrific twist on an Italian dessert featuring a flavor combination my husband and I just can't resist. A litttle too rich for you? Try lightening it up with reduced-fat whipped topping and cream cheese.

—ANNA GINSBERG AUSTIN, TX

START TO FINISH: 30 MIN.
MAKES: 15 SERVINGS

- **2 cups heavy whipping cream**
- **1 package (8 ounces) cream cheese, softened**
- **½ cup (4 ounces) mascarpone cheese**
- **9 ounces white baking chocolate, melted and cooled**
- **1 cup confectioners' sugar, divided**
- **1 teaspoon vanilla extract**
- **2 packages (3 ounces each) ladyfingers, split**
- **⅔ cup orange juice**
- **4 cups sliced fresh strawberries**
  Chocolate syrup, optional

1. In a large bowl, beat cream until soft peaks form. In another bowl, beat cheeses until light and fluffy. Beat in cooled chocolate, ½ cup confectioners' sugar and vanilla. Fold in 2 cups of the whipped cream.
2. Brush half of ladyfingers with half of the orange juice; arrange in a 9x13-in. dish. Spread with 2 cups of cream cheese mixture; top with half of the strawberries. Brush the remaining ladyfingers with remaining orange juice; arrange over berries.

3. Gently stir remaining confectioners' sugar into remaining cream cheese mixture; fold in remaining whipped cream. Spread over ladyfingers. Top with remaining strawberries. Refrigerate until serving. If desired, drizzle with chocolate syrup before serving.

Dirt Dessert

My mom used to serve me this yummy dessert, and I just loved it. It's so fun to eat, and a snap to make. Add some gummy worms on top for the kids if you like.

—KRISTI LINTON BAY CITY, MI

PREP: 30 MIN. + CHILLING
MAKES: 20 SERVINGS

- **1 package (8 ounces) cream cheese, softened**
- **¼ cup butter, softened**
- **1 cup confectioners' sugar**
- **3½ cups cold 2% milk**
- **2 packages (3.4 ounces each) instant vanilla pudding mix**
- **1 carton (12 ounces) frozen whipped topping, thawed**
- **1 package (15½ ounces) Oreo cookies, crushed**
  Shaved white chocolate, optional

1. In a large bowl, beat the cream cheese, butter and confectioners' sugar until smooth. In another bowl, whisk milk and pudding mixes for 2 minutes; let stand 2 minutes or until soft-set. Gradually stir into cream cheese mixture. Fold in the whipped topping.
2. Place 1⅓ cups crushed cookies in an ungreased 9x13-in. dish. Layer with half of pudding mixture and half of remaining cookies. Repeat layers. Chill at least 1 hour before serving. Serve with white chocolate if desired.

Pretzel Dessert

My recipe makes a big batch of this sweet and salty, creamy and crunchy treat. That's fine with my family, because any leftovers are super the next day, too.

—**RITA WINTERBERGER** HUSON, MT

PREP: 20 MIN. + CHILLING
MAKES: 16 SERVINGS

- 2 **cups crushed pretzels, divided**
- ¾ **cup sugar**
- ¾ **cup butter, melted**
- 1 **package (8 ounces) cream cheese, softened**
- 1 **cup confectioners' sugar**
- 1 **carton (8 ounces) frozen whipped topping, thawed**
- 1 **can (21 ounces) cherry pie filling**

1. In a large bowl, toss 1½ cups pretzels with sugar and melted butter. Press into an ungreased 9x13-in. dish.
2. In a large bowl, beat the cream cheese and confectioners' sugar until smooth. Fold in the whipped topping.
3. Spread half of mixture over pretzel layer. Top with pie filling; spread with remaining cream cheese mixture. Sprinkle with remaining pretzels. Refrigerate overnight before serving.

TOP TIP

To crush pretzels or cookies without making a mess, place food in a resealable plastic bag or a clean cereal bag (these are strong and won't puncture). Crush with a rolling pin or can.

Blueberry-Pecan Crisp

Here's the perfect marriage of cake and pie, with the toasted pecans adding an addictive crunch. Be prepared to serve seconds.

—**SHARON PARMA** VICTORIA, TX

PREP: 15 MIN. • **BAKE:** 40 MIN.
MAKES: 15 SERVINGS

- 1 **can (20 ounces) unsweetened crushed pineapple, undrained**
- ½ **cup packed brown sugar**
- 1 **teaspoon ground cinnamon**
- 1 **can (21 ounces) blueberry pie filling**
- 1 **package yellow cake mix (regular size)**
- 1 **cup pecan halves, chopped**
- 1 **cup butter, melted**
  Vanilla ice cream, optional

1. Pour pineapple into a greased 9x13-in. baking dish. Combine brown sugar and cinnamon; sprinkle over pineapple. Top with pie filling. Sprinkle with cake mix and pecans; drizzle with butter.
2. Bake at 350° for 40-50 minutes or until filling is bubbly and topping is golden brown. Serve with ice cream if desired.

Chocolate Almond Dessert

Who wouldn't love this rich and decadent finale? It's absolutely perfect for any special occasion.
—**HEIDI HALL** NORTH SAINT PAUL, MN

PREP: 20 MIN.
COOK: 10 MIN. + CHILLING
MAKES: 15 SERVINGS

- 1 prepared angel food cake (8 to 10 ounces), cut into 1-inch cubes
- 4 cups cold 2% milk
- 2 packages (3.4 ounces each) cook-and-serve chocolate pudding mix
- 1 milk chocolate candy bar (1.55 ounces), chopped
- ¾ cup sliced almonds, toasted, divided
- 1 cup heavy whipping cream, whipped

1. Arrange half of the cake cubes in an ungreased 9x13-in. dish; set aside. In a large saucepan, whisk milk and pudding mixes. Add candy bar. Cook and stir over medium heat until mixture comes to a boil. Cook and stir 1-2 minutes longer or until thickened.

2. Pour half of the pudding over cake cubes. Sprinkle with half of the almonds; cover and refrigerate. Transfer remaining pudding to a small bowl; cover and refrigerate until chilled.

3. Arrange remaining cake cubes over dessert. Whisk chilled pudding; fold in whipped cream. Spread over top and sprinkle with remaining almonds. Cover and refrigerate for at least 1 hour. Cut dessert into squares.

Old-Fashioned Cherry Torte

When my mom was a little girl, my Great-Grandma Alice would make this easy dessert. The torte, with its sweet-salty combination of cherries, meringue and a saltine crust, is still a favorite in our family today.
—**DANIELLE BRANDT** RUTHTON, MN

PREP: 30 MIN. + CHILLING
MAKES: 12 SERVINGS

- 1 cup crushed saltines
- ½ cup butter, melted
- 4 large egg whites
- 1 teaspoon white vinegar
- 1 teaspoon vanilla extract
- ½ cup sugar
- 1 can (21 ounces) cherry pie filling
- 1¾ cups heavy whipping cream, whipped

1. Combine cracker crumbs and butter; press onto the bottom of a greased 9x13-in. baking dish.

2. In a large bowl, beat the egg whites, vinegar and vanilla on medium speed until soft peaks form. Gradually beat in sugar, 1 tablespoon at a time, on high until stiff glossy peaks form and sugar is dissolved. Spread meringue evenly over crust. Bake at 400° for 10 minutes or until golden brown. Cool completely on a wire rack.

3. Spread pie filling over meringue. Top with whipped cream. Refrigerate for at least 2 hours.

Peanut Butter Custard Blast

"Ooey, gooey, great!" is how friends and family describe this chocolate-peanut butter dessert. I appreciate the chilly treat's make-ahead convenience.

—MARILEE EVENSON
WISCONSIN RAPIDS, WI

PREP: 30 MIN.
COOK: 25 MIN. + CHILLING
MAKES: 15 SERVINGS

- 2 **cups Oreo cookie crumbs**
- 2 **tablespoons sugar**
- ⅓ **cup butter, melted**

FILLING

- 1½ **cups sugar**
- ⅓ **cup cornstarch**
- 2 **tablespoons all-purpose flour**
- ½ **teaspoon salt**
- 6 **cups 2% milk**
- 6 **large egg yolks, beaten**
- 1 **cup creamy peanut butter**

TOPPING

- 2 **cups heavy whipping cream**
- 1 **tablespoon confectioners' sugar**
- 6 **peanut butter cups, chopped**
- ½ **cup chopped salted peanuts**
- 2 **tablespoons chocolate syrup**

1. Preheat oven to 375°. In a small bowl, combine cookie crumbs and sugar; stir in butter. Press onto bottom of a greased 9x13-in. baking dish. Bake for 8 minutes or until set. Cool on a wire rack.

2. For filling, in a large saucepan, combine sugar, cornstarch, flour and salt. Stir in milk until smooth. Cook and stir over medium-high heat until thickened and bubbly. Reduce heat; cook and stir 2 minutes. Remove from heat. Stir a small amount of hot mixture into egg yolks; return all to pan, stirring constantly. Bring to a gentle boil; cook and stir 2 minutes.

3. Remove from heat. Stir 1 cup into peanut butter until smooth. Gently stir peanut butter mixture into the pan. Pour over crust. Cool to room temperature. Cover and refrigerate at least 2 hours.

4. In a large bowl, beat cream until it begins to thicken. Add confectioners' sugar; beat until stiff peaks form. Spread over peanut butter mixture. Sprinkle with peanut butter cups and peanuts. Drizzle with the chocolate syrup.

⑤ INGREDIENTS

Black Forest Dump Cake

I make a Black Forest cake the easy way: Dump everything into a dish and let the magic happen. Give it a creamy, pretty topping by reserving two tablespoons of juice from the canned cherries and stirring it into some whipped cream.

—MEGHAN MCDERMOTT
SPRINGFIELD, MO

PREP: 10 MIN. • **BAKE:** 40 MIN.
MAKES: 12 SERVINGS

- 1 can (21 ounces) cherry pie filling
- 1 can (15 ounces) pitted dark sweet cherries, undrained
- 1 chocolate cake mix (regular size)
- ½ cup sliced almonds
- ¾ cup butter, cubed

1. Preheat oven to 375°. Spread pie filling into a greased 9x13-in. baking dish; top with undrained cherries. Sprinkle with cake mix and almonds. Top with cubed butter.

2. Bake 40-50 minutes or until topping is set. Serve warm or at room temperature.

Caramel-Mocha Ice Cream Dessert

You can use any kind of ice cream in this frosty dessert—the possibilities are endless! To keep things simple, substitute chocolate and vanilla for coffee and dulce de leche.

—SCARLETT ELROD NEWNAN, GA

PREP: 45 MIN. + FREEZING
MAKES: 20 SERVINGS

- 10 whole graham crackers
- 1 cup butter, cubed
- 1 cup packed brown sugar
- 1 cup chopped pecans

FILLING

- 1 quart dulce de leche ice cream, softened
- 1 jar (16 ounces) hot fudge ice cream topping, warmed
- 1 quart coffee ice cream, softened
- 1½ cups heavy whipping cream
- ⅓ cup coffee liqueur
  Chocolate curls

1. Arrange crackers in a single layer in a greased 15x10x1-in. baking pan. In a saucepan, melt butter over medium heat. Stir in brown sugar. Bring to a gentle boil; cook and stir for 2 minutes. Remove from the heat and stir in pecans. Pour over crackers; spread to cover crackers.

2. Bake at 350° for 8-10 minutes or until bubbly. Cool completely on a wire rack.

3. Crush cracker mixture into coarse crumbs; sprinkle half into an ungreased 9x13-in. dish. Spread with dulce de leche ice cream. Cover and freeze 1 hour or until firm.

4. Drizzle with ice cream topping and sprinkle with remaining crumb mixture. Cover

and freeze 30 minutes or until ice cream topping is set.

5. Spread with coffee ice cream; freeze. In a small bowl, beat cream until stiff peaks form. Fold in coffee liqueur. Spread over top of dessert. Cover and freeze 4 hours or until firm.

6. Remove from freezer 15 minutes before serving. Garnish with chocolate curls.

Butterfinger Delight

I got the recipe for this wonderful no-bake treat from my mother-in-law—it's my husband's favorite. Friends and family often ask me to bring it to get-togethers, where it's always a big hit.

—LINDA WINTER ENID, OK

PREP: 30 MIN. + CHILLING
MAKES: 12-15 SERVINGS

- 1 cup crushed Ritz crackers (about 30 crackers)
- 1 cup graham cracker crumbs
- 4 Butterfinger candy bars (2.1 ounces each), crushed
- ¾ cup butter, melted
- 1½ cups cold milk
- 2 packages (3.4 ounces each) instant vanilla pudding mix
- 1 quart reduced-fat chocolate frozen yogurt, softened
- 1 carton (12 ounces) frozen whipped topping, thawed, divided

1. In a large bowl, combine the first four ingredients; set aside ½ cup for topping. Press remaining crumb mixture into an ungreased 9x13-in. dish. Chill for 5 minutes.

2. Meanwhile, in a large bowl, whisk milk and pudding mixes for 2 minutes. Let stand for 2 minutes or until set (mixture will be thick). Stir in the frozen yogurt and 1 cup whipped topping until smooth. Spread over crust.

3. Top with remaining whipped topping. Sprinkle with reserved crumb mixture. Refrigerate for 8 hours or overnight.

Cream Puff Cake

With its light, golden crust and yummy filling, this party-size cream puff is one gorgeous crowd-pleaser. Take it to a potluck. Watch friends line up for seconds.

—**KIMBERLY WALLACE** DENNISON, OH

PREP: 25 MIN.
BAKE: 25 MIN. + CHILLING
MAKES: 15 SERVINGS

- 1 **cup water**
- ½ **cup butter, cubed**
- 1 **cup all-purpose flour**
- 4 **large eggs**

FILLING

- 1 **package (8 ounces) cream cheese, softened**
- 2½ **cups 2% milk**
- 3 **packages (3.3 ounces each) instant white chocolate or vanilla pudding mix**
- 1 **carton (8 ounces) frozen whipped topping, thawed**

1. Preheat oven to 400°. In a large saucepan, bring water and butter to a boil. Add flour all at once and stir until a smooth ball forms. Remove from heat; let stand 5 minutes. Add eggs, one at a time, beating well after each addition. Continue beating until smooth and shiny.

2. Transfer to a greased 9x13-in. baking dish. Bake 22-26 minutes or until puffed and golden brown. Cool completely on a wire rack.

3. For filling, in a large bowl, beat cream cheese, milk and pudding mixes until smooth. Spread over crust; refrigerate 20 minutes. Spread with whipped topping. Chill until serving.

Patriotic Dessert

I took this beauty to a luncheon and came home with dozens of requests for the recipe! It was quite a success. People told me it tasted as good as it looked .

—**FLO BURTNETT** GAGE, OK

PREP: 40 MIN. + CHILLING
MAKES: 12-15 SERVINGS

- 1 **cup all-purpose flour**
- 1 **cup finely chopped pecans**
- ½ **cup butter, softened**
- 1 **package (8 ounces) cream cheese, softened**
- 1 **cup confectioners' sugar**
- 1 **carton (8 ounces) frozen whipped topping, thawed, divided**
- 1-½ **cups cold milk**
- 1 **package (5.1 ounces) instant vanilla pudding mix**
- 3 **cups fresh strawberries, halved**
- ½ **cup fresh blueberries**

In a bowl, combine flour, pecans and butter. Press into an ungreased 9x13-in. baking pan. Bake at 350° for 20 minutes. Cool on a wire rack.

4. In a bowl, beat cream cheese and confectioners' sugar. Fold in half of the whipped topping; spread over crust. In a bowl, whisk milk and pudding mix for 2 minutes. Let stand for 2 minutes or until soft-set.

5. Spread over cream cheese layer. Cover with remaining whipped topping. Decorate with strawberries and blueberries to resemble a flag. Chill for at least 1 hour before serving.

Banana Sundae Dessert

You get a taste of chocolate, banana and cherries in every bite of this frosty treat. It does take a while to assemble, but in my book, it's well worth a bit of time!

—CAROLINE WAMELINK
CLEVELAND HEIGHTS, OH

PREP: 25 MIN. + FREEZING
MAKES: 16 SERVINGS

- 1 package (12 ounces) vanilla wafers, crushed
- ½ cup butter, melted
- 2 tablespoons sugar
- 6 cups chocolate chip ice cream, softened if necessary
- 4 large firm bananas, sliced
- 2 jars (11¾ ounces each) hot fudge ice cream topping, divided
- 6 cups strawberry or cherry vanilla ice cream, softened if necessary
  Whipped cream and maraschino cherries

1. In a bowl, mix wafer crumbs, melted butter and sugar; press onto bottom of a 9x13-in. dish. Freeze 15 minutes.

2. Spread chocolate chip ice cream over crust. Layer with bananas and 1½ jars fudge topping (about 1½ cups). Freeze, covered, at least 30 minutes.

3. Spread strawberry ice cream over top. Freeze, covered, 6 hours or overnight.

4. Remove from the freezer 10 minutes before cutting. Warm remaining fudge topping; drizzle over top. Serve with whipped cream and cherries.

Walnut Apple Dessert

The neighbor who shared this recipe with me predicted that I'd serve it often, just as she has for more than 30 years. It's easy to put together and wonderfully fruity. I like to serve it with ice cream or a dollop of whipped cream.

—DIANN MALLEHAN KENTWOOD, MI

PREP: 15 MIN. • **BAKE:** 45 MIN.
MAKES: 12-16 SERVINGS

- 8 cups sliced peeled tart apples (about 6 medium)
- 2¼ cups packed brown sugar, divided
- 2 teaspoons ground cinnamon
- 1 cup butter, softened
- 2 large eggs
- 2 cups all-purpose flour
- 1 cup finely chopped walnuts, divided
  Vanilla ice cream, optional

1. Place apples in a greased 9x13-in. baking dish. Sprinkle with ¼ cup brown sugar and cinnamon. In a bowl, cream butter and remaining brown sugar. Beat in the eggs. Stir in flour and ½ cup walnuts. Spread over apples. Sprinkle with remaining walnuts.

2. Bake at 350° for 45-55 minutes or until the apples are tender. Serve warm with ice cream if desired.

Cherry-Blackberry Crisp

I've also used mulberries instead of blackberries in this old family recipe. Whichever you choose, it's a mouthwatering treat.

—WANDA ALLENSWORTH
WEBSTER CITY, IA

PREP: 20 MIN. + STANDING
BAKE: 55 MIN. • **MAKES:** 15 SERVINGS

- ⅔ cup packed brown sugar
- 2 tablespoons quick-cooking tapioca
- ½ teaspoon almond extract
- ¼ teaspoon ground cinnamon
- 4 cups frozen pitted tart cherries, thawed
- 2 cups frozen unsweetened blackberries, thawed

TOPPING
- 1½ cups all-purpose flour
- 1½ cups sugar
  Dash salt
- ⅔ cup cold butter
- 1½ cups finely chopped walnuts
  Whipped cream

1. In a large bowl, combine the brown sugar, tapioca, extract and cinnamon. Gently stir in cherries and blackberries. Allow to stand for 10 minutes. Pour into a greased 9x13-in. baking dish.

2. In another bowl, combine the flour, sugar and salt. Cut in butter until crumbly. Add walnuts; sprinkle over fruit. Bake, uncovered, at 350° for 55-60 minutes or until topping is golden brown and filling is bubbly. Serve warm with whipped cream.

Autumn Harvest Cobbler

Saying goodbye to summer's peach crisps doesn't have to be sorrowful when there's a delicious fall cobbler waiting for you.

—**NANCY FOUST** STONEBORO, PA

PREP: 35 MIN. • **BAKE:** 15 MIN.
MAKES: 12 SERVINGS

- ½ **cup sugar**
- 1 **teaspoon ground cinnamon**
- ½ **teaspoon salt**
- ½ **teaspoon ground nutmeg**
- 2 **cups cold water, divided**
- 6 **large tart apples, peeled and thinly sliced**
- 1 **cup golden raisins**
- 1 **cup dried apricots, halved**
- 1 **tablespoon lemon juice**
- 2 **tablespoons cornstarch**

TOPPING

- 2 **cups biscuit/baking mix**
- ¾ **cup 2% milk**
- 1 **tablespoon coarse sugar**
- 2 **teaspoons grated lemon peel**
  Whipped cream

1. In a large saucepan, combine the sugar, cinnamon, salt, nutmeg and 1¾ cups water. Bring to a boil. Stir in the apples, raisins, apricots and lemon juice. Return to a boil. Reduce heat; simmer, uncovered, 10 minutes, stirring occasionally.

2. Combine cornstarch and remaining water until smooth. Stir into pan. Bring to a boil; cook and stir for 2 minutes or until thickened. Transfer to a greased 9x13-in. baking dish.

3. In a small bowl, combine biscuit mix and milk just until blended. Drop by tablespoonfuls onto hot apple mixture. Sprinkle with coarse sugar and lemon peel.

4. Bake the cobbler at 400° for 15-20 minutes or until topping is golden brown. Serve warm with whipped cream.

Cranberry-Pear Apple Crisp

PREP: 20 MIN. • **BAKE:** 1 HOUR
MAKES: 12-14 SERVINGS

- 8 **medium pears, peeled and sliced**
- 4 **medium tart apples, peeled and sliced**
- 2 **cups fresh or frozen cranberries, thawed**
- 1 **cup sugar**
- ¾ **cup all-purpose flour**

TOPPING

- 1 **cup packed brown sugar**
- ¾ **cup all-purpose flour**
- ¾ **cup quick-cooking oats**
- ¼ **teaspoon ground cinnamon**
- ½ **cup butter**

1. In a large bowl, toss the fruit, sugar and flour. Pour into a greased 9x13-in. baking dish. For topping, in a bowl, combine the brown sugar, flour, oats and cinnamon. Cut in butter until mixture resembles coarse crumbs. Sprinkle over the fruit mixture.

2. Bake at 350° for 60-65 minutes or until fruit is tender and topping is golden brown.

TOP TIP

When making biscuits, pie crusts or other baked goods, use your potato masher to cut the butter or shortening into the dry ingredients. It works quickly.
—**DONNA L.** ANTWERP, NY

Crunchy Ice Cream Delight

Four generations of home cooks swear by these amazing ice cream bars. If you love nuts as much as my family does, double the butter and almonds, and save half to sprinkle on top.
—**ANGIE RICKLEFS** SIOUX CITY, IA

PREP: 20 MIN. + FREEZING
MAKES: 15 SERVINGS

- 2 **tablespoons butter**
- ½ **cup slivered almonds**
- 1 **cup crushed Rice Chex**
- ½ **cup flaked coconut**
- ½ **cup packed brown sugar**
- ⅛ **teaspoon salt**
- 1 **carton (1¾ quarts) vanilla bean ice cream, softened if necessary**

1. Preheat oven to 375°. In a large skillet, melt butter over medium heat. Add almonds; cook and stir 2-3 minutes or until toasted. Stir in Rice Chex, coconut, brown sugar and salt. Press onto bottom of an ungreased 9x13-in. baking dish. Bake 5-6 minutes or until edges are golden brown. Cool 10 minutes; place in freezer 30 minutes.

2. Gently spread ice cream over crust. Cover and freeze overnight. Cut into bars.

The lovely, crunchy topping and flavorful blend of tart cranberries with sweet apples and pears make this dessert a sublime finish to a hearty fall or winter meal. —**LOIS GELZER** STANDISH, ME

Benjamin's Chocolate Cheesecake

When I have time, I enjoy making cheesecakes. In fact, I've come up with a couple of my own recipes. I like this foolproof one because it has just the right mix of ingredients to make it a pleasure for any palate.

—**BENJAMIN CLARK** WARSAW, NY

PREP: 20 MIN.
BAKE: 40 MIN. + CHILLING
MAKES: 24 SERVINGS

- 1 **package (18 ounces) ready-to-bake refrigerated triple-chocolate cookie dough**
- 1 **package (8 ounces) milk chocolate toffee bits**
- 1 **package (9½ ounces) Dove dark chocolate candies**
- 3 **packages (8 ounces each) cream cheese, softened**
- 1 **can (14 ounces) sweetened condensed milk**
- ¾ **cup (6 ounces) vanilla yogurt**
- 4 **eggs, lightly beaten**
- 1 **teaspoon vanilla extract Whipped cream**

Let dough stand at room temperature for 5-10 minutes to soften. Press nine portions of dough into an ungreased 9x13-in. baking dish (save remaining dough for another use). Set aside 2 tablespoons toffee bits for garnish; sprinkle remaining bits over dough.

1. In a microwave, melt chocolate candies; stir until smooth. In a large bowl, beat the cream cheese, milk and yogurt until smooth. Add eggs; beat on low speed just until combined. Stir in vanilla and melted chocolate. Pour over crust.

2. Bake at 350° for 40-45 minutes or until center is almost set. Cool on a wire rack. Refrigerate for 4 hours or overnight. Garnish with whipped cream and reserved toffee bits.

⑤ INGREDIENTS
Watermelon Sorbet

You don't need an ice cream maker for this blissfully simple sorbet. My family loves it so much that I can never keep enough watermelon in the house to meet the demand!

—**KORY FIGURA** WAVERLY, IA

PREP: 35 MIN. + FREEZING
MAKES: 1½ QUARTS

- 1 **cup sugar**
- 1 **cup water**
- 8 **cups cubed seedless watermelon**
- 2 **tablespoons lemon juice**

1. In a small saucepan, bring sugar and water to a boil. Cook and stir until sugar is dissolved; set aside.

2. In a blender or food processor, process the watermelon in batches until pureed. Transfer to a large bowl; stir in the sugar syrup and lemon juice.

3. Pour into a 9x13-in. dish; cover and freeze for 8 hours or until firm. Just before serving, puree watermelon mixture in batches again until smooth.

TOP TIP

When making sorbet, don't skimp on the amount of sugar in the recipe: The high sugar content keeps it from freezing into a block of ice. Sugar also helps give sorbet its smooth texture, so keep things sweet and enjoy.

Two-Layered Apple Crisp

I feel blessed to have had the opportunity to bake this for a local women's shelter. I like to make it with Honeycrisp or Golden Delicious apples, or a blend of the two.

—CHAR MORSE WHITEHALL, MI

PREP: 30 MIN. • **BAKE:** 45 MIN.
MAKES: 12 SERVINGS

- ¾ cup butter, softened
- 1½ cups packed brown sugar
- 2 teaspoons ground cinnamon
- ½ teaspoon salt
- 2 cups all-purpose flour
- 2 cups old-fashioned oats

FILLING

- 1 cup sugar
- ¾ cup all-purpose flour
- ¼ cup packed brown sugar
- 1 teaspoon ground cinnamon
- ⅛ teaspoon ground nutmeg
- 3 large Honeycrisp or Golden Delicious apples, peeled and sliced (about 6 cups)
- 3 teaspoons vanilla extract
- 1 tablespoon butter
  Optional toppings: ice cream, caramel sauce and pecans

1. In a large bowl, beat the butter, brown sugar, cinnamon and salt until crumbly. Add flour and oats; mix well. Press 3 cups oat mixture into the bottom of a greased 9x13-in. baking dish.
2. In another bowl, mix the first five filling ingredients. Add apples and vanilla; toss to combine. Spoon over oat layer. Dot with butter; sprinkle with remaining oat mixture.
3. Bake, uncovered, at 350° for 45-50 minutes or until golden brown and apples are tender. If desired, serve with toppings.

Strawberry-Rhubarb Cream Dessert

A neighbor shared this recipe with me, and I created my own variation using garden-fresh rhubarb and strawberries. The cookie crust and creamy sweet-tart layers went over big at a family party: Not a crumb was left!

—SARA ZIGNEGO HARTFORD, WI

PREP: 1 HOUR + CHILLING
MAKES: 12 SERVINGS

- 2 cups all-purpose flour
- 1 cup chopped pecans
- 1 cup butter, melted
- ¼ cup sugar

TOPPING

- 1 cup packed brown sugar
- 3 tablespoons cornstarch
- 5 cups chopped fresh or frozen rhubarb
- 1 cup sliced fresh strawberries
- 1 package (8 ounces) cream cheese, softened
- 1 cup confectioners' sugar
- 1¼ cups heavy whipping cream, whipped, divided
  Additional brown sugar, optional

1. In a small bowl, combine the flour, pecans, butter and sugar. Press into a greased 9x13-in. baking dish. Bake at 350° for 18-20 minutes or until golden brown. Cool on a wire rack.
2. In a large saucepan, combine brown sugar and cornstarch. Stir in rhubarb until combined. Bring to a boil over medium heat, stirring often. Reduce heat; cook and stir for 4-5 minutes or until thickened. Remove from the heat; cool. Stir in strawberries.
3. In a large bowl, beat cream cheese and confectioners' sugar until smooth. Fold in 1 cup whipped cream. Spread over crust; top with rhubarb mixture. Spread with remaining whipped cream. Refrigerate for 3-4 hours before serving. Garnish with additional brown sugar if desired.

Chocolate Chip Cookie Dessert

This frosty family favorite couldn't be much easier to prepare, especially on hot days when I don't like turning on the oven. My husband and three sons love it so much that we even use our grill to make it on camping trips.

—**CAROL MARNACH** SIOUX FALLS, SD

PREP: 40 MIN. + FREEZING
MAKES: 15 SERVINGS

- 1 tube (16½ ounces) refrigerated chocolate chip cookie dough
- ½ cup caramel ice cream topping
- ½ cup cold 2% milk
- 1 package (3.4 ounces) instant vanilla pudding mix
- 1 carton (8 ounces) frozen whipped topping, thawed
- ¾ cup chopped nuts
- ¾ cup English toffee bits or almond brickle chips
- 3 ounces semisweet chocolate, chopped
- 3 tablespoons butter

1. Let dough stand at room temperature for 5-10 minutes to soften. Press into an ungreased 9x13-in. baking pan. Bake at 350° for 13-15 minutes or until golden brown. Cool completely.
2. Spread caramel topping over crust. In a large bowl, whisk milk and pudding mix for 2 minutes (mixture will be thick). Fold in whipped topping, nuts and toffee bits. Spread over caramel layer. Freeze 4 hours or until firm.
3. In a microwave, melt chocolate and butter; stir until smooth. Drizzle over pudding layer. Cut into squares.

Pears and Cranberries Poached in Wine

An elegant dessert doesn't have to take tons of work. Tart and refreshing, this simple-to-make treat is a memorable dinner finale.

—**EVA AMUSO** CHESHIRE, MA

PREP: 15 MIN. • **BAKE:** 30 MIN.
MAKES: 12 SERVINGS

- 6 medium pears, halved and cored
- 2 cups fresh or frozen cranberries, thawed
- 1½ cups white wine or white grape juice
- ½ cup sugar
- ½ cup cranberry juice
- 2 tablespoons butter
- 2 teaspoons grated lemon peel
  Creme fraiche or whipped cream

1. Preheat oven to 375°. Place pears in a greased 9x13-in. baking dish, cut side up. Top with cranberries.
2. In a small saucepan, combine wine, sugar, cranberry juice, butter and lemon peel; bring to a boil. Cook and stir until sugar is dissolved; spoon over pears.
3. Bake, covered, 30-35 minutes or until pears are tender, basting occasionally. Serve with creme fraiche.

Lemon Fluff

Get this mouthwatering dessert started with just a few pantry ingredients. You can also make it a day ahead for convenience.

—LEOLA MCKINNEY

MORGANTOWN, WV

PREP: 25 MIN. + CHILLING
MAKES: 12 SERVINGS

1 can (12 ounces) evaporated milk
1 package (3 ounces) lemon gelatin
1 cup sugar
1⅓ cups boiling water
¼ cup lemon juice
1¾ cups graham cracker crumbs
5 tablespoons butter, melted

1. Pour milk into a small metal bowl; place mixer beaters in the bowl. Cover and refrigerate for at least 2 hours.

2. Meanwhile, in a large bowl, dissolve gelatin and sugar in boiling water. Stir in lemon juice. Cover and refrigerate until syrupy, about 1½ hours.

3. In a small bowl, combine crumbs and butter; set aside 2 tablespoons for garnish. Press remaining crumbs onto the bottom of a 9x13-in. dish. Beat chilled milk until soft peaks form. Beat gelatin until tiny bubbles form. Fold milk into gelatin. Pour over prepared crust. Sprinkle with reserved crumbs. Cover and refrigerate until set. Cut into squares.

Humble rice pudding gets a Cinderella makeover with this upscale recipe. It's just the right thickness for soaking up a hot caramel topping.

—JANICE ELDER CHARLOTTE, NC

Toffee Rice Pudding with Caramel Cream

PREP: 45 MIN.
BAKE: 35 MIN. + COOLING
MAKES: 16 SERVINGS

- 3 **cups water**
- 1 **cup uncooked medium grain rice**
- ¼ **teaspoon salt**
- 3 **cups pitted dates, chopped**
- 3 **cups 2% milk**
- 2 **teaspoons vanilla extract**
- 1 **cup packed brown sugar**
- 1½ **cups heavy whipping cream, divided**
- ¼ **cup butter, cubed**
- ½ **cup sour cream**
- ¼ **cup hot caramel ice cream topping**

1. In a large saucepan, bring the water, rice and salt to a boil. Reduce heat; cover and simmer for 12-15 minutes or until rice is tender. Add dates and milk; cook and stir for 10 minutes. Remove from the heat; stir in vanilla. Set aside.

2. In a small saucepan, combine the brown sugar, 1 cup cream and butter. Bring to a boil. Reduce heat; simmer, uncovered, for 2 minutes, stirring constantly. Stir into rice mixture. Transfer to a greased 9x13-in. baking dish. Bake, uncovered, at 350° for 35-40 minutes or until bubbly. Cool for 15 minutes.

3. Meanwhile, in a small bowl, beat the sour cream, caramel topping and remaining cream until slightly thickened. Serve with warm rice pudding. Refrigerate leftovers.

⑤ INGREDIENTS
Shattered Crystal Ball

Kids love the sweet gelatin and fluffy whipped topping in this irresistible dessert. Use different flavors and colors of gelatin for variety.
—*TASTE OF HOME* **TEST KITCHEN**

PREP: 25 MIN. + CHILLING
MAKES: 12-15 SERVINGS

- 2 **packages (3 ounces each) lime gelatin**
- 6 **cups boiling water, divided**
- 2 **packages (3 ounces each) orange gelatin**
- 2 **envelopes unflavored gelatin**
- ⅓ **cup cold water**
- 1½ **cups white grape juice**
- 1 **carton (12 ounces) frozen whipped topping, thawed**

1. In a bowl, dissolve the lime gelatin in 3 cups boiling water. Pour into an 8-in.-square dish coated with cooking spray. In another bowl, dissolve orange gelatin in remaining boiling water. Pour into another 8-in.-square dish coated with cooking spray. Refrigerate gelatins for 4 hours or until very firm.

2. In a small saucepan, sprinkle unflavored gelatin over cold water; let stand for 1 minute. Add grape juice. Heat over low heat, stirring until gelatin is completely dissolved. Pour into a large bowl; refrigerate for 45 minutes or until slightly thickened. Fold in whipped topping.

3. Cut green gelatin into ½-in. cubes and orange gelatin into 1-in. cubes. Set aside 8-10 cubes of each color for garnish. Place 2 cups whipped topping mixture in a bowl; fold in remaining green cubes. Spread into a 9x13-in. dish coated with cooking spray. Fold remaining orange cubes into remaining whipped topping mixture; spread over bottom layer. Sprinkle with reserved green and orange gelatin cubes. Refrigerate for 2 hours or until set. Cut into squares.